Jesus as Man, Myth, and Metaphor

Jesus as Man, Myth, and Metaphor
Beyond the Jesus of History Debate

BENJAMIN W. FARLEY

Wipf & Stock
PUBLISHERS
Eugene, Oregon

JESUS AS MAN, MYTH, AND METAPHOR
Beyond the Jesus of History Debate

Copyright © 2007 Benjamin W. Farley. All rights reserved. Except for brief quotations in critical publications or reviews, no part of this book may be reproduced in any manner without prior written permission from the publisher. Write: Permissions, Wipf and Stock, 199 W. 8th Ave., Eugene, OR 97401.

ISBN 13: 978-1-55635-477-9

Unless otherwise noted, Scripture quotations are from the New Revised Standard Version Bible™, Copyright © 1989, Division of Christian Education of the National Council of the Churches of Christ in the United States of America; reprinted with permission. All rights reserved.

Quotations from *The Gospel of Thomas*, unless otherwise specified, are reprinted with permission of Scribner, an imprint of Simon & Schuster Adult Publishing Group, from *The Five Gospels: What Did Jesus Really Say?* by Robert W. Funk, Roy W. Hoover with the Jesus Seminar. Copyright © 1993 by Polebridge Press. All rights reserved.

Manufactured in the U.S.A.

For
Alice Anne, John, and Bryan

In memory of
Lewis Bevens Schenck,
Donald G. Miller,
Henry Brimm,
and
Balmer Kelly

He who increases knowledge increases sorrow.
—Eccl 12:18 (RSV)

*Foxes have holes, and birds of the air have nests;
but the Son of Man has nowhere to lay his head.*
—Matt 8:20

Contents

Acknowledgements / ix

1. Defining the Jesus of History / 1
2. Other Historical Figures and Movements and Their Impact on Mankind / 19
3. The Elements of Myth / 37
4. Mythical Dimensions in the Life of the Pre-Easter Jesus / 51
5. Parable, Metaphor, and Myth / 65
6. Children, Women, Prostitutues, Publicans, and Beggars / 75
7. The Hero as Universal Archetype / 85
8. Archetypes of the East / 95
9. Nativity, Transfiguration, and the Cross / 103
10. The Resurrection / 119
11. Jesus as Metaphor / 131
12. Jesus as Shaman, Magician, and Healer / 149
13. The Pre-Easter Jesus as Wonderful Counselor and Prince of Peace / 155
14. The Chief Priests, Scribes, Elders, Pharisees, and Essenes / 165
15. Jesus and the Sabbath / 169
16. The Historical Jesus and the Apostle Paul / 173
17. The Pre-Easter Jesus and the Creeds of the Church / 181
18. The Historical Jesus and the Reformed Tradition / 187

19 Intrigue, Conspiracies, and Plots / 195

20 Conclusion: The Five Trees of Paradise / 201

Bibliography / 207

Scripture Index / 211

Acknowledgements

I wish to acknowledge my gratitude to Donald McKim of Westminster/John Knox Press, John Loudon of Rowan and Littlefield Publishers, and James Ernest of Baker Academic Books for their encouragement and interest during my research on this work. To each I am deeply grateful.

Above all, I wish to thank Lisa White for her editorial assistance, Georgene Clower for her keen eye and helpful suggestions, and Libby Case, who painstakingly proofed each chapter and offered invaluable feedback, all of which I welcomed.

1

Defining the Jesus of History

THE PAST century and more has witnessed a plethora of quests of the historical Jesus. They range from Schweitzer's to Bultmann's, from Bultmann's to Bornkamm's, and from the latter to the current sea of works undertaken by such scholars as Marcus Borg, Burton Mack, Geza Vermes, and John Dominic Crossan. Crossan's monumental *The Historical Jesus: The Life of a Mediterranean Jewish Peasant* and its sequel, *The Birth of Christianity*, attest to New Testament research at its best. But much of this has come at a diminution of the so-called Christ of Faith, or problematic for understanding the role of the post-Easter Jesus. Can the Christ of Faith survive in light of the current critical perception that presents Jesus as a social revolutionary, or a peasant Cynic, who became something of a cult figure from both a political and religious perspective?

Certainly, the above studies constitute welcomed resources for exploring the life of Jesus. They provide essential windows into its historicity and Jesus' authentic sayings, deeds, and identity. Such works also attempt to analysis the tantalizing transition from Jesus the historical person to Jesus the risen Savior and Lord of the world. Nonetheless, the question remains: why study Jesus, if he were merely a Cynic, or a popular peasant revolutionary? Moreover, that the Apostolic and Post-Apostolic Ages found his version of Yahwistic piety and his symbolism as a *soter* figure superior to Roman imperialism's gods and goals, does not suffice, necessarily, to render him, or early Christianity's views, tenable today. This seems especially apparent in view of the intense research to recover the historical Jesus before that transition occurred.

Furthermore, compounding all this is the fact that the modern era no longer believes in the ancient world's superstitions, theocracies, political philosophies, etc. We admire their art, literature, architecture, and myths. For these provide insight into their concepts of self, politics, religion, philosophy, and universal longings. However, their respective answers and achievements for their day cannot substitute for modern mankind's efforts, nor can their beliefs be embraced without critical reflection. There has to be a more compelling reason for Jesus studies and adherence to Christian beliefs, beyond the fact that he challenged his Palestinian hearers to rethink their religious and political heritage. In truth, that he might represent the best that one can become, or save one from personal and collective sin, or insure a believer of a life in a world hereafter, strikes the agnostic contemporary world as delusional, at best. The present time frame encourages a person to become only that unique self he or she chooses to become in the process of individuation. Psychiatry has demonstrated the value of this quite successfully for over a century now. Moreover, the current worldview looks unkindly on someone else doing for an individual what an individual must do alone for oneself. The Buddha taught that one is one's only savior; that it is an illusion to expect redemption to come from without. Jesus said: "The kingdom of God is within you" (Luke 9:35). It is not outside but inside human beings. Nonetheless, having said that, Jesus did not discourage faith in the transcendent God of his forebears. As for a life beyond the grave, Gilbert Ryle's famous "Ghost in the Machine" made it painfully clear that mankind's conscious episodes are impossible without brain waves and the latter impossible without physiological underpinnings. There are no two, separate selves, one inner and destined for eternity, the other outer and limited by death and decay. Inner and outer are only two aspects of the same self. To reason otherwise is to create a "category mistake." His arguments, along with others,' sought to end that long noetic trail from Plato through Descartes that favored a dualistic, two-substance approach.

The challenge is rightfully to be asked: How are we to assess this historical figure today? Is his value like the Buddha's, or Lao Tzu's and his Taoist principles in general? That is at least one question worth pursuing. A second has to do with Jesus' timeframe and its mythic worldview. Jesus' Jewish faith repudiated the classical world's concepts of deity and multiple gods. Yet, within a few years following Jesus' crucifixion, classical Christianity began utilizing Greco-Roman perceptions of divinity with respect to the life of Jesus, interpreting his appearance as a God-Man, or Son of God, born of a divine spiritual essence that had "overshadowed" (Luke 1:35) his Galilean mother, Mary. This "mythologization" of the historical Jesus as the Sophia of the universe become flesh is preserved in all four Gospels, whether implicitly or explicitly, and cannot be ignored. Also, Plato's dualistic view of spirit versus flesh dominates Paul's theology, and many of Paul's recommended virtues are Stoic in content and form. Is it still possible for one to find his or her spiritual needs fulfilled by this post-Easter figure whose universal purpose and divine status contrasts so sharply with the Jesus of history? If so, how and why? I realize that my interpretations may be viewed, at best, as only tentative, or idiosyncratic, and will represent only one scholar's viewpoint. Perhaps they will generate more incisive and critical approaches, or more successfully argued positions. In truth, as Schweitzer knew so well, every generation must conclude for itself the significance of Jesus and his lasting value for believers, as well as nonbelievers.

First a brief review of some of history's more salient appraisals of the historical Jesus is in order. As appropriate, Albert Schweitzer deserves first mention.

Albert Schweitzer (1875–1965)

Albert Schweitzer's *Quest of the Historical Jesus* left him both disillusioned and mesmerized. What disillusioned him? German liberal theology's assessment and reconstruction of Jesus, because it was the product of an unbridled attempt to render Jesus as a perfectly understandable phenomenon of history. Writes Schweitzer:

> There is nothing more negative than the result of the critical study of the Life of Jesus. . . .The Jesus of Nazareth who came forward publicly as the Messiah, who preached the ethic of the Kingdom of God, who founded the Kingdom of Heaven upon earth, and died to give His work its final consecration, never had any existence. He is a figure designed by rationalism, endowed with life by liberalism, and clothed by modern theology in an historical garb.[1]

After much agonizing of his own, Schweitzer ventured that the Jesus of history was a mistaken apocalyptic who, aflame with eschatological fervor, sought to hasten the coming of God's kingdom by taking matters into his own hand and by dying as a martyr to insure God's intervention in history. Regrettably, such did not happen.

As for the liberal view of his day, Schweitzer rejected its Jesus altogether. Such a modern Jesus as they perceived him was too small to serve mankind, and his portrayal as such missed the whole mark. In Schweitzer's view, Jesus, "as a man like ourselves," never existed. Moreover, such a Jesus "cannot call spiritual life into existence." For Schweitzer, it is far wiser "to leave the individual man alone with the sayings of Jesus . . ." Furthermore, "it is not Jesus as historically known, but Jesus as spiritually arisen within men, who is significant for our time and can help it." It is his spirit that

---

1. Albert Schweitzer, *Quest of the Historical Jesus*, New York, 1964, p. 398.

"goes forth from Him and in the spirits of men strives for new influence and rule, is that which overcomes the world."[2] Sounding Platonic and Gnostic to the core, he adds:

> The abiding and eternal in Jesus is absolutely independent of historical knowledge and can only be understood by contact with His spirit which is still at work in the world. In proportion as we have the Spirit of Jesus we have the true knowledge of Jesus.[3]

The historical Jesus "influenced individuals by the individual word," one on one. Identifying him with the Messiah, or Son of God, complete with a rationalistic system of doctrine and dogma, only obscures his appeal and value. Finally, Schweitzer found the words within himself that best summed up the historical Jesus for him. His summary has never been superceded.

> He comes to us as One unknown, without a name, as of old, by the lake-side. He came to those men who knew Him not. He speaks to us the same word: "Follow thou me!" and sets us to the tasks which He has to fulfil for our time. He commands. And to those who obey Him, whether they be wise or simple, He will reveal Himself in the toils, the conflicts, the sufferings which they shall pass through in His fellowship, and, as an ineffable mystery, they shall learn in their own experience Who He is.[4]

Such a Jesus inspirited Schweitzer to re-equip himself as a medical missionary and to lose himself in the great Unknown of Africa's jungles as one whose soul had come to know Who He was, in the ineffable mystery of obedience and suffering. Only Gandhi, Mother Teresa, and the Dalai Lama have followed in Schweitzer's footsteps in similar paths of obedience, conflict, and suffering.

Rudolf Bultmann (1884–1976)

Rudolf Bultmann is best remembered for his demythologization program and form critical analysis, which he shared with Martin Dibelius. By recognizing the three-storied universe into which Jesus and his disciples were born, and its mythological structures (heaven, God, and angels above, earth in the middle, and the devil, disease, and evil spirits below), Bultmann hoped to capture a more historically accurate portrait of Jesus.

2. Ibid., p. 400.
3. Ibid.
4. Ibid., p. 403.

His methodology sought to discover the *Sitz im Leben* (setting in life) of Jesus' sayings, along with each unit's literary form and usage in the early Christian community. This led Bultmann and Dibelius to identify five primary types of literary forms that, hopefully, would shed light on Jesus' mission and message. The five are: pronouncement stories, legends, sayings, miracles, and the passion narrative. Once a reader dismisses the early Church's Hellenization of Jesus, in which it turned the historical Jesus into a divine figure sent from God to save the world, a closer view of Jesus as a radical Jewish interpreter of God's will emerges. Since, however, this wisdom of old no longer grasps a modern humanity, Bultmann sought to render Jesus' message and life meaningful by interpreting both along existentialist lines. The cross and resurrection remain paramount for Bultmann, but for existentialist reasons.

> The historical event of the cross acquires cosmic dimensions. . . . For if we see in the cross the judgment of the world and the defeat of the rulers of this world . . . , the cross becomes *the judgment of ourselves* as fallen creatures enslaved to the powers of the "world."
>
> By giving up Jesus to be crucified, God has set up the cross *for us*. To believe in the cross of Christ does not mean to concern ourselves with a mythical event . . . , but rather to make the cross of Christ *our own, to undergo crucifixion with him*. The cross . . . is not just an event of the past . . . , but . . . *an ever-present reality.*[5]

As for the resurrection, it is "not an event of past history." It is an article of faith, just as the saving efficacy of the cross is an article of faith. The meaning of the resurrection expresses the "truth in the affirmation that the Crucified was not holden of death, but rose from the dead."[6] "Cross and resurrection form a single, indivisible cosmic event which brings judgement to the world and opens up for men the possibility of authentic life."[7]

If Schweitzer's twofold view of Jesus emphasizes (1) a failed human attempt to usher in the Kingdom of God, but one which nevertheless (2) retains a haunting and esoteric quality for Christ's admirers because of Jesus' capacity for sustaining a personal and mystical relationship with God, Bultmann's Jesus opens the way for each individual to accept freedom from his/her existential fallenness, or forfeiture, and freedom for a new beginning of hope and partnership with God and man in one's present time.

---

5. R. Bultmann, *Kerygma and Myth*, New York, 1953, p. 36. Italics for emphasis.
6. Ibid., p. 38.
7. Ibid., p. 39.

Gunther Bornkamm

Gunther Bornkamm would take a different approach while still drawing upon Bultmann's form critical work. For Bornkamm, the historical Jesus can be discerned *in* the Church's kerygma or proclamation about Jesus, and the kerygma can be *seen in* the Church's Gospels about *Jesus*. Granted, "no one is any longer in the position to write a life of Jesus,"[8] the life of Jesus can, nonetheless, be seen in its broad strokes from the Church's Gospels. What we find there is the Church's belief that Jesus is risen and that his message about the Kingdom is relevant for the present.

> In the relating of past history [the Gospels] proclaim who he is, not who he was. What the passion narratives show applies also to the Gospels as a whole: what belongs to the past in the history of Jesus should always be investigated and understood in relation to its significance for the present time today and the coming time of God's future.[9]

Because of this, Jesus' words have to do with the present, just as they did for the early Church. In those Gospels "the word of Jesus is preserved," but with immense freedom, as each evangelist applies that word in a manner best suited for his community. To that extent, Bornkamm is unwilling to sever Jesus' message from its historical context and interpret it only along existentialist lines. We are not dealing with a timeless mythic event but with history. If anything, "the Gospels are the rejection of myth." They do not represent "a historical interest apart from faith."[10]

What, then, are "the rough outlines of Jesus' person and history" that emerge in a critical but sympathetic reading of the Gospels? For Bornkamm, Jesus' father and mother were Joseph and Mary. He was of Jewish origin. His father was a carpenter, and in all likelihood, he was too. He had at least four brothers: James, Joses, Judas, and Simon (Mark 6:3). He spoke Aramaic but surely knew Hebrew. He might have known Greek. Nevertheless, Borhkamm concludes: "we find in Jesus no trace of the influence of Greek philosophy or of the Greek manner of living."[11] At about the age of 30, Jesus was baptized by John. What this might have meant to him, however, is beyond our capacity to know. Nor do we know how long Jesus' work and ministry lasted. Certainly, we may think of him

---

8. G. Bornkamm, *Jesus of Nazareth*, New York, p. 13.
9. Ibid., p. 17.
10. Ibid., p. 23.
11. Ibid., p. 54.

Defining the Jesus of History

as a rabbi, steeped in the ancient knowledge of the Old Testament. He believed in the coming Kingdom of God and wished to prepare his people for it. The decisive turning point in his life occurred when he decided to go to Jerusalem to confront its religious and political leaders of this imminent event. It resulted in his cross and death. From these "meager, indisputable facts" today's historians and theologians must piece together "the life story of Jesus and its stages." The remainder of Bornkamm's book is devoted to this task. What Bornkamm basically distills may be summarized as this: Jesus is of this world, yet an "unmistakable otherness" hovers over Jesus. It is like Schweitzer's shadow has spellbound Bornkamm, or, if not Schweitzer's, it is Jesus' own "insoluble mystery" that pervades every nuance of the Gospels' texts. Something confronts us in Jesus that won't be dismissed. He is a prophet of God's coming kingdom, yet he is more than that. He never speaks of his own calling, claims no specific authority, mentions no ecstatic states, visions, or secret revelations that might explain his actions and purpose. He never justifies himself. But all who hear him are thrilled or troubled. Bornkamm finds nothing objectionable about designating Jesus as a *rabbi* who proclaims the divine law, teaches in synagogues, gathers disciples, and debates with other scribes in the manner of their profession, under the authority of scripture.[12] Beyond what Jesus might have said, versus how tradition couches it, what grips the reader is Jesus' "astounding sovereignty." For Bornkamm, it is this authority that contains "the mystery of Jesus' personality and influence." Men and women are forced to step outside themselves to see themselves as they are. Jesus' program is a "passionate tackling" of life. We witness this in both his words and deeds—however the latter might be influenced by tradition. As a result, Jesus makes "the reality of God present," which is the essential mystery of Jesus.

Basically, this is the heart of Bornkamm's interpretation of Jesus' historical purpose. His life, words, and deeds witness to the presence of God's reign now. The long fervent hope of Israel's prophets, that this puzzling world is not beyond redemption but belongs to God's Lordship, is vindicated in the words and deeds of Jesus. The world is no longer under the power of demonic forces but ripples with the presence of God. The new eon has already begun. "Blessed are the poor now, those who hunger now, those who weep now" (Luke 6:20f.). The kingdom is more than an apocalyptic, cosmic, yet-to-occur event. God reigns now. His kingdom is already dawning. Jesus is the sign of its reality. His words and actions testify to its presence. Like the mustard seed, its beginning is almost insig-

---

12. Ibid., p. 57.

nificant, hidden like the buried treasure in the field, undetected by most eyes. The kingdom comes by its own power: that is its miracle, and it requires human patience, humility, and total trust in God. Through Jesus' parables and Beatitudes, the hungry, poor, and mournful, the blind, the lame, and the outcast, are lifted by grace to see that God has and is coming to them. Thus Jesus' preaching opens their lives to hope and joy. All preconceived social limitations are shaken, if not abolished, by the good news of the coming Kingdom. Bornkamm's Jesus unmistakably challenges the religious and political powers of his time. Without sentimentality or "romantic predilection," Jesus brings hope to the "people on the fringe of society," to those who are viewed as marked, sick, and deserving of retribution, or condemned and powerless, along with women and children whose status is minimal anyway. They are the ones with whom Jesus sits at table and breaks bread. Will those who have eyes to see and ears with which to hear repent? For "repentance" means "to lay hold on the salvation which is already at hand, and to give up everything for it."[13] It is God's invitation to them through the good news of his coming kingdom, therefore it comes to them as grace. The lost become saved and the saved become lost (Mark 8:35). This is mankind's future that God has willed, thus now is the hour of decision.

Bornkamm does not doubt that Jesus was crucified, but the early Church's portrayal of Jesus as the Son of Man, as the Messiah, and Suffering Servant belong to the Church's message, not claims that the historical Jesus made himself. His resurrection lies beyond the realm of historical scholarship. But his disciples believed and acknowledged his risenness. The Easter stories are evidence of this faith. They are not "records and chronicles" of what happened. In the final analysis, it is the *message* of Easter that is to be sought in the Easter *stories*. And it is that message, with its vindication of the life of Jesus, that testifies to the grace of God that provides redemption and a future to all who accept God's invitation to repent and commence the process of life's transformation.

If Schweitzer, Bultmann, and Bornkamm interpret Jesus as a proponent of an apocalyptic vision of the Kingdom of God—however much they may spiritualize, existentialize, or soften its eschatological content––the next three scholars totally de-emphasize any apocalyptic dimension in favor of a "sapiential eschatology." The difference between the two may be summed up as follows: apocalyptic eschatology has to do with waiting for God to intervene in history; sapiential eschatology has to do with Christ's followers supporting, advancing, and incarnating God's purposes

---

13. Ibid., p. 82.

now. Mack, Borg, and Crossan each advocate interpreting the work and sayings of Jesus from this viewpoint.

This approach did not emerge out of a vacuum, but it developed out of a long history of scholarship devoted to Jesus' sayings, or the *Gospel of Q*—the now recognized hypothetical collection of Jesus' sayings, which Matthew and Luke used, and which the *Gospel of Thomas* equally mirrors. Let us review these three scholars' work in turn, along with Vermes's.

Burton Mack

In his book, *The Lost Gospel of Q*, Burton Mack draws on James Robinson's work on Q and his thesis that Jesus' era's teachers utilized a variety of aphorisms and maxims to promulgate their "philosophies." Mack also draws on John Kloppenborg's analysis of Q as a repository of such material, and thus advances the argument that Jesus was a "sapiential instructor" who endorsed a similar, but unique, approach of his own. According to Mack, Jesus' followers collected his instructions, which later underwent no less than three enlargements or expansions. Only the first collection captures the historical Jesus' teachings, whereas the latter two contain his followers' expansions and adumbrations, not part of Jesus' original wisdom. Jesus' own words never pointed to himself. They had to do with God's rule, with Nature as a manifestation of divine order, and with Israel's epic history as an example of God's rule.[14]

In Mack's view, the historical Jesus may best be seen as a mendicant sage, or wandering Cynic. As such, he shocked his Palestinian neighbors and overlords with his pithy, abrupt, and abrasive wisdom, which called for rustic simplicity and ruthless honesty, in keeping with the true meaning of God's will for his people. He did this by means of jolting aphorisms and maxims, which challenged his hearers to transform their lives.

Mack believes that Jesus' followers thought of him as a "Cynic-like sage."[15] "Cynics were known for begging, voluntary poverty, renunciation of needs, severance of family ties, fearless and carefree attitudes, and troublesome public behavior."[16] This description certainly fits the Synoptic Gospels' frequent depiction of Jesus. Moreover, the Cynics' themes focused on critiquing the rich, their pretensions and multiple forms of social, religious, and political hypocrisy. Again, enter, Jesus of Nazareth!

---

14. B. Mack, *The Lost Gospel of Q*, San Francisco, 1993, p. 122.
15. Ibid., p. 115.
16. Ibid.

Mack believes that the original layer of Q contained two types of discourse that reveal the heart of the historical Jesus' (1) approach and (2) injunctions. In his *approach*, Jesus used "aphoristic maxims." Examples include: How fortunate the poor! Everyone who asks receives! Life is more than food! If salt is saltless, it is good for nothing! Mack refers to Jesus' *injunctions* as "aphoristic imperatives." They follow from Jesus' maxims. Examples: Love your enemies! Judge not and you won't be judged! Carry no money, bag, or sandals! In turn, these Cynic-like views encouraged *a life style*, which Jesus' first followers sought to embrace and which they preserved in Q's first edition, or first layer. This life style would have engendered such goals as: voluntary poverty, non-retaliation, rules for begging, renunciation of needs, and confidence of God's care.

As time went by, layer two, or Q^2 was created to defend the community's collection of Jesus' sayings, along with his way of life. In fact, Mack believes the authors of Q^2 recast Jesus, the wisdom teacher, into a kind of prophet, whose work was rejected but who nonetheless delivered judgments in an "apocalyptic idiom."[17] Once out of their hands, layer three, or Q^3 added further interpretations. The latter exceeded anything the historical Jesus said, enjoined, or condoned, and would have been rejected by Jesus' first followers as containing false views and statements.

Once Matthew and Luke incorporated Q in their respective Gospels, copies of the *Gospel of Q* fell into disuse and eventual oblivion. There was no further need for them. Matthew and Luke had not only preserved Jesus' sayings, but had set them within the context of a Christ Cult interpretation, thereby giving them a totally different meaning as well as a specificity of time and place they had lacked in their earlier form.

Mack's analysis of Jesus as a Cynic-like wisdom teacher sets Jesus apart from any possible connection with institutional Judaism. This being the case, he cannot quality as Bornkamm's "rabbi." He is more of an outsider, an unwanted agitator. As a result of his own choice, he became a freethinker, a gadfly, like Socrates, or a prophet, similar to the great prophets of Israel's epic past. He had taken on the role of an independent critic of his nation, its people, its leaders, and the direction toward which his people were stumbling away from their heritage.

Mack is adamant; the existence of Q displays that the Synoptic Gospels do not record the historical events that generated Christianity. The Jesus movements that produced Q were not motivated by a Christ Cult's interests, or by an emphasis on Jesus' death and resurrection as the personal savior of the world. In fact, Jesus' first followers knew nothing of

---

17. Ibid., p. 154.

the events upon which the Synoptic Gospels depend. They knew nothing of his baptism, of his conflict with Jewish officials and their plot to kill him, or of his instructions to the twelve, his transfiguration, journey to Jerusalem, his last supper, trial, crucifixion "as king of the Jews," or of his resurrection, or any stories about an empty tomb. All this is the work of later Jesus traditions that interpreted the historical Jesus along lines that furthered their own needs and goals. Many of these traditions were foreign to Judah's soil and originated in Syrian and Pauline circles.

In Mack's view, the discovery of Q forces the Church (1) to rethink its vision of Jesus and (2) the dogma that the Church created across the centuries. Blind adherence to a conception of Jesus, such as the narrative gospels present, must be recognized for what it is and new perceptions ventured.

Marcus Borg

Marcus Borg's Jesus is less strident and less rules-centered than Mack's (see Borg's *Meeting Jesus Again for the First Time*, 1994). As one of the founding members of the Jesus Seminar, Borg, like Mack, takes a non-apocalyptic approach to Jesus. Basing his research on the Seminar's emphasis of Jesus as a teacher, who used aphorisms and parables to proclaim his message and to advance his cause, Borg holds to the distinction between a pre-Easter Jesus and a post-Easter Jesus. The Gospels contain memories of both these Jesuses. In them we hear two voices: "the voice of the pre-Easter Jesus and the voice of the community in the post-Easter setting."[18]

What do we know of this pre-Easter Jesus? Borg provides a long and helpful list. He was deeply Jewish. His Bible was the Jewish Scripture. He had no intention of establishing a new religion. His audience was Jewish; so were his first hearers. The stories of his birth and childhood are not historical. They are rather symbolic narratives created by the Christian movement. That they attest to Jesus as "an extraordinary person" is beyond doubt.

Jesus was probably born near the close of Herod the Great's reign. His mother and father were Mary and Joseph; he had four brothers and a number of sisters. He grew up in Nazareth, near the city of Sepphoris, which had boasted a population of 40,000 before being destroyed by the Romans in 4 BC. The latter occurred as a result of the civil disturbances that followed Herod's death. The city was rebuilt during Jesus' youth. This means that Jesus was reared in a cosmopolitan environment. Gentiles and Greeks mingled here and both Aramaic and Greek were spoken.

---

18. M. Borg, *Meeting Jesus Again for the First Time*, San Francisco, 1994, p. 21.

Jesus as Man, Myth, and Metaphor

What can be assumed about Jesus' earlier years? Borg surmises that Jesus went to school in the synagogue in Nazareth, where the Torah served as his primer. He probably became a woodworker (*tekton* in Greek), making wood products for the building boom taking place in and around Sepphoris. Borg notes that a *tekton* ranked at the lower end of the peasant class, belonging to a family that had lost its familial lands.

If his family were devout at all, he would have engaged in the common Judaism of his day, participated in its rites, and observed its holy days, certainly at least the Passover in the spring, Pentecost fifty days later, and Tabernacles in the fall.

At some point in his life, Jesus became a "religious seeker." At about age 30, he left Nazareth and became a follower of John the Baptist. He probably underwent a "conversion experience"—however sudden or gradual, which led to an "internal transformation" and inspired the ministry he embraced. Once John was arrested, Jesus continued the Baptizer's mission, or his own version of the same.

Other claims can be ventured. In all likelihood, Jesus' self-understanding and message were *nonmessianic*. His message had nothing to do with himself. He pointed at all times to God. Likewise, the pre-Easter Jesus' message was *noneschatological*. He never espoused a world-ending vision or a supernatural intervention of the Kingdom of God.

From a positive point of view, Borg offers four ways of assessing the historical Jesus' personality and mission: 1) He was a *spirit person*, a mediator of the sacred. He had a vivid sense of seeing into a higher layer of reality. He sensed that there is more to reality than the world of ordinary experience. His awareness of the sacred was *noetic* (a form of knowing) and not simply ecstatic. 2) As a spirit person, Jesus became a kind of conduit for the love, power, and wisdom of God. He perceived God's power and love as being present, not out there somewhere, but within and around his hearers. This consciousness of God dominated his role as a *teacher of wisdom*. 3) Jesus was *a social prophet* as well. He criticized the social, class, political, and economic conditions of his time. He was an advocate for justice; consequently, his work and message involved him in conflict with those in power. Finally, 4) Jesus was a *movement founder*. His activities and pronouncements challenged the structures of his day and created a movement that became the Christian Church.

Jesus' verbal talents remain unequalled. His use of metaphor, poetry, wit, imagination, and "dramatic public actions," such as eating with prostitutes and sinners, put him in the forefront. He was clearly intelligent, progressive, daring, and brave. He could show compassion as well as strength.

His presence had a healing effect. Writes Borg: "more healing stories are told about him than about anybody else in the Jewish tradition."[19] That there was something compelling about him is undeniable. He angered many among the elite and powerful. As a result, his life was short and his public mission brief. Unlike Lao Tzu or the Buddha, he never lived into old age. At best he died in his early 30s. How could his followers forget him? They couldn't. Thus he became material for the wants and sorrows of a world that gradually elevated him to the status of the Son of God, the Messiah, the Christ who takes away the sins of the world. The road form history to myth passed straight from Jerusalem to Damascus, then to Antioch, Tarsus, Corinth, and, ultimately, to Rome. Let him who has ears to hear, hear what his spirit is saying!

Borg's is an inspirational, as well as an informative, picture of the historical Jesus. It savors something of Schweitzer's "One Unknown," along with Bornkamm and Mack's sobering conclusions: that Jesus was a man, much like any human being, whose heart and soul yielded to a vision that dared to transform his world. It cost him his life. Any who would "take up their cross" to follow him, will surely find that path of self-transformation and openness to the sacred, just as costly and just as fulfilling.

John Dominic Crossan

No one has stepped forward to flesh out the Jesus of History as methodically and accurately, from the viewpoint of modern historical analysis, as John Dominic Crossan. He labels his work "a reconstruction" and describes his approach as "interactivism." By "reconstruction" he means a work that must be done over and over again. This is owing to the fact that every generation brings itself into the past it studies. This "interaction" is unavoidable. Past and present interact with each other; they challenge and change each other. If anything, this is what postmodernism has taught philosophers, historians, and theologians alike. Furthermore, Crossan prefers the term "reconstruction" to the phrase "the search for the historical Jesus," or "the quest of the historical Jesus." These older searches and quests implied that one was "going to attain an answer once and for all forever."[20] Because of the way past and present interact, the process of reconstruction is every generation's task. It never ends.

Crossan makes a further distinction between two New Testament views concerning flesh and spirit. One is Hellenistic and existed before

---

19. Ibid., p. 31.
20. John D. Crossan, *The Birth of Christianity*, San Francisco, 1998, pp. 43–44.

Christianity came along. It denigrates the flesh in favor of the spirit and mirrors Plato's dualism. The other is monistic and preserves the unity of flesh and spirit. It is more ancient and Jewish than the former. For Crossan, Paul's theology borders on the Platonic and introduces a "slippery slope" into his theology and an unnecessary "inconsistency." He calls this approach, or sensibility, *sarcophobia*—fear of the flesh, a *phobus* of *sarx*. The opposite and more biblical sensibility he calls *sarcophilia*—or love of the flesh, or appreciation of the unity of one's human essence as soul and flesh. The latter sensibility best provides a normative principle for grappling with the historical Jesus. Otherwise, one drifts into Gnosticism and ceases to view Jesus as "human," or as an historical figure. From a preliminary point of view, Crossan remarks: "If you begin with Paul, you will interpret Jesus incorrectly; if you begin with Jesus, you will interpret Paul differently."[21]

Crossan also rejects the distinction between a "pre-Easter Jesus" and a "post-Easter Jesus." Writes Crossan: "There is . . . only one Jesus, the embodied Galilean who lived a life of divine justice in an unjust world, who was officially and legally executed . . . and whose continued empowering presence indicates, for believers, that God is not on the side of injustice."[22] Moreover:

> There are not two Jesuses—one pre-Easter and another post-Easter, one earthly and another heavenly, one with a physical and another with a spiritual body. There is only one Jesus, the *historical* Jesus who incarnated the Jewish God of justice for a believing community committed to continuing such incarnation ever afterward.[23]

Interestingly enough, all the above statements are found in Crossan's *The Birth of Christianity*, the book that followed his work on the historical Jesus. They express his theological presuppositions, which appear to have grown out of his research of the historical Jesus. They are theological and not scientific from an epistemological point of view. Historians, therefore, may wish to question Crossan's rejection of *his defined* "two Jesuses." His definition supports his theological views, but a two-Jesuses theory can be defined differently, one belonging to the category of history, the other to the category of faith, language, and literature. Let me explain.

The *historical Jesus* is dead; his body was in all likelihood thrown into a lime pit, or left exposed for crows and dogs to eat. That Jesus' life came to an end that horrible Friday afternoon in April, AD 27 or 28. That Jesus

21. Ibid., p. xxi.
22. Ibid., p. xxx.
23. Ibid.

will never live again. The *risen Jesus,* on the other hand, is a Jesus of faith. The Son of Man, Messiah, and Son of God Jesus is clearly an extension of the historical Jesus' life and its meaning for his first followers. But this is a Jesus of interpretation, of reflection and typology, based on studying the *Septuagint,* not the physical Jesus of Galilee who taught them his aphorisms and parables, or cast out demons in their midst. They may well have "experienced" his "presence" with them and for them, but *categorically,* this was a different Jesus than the Jesus of spirit and flesh. We have, then, one Jesus, one historical life, which was experienced in two *categorically* different ways. During his life, he was experienced, remembered, and known as one who truly lived and truly died. After his death, this same Jesus was interpreted, experienced, and hallowed as the Suffering Servant and embodiment of God, or, at least, the embodiment of God's wisdom and righteousness. That first Jesus belongs to the category of history; the second to the category of faith, myth, and metaphor—true, not two Jesuses, but two *categorically* different ways of relating to the historical Jesus. This distinction, however, has carried us into new material and beyond our present chapter. We will return to the above discussion later. But for now, how does Crossan picture the Jesus of history, based on his monumental, thorough, and detailed study?

Crossan concludes that Jesus must be seen against a background of "inclusive Judaism," but not the type representative of an "elite, literary, and philosophical synthesis of a Philo of Alexandria." His was rather a "peasant, oral, and popular philosophical praxis of what might be termed . . . a Jewish Cynicism."[24] Jesus' emphasis fell on practice and life-style, not simply theory. Jesus' praxis was opposed to the cultural Mediterranean civilization of his day that was based on honor, shame, patronage, and clientage. He looked, dressed, ate, and lived differently. He included groups, genders, and classes relegated to the absolute social and political margins by his own culture's rules. Against a political climate noted for its share of bandits, revolutionaries, messianic claimants, and apocalyptical and millennial prophets, Jesus' modus of operation was closer to that of a nonviolent protester's. His work united "two disparate elements: healer and Cynic, magic and meal." Hence, Jesus may be viewed as "a peasant Jewish Cynic."[25] His home setting was the area about Sepphoris, but his activity carried him to the farms and villages of Lower Galilee. "His strategy . . . was the combination of free healing and common eating, a religious and economic egalitarianism that negated alike and at once the hierarchical

---

24. John D. Crossan, *The Historical Jesus,* San Francisco, 1991, p. 421.
25. Ibid.

and patronal normalcies of Jewish religion and Roman power." He kept on the move, never settling down. He did not claim to be a broker or mediator between himself and man or between himself and God. His use of parable and miracle, healing and eating, was "calculated to force individuals into unmediated physical and spiritual contact with God and unmediated physical and spiritual contact with one another." His was a "brokerless kingdom of God."[26] After all, the kingdom of God is within you; it has come near; it is present now (Q, Luke 17:20–21, *Gospel of Thomas* 113; *The Five Gospels*).

For Crossan, Jesus' ministry was one of "open commensality," meaning no one was excluded; all were welcomed alike. His was a mission that conjoined "magic and meal, miracle and table, compassion and commensality."[27] All three of these themes are found in sufficient, independent (Gospel) sources to guarantee the standard of multiple attestation (central to Crossan's methodology as well as the Jesus Seminar's). It is not surprising, therefore, that these same themes appear throughout Paul's letters, in the Acts of the Apostles, in Q, and in the *Didache* as well. Nor is it surprising that these themes underlie the transition from the historical Jesus to the Jesus of faith, whose "presence" in the breaking of the bread empowers his followers to become incarnations of his spirit, dedicated to his and their on-going mission. If the "risen Jesus" is anywhere, there he is!

Crossan doubts that the passion narratives have anything to do with the historical Jesus' last meal, arrest, trial, execution, or resurrection. He dubs this tradition the "historicizing of prophecy." As the Church reflected on Jesus' execution, passages in Isaiah, Malachi, and the Psalms provided insight that turned Jesus' death into a new vision of his living and embodied purpose and presence among his followers.

This review hardly scratches the surface of Crossan's lengthy and tightly argued case for the historical Jesus as "a peasant Jewish Cynic," but it certainly illumines the contemporary quest for a Jesus who fits the political, cultural, and religious parameters of his time, and that seeks to free Jesus studies from, what some have called, "the tyranny of dogma."

Geza Vermes

Vermes, Professor Emeritus of Jewish Studies at Oxford, adopts an approach much like Crossan's and others,' insofar as he seeks to strip as many

---

26. Ibid., p. 422.
27. Ibid., p. 332.

creedal and mythical elements from the Gospel narratives as possible, while relying on double attestation, ancient historical sources, and the principle of coherence to flesh out the authentic Jesus and his words.

For Vermes, we know practically nothing about Jesus' historical background. At best, he was from Nazareth and followed his father Joseph's trade as a *tekton*. His mother was Maria (in Hebrew). He had four brothers and several sisters, but, for Jesus, his real family consisted in those who shared his belief in the word of God and who sought to do God's will. As a result, Jesus was not on good terms with his family and encountered resistance from his relatives and neighbors. He was not fond of urban life and preferred the Galilean countryside. Early on, he became attracted to John the Baptist's movement and considered him his source of inspiration.

His public activity was threefold: he cured the sick, freed the demon possessed, and preached repentance, or Jewish *teshuvah* (turning), in light of the nearness of the coming Kingdom. His charismatic style and penchant for dramatic speech and hyperbole amazed his people, which is why they hailed him as one who spoke with "authority." His main concern was for Jews, though he occasionally spoke to and about Gentiles. His message was devoid of political rhetoric. He saw himself as something of "a representative of God, a latter-day prophet."[28] He devoted himself to God, God's Torah, and Kingdom. He embraced the life-style of a mendicant, eschewed wealth, and disliked honorific titles. He never called himself "Messiah" or "Son of God."

If anything, Jesus perceived himself as a champion of the poor, despised, disabled, and weak. He admired repentant tax-collectors and prostitutes. He loved children and held them up as models of belief in parental good will. He could be both convivial and enjoy a feast, as well as austere. He loved to use exaggeration and imagery in his speech. While being kind and compassionate, he could also display impatience with sloth and compromise. He was not necessarily the "meek and mild figure of pious Christian imagination."[29]

Jesus' tragic death was the result of his prophetic zeal. He did not anticipate it, nor expect it that last week of his life. Since the Jewish authorities resented his activities and feared that his presence in Jerusalem might start a rebellion, they appealed to Pilate to silence him. Pilate did not hesitate to execute this so-called "king of the Jews."

Vermes has a high regard for Jesus' message, motivation, and commitment to serve God. For Jesus, his trust in God was paramount, and he

---

28. Vermes, *The Authentic Gospel of Jesus*, London, Penguin Books, 2003, p. 401.
29. Ibid., p. 404.

sought and expected the same trust and belief in God from others. To do God's will was his highest purpose.

For Further Reflection

It would be insane to attempt a consensus of the above views, as if a working, definitive assessment of the historical Jesus could be given. As a generalist, whose field is actually Calvin Studies, but whose career involved teaching courses in philosophy, religion, and Bible, my own view of the historical Jesus wavers somewhere between Bornkamm's and the Borg-Crossan-Vermes reconstruction. I think it is impossible *totally* to separate the historical Jesus from the narratives that preserve the Church's understanding of him. We are forced to see Jesus as a human being whose preservation in texts hinges on his followers' interpretations of him. We do not have to accept their interpretations or texts as the final word, though we cannot resolve the matter without them. In the case of John and Paul, Jesus is viewed as the incarnated presence of the mystery of God, as well as being the world's redeemer. In accordance with the Synoptic Evangelists, Jesus is seen as the flesh-and-blood, long-awaited Messiah and Messianic Suffering Servant of Isaiah 53. These interpretations emerged, following Jesus' death, between the years of his execution and Paul's first letters (i.e. from AD 28–50). Furthermore, I believe that the current methodology of focusing almost entirely on Jesus' sayings, whether in Q or the *Gospel of Thomas*, skews the "quest," whether we like the term or not. Why? Because a radical, peasant, Jewish Cynic, whose life-style and philosophy addressed primarily social, class, and political wounds, without awakening his hearers' longings for the Eternal, would not have engendered a Way that cherished him as a symbol of wholeness, goodness, and compassion—which is why the memory of his "sayings" survived. Was he political? Yes. But he was far more! He was a manifestation of the mystery that redeems and heals life. Whether that came from within himself, or from God, I do not know. I wager that it was this sense of redemptive healing and hope that his words and presence evoked that captivated his hearers, or "astonished" them in Bornkamm's view, that appealed to his followers and led to Christianity as we know it. This is the historical Jesus, who still comes to us as "One Unknown," whose encounter with us can still transform lives and speak to that inner restlessness, to those hidden uncertainties and inner demons that we all possess and fear will be exposed.

2

Other Historical Figures and Movements and Their Impact on Mankind

The Historical Buddha

AT ONCE, the life of the Buddha springs to mind. Few historical figures, apart from Jesus of Nazareth, have inspired human lives as profoundly as the Nepalese Prince, known as Siddhartha Gautama, or Siddhatta Gotama in his native Pali language. From the moment he left home in search of the riddle of life's mystery, to his influence on the current Dali Lama, the Buddha's impact on one's self-understanding, relationship to others, and the universe, has been immeasurable. He stands beside the Jesus of history as one of its greatest fulcrums of change.

Nonetheless, a study of his life confronts researchers with a list of obstacles similar to those that Jesus research encounters. How does one separate the historical man from the ancient texts that preserve his words, deeds, and story? They, too, are the consequence of faith and have their own history of textual problems. Many were not set to writing until one hundred years following his death. The *Tripitaka*, or scriptures of Buddhism, contain a fascinating compendium of texts and commentaries that span several hundred years in the making. It would be like adding to the New Testament the first three hundred years of the works of the early Christian Fathers. As the Buddhist scholar Sangharakshita has warned, past methodological approaches have done more to obscure the Buddha than to promote enlightenment. He identifies three such approaches. The first, he labels as *sectarian*, which speaks for itself; the second as *fundamentalist*, which is the search for what the Buddha "really" said; and the third as *encyclopedic*, which diverts attention from the goal of experiencing Enlightenment. Instead, it substitutes information about the Buddha in place of the Enlightenment experience.[1] In spite of all this, what can be said about the historical Buddha?

Drawing upon Sangharakshita's own "reconstruction," the future Buddha (the one who woke up and saw things as they are) was born near Kapilavastu, Nepal around 563 BC, into a proud and independent clan: the Sakyas. Their republic was prosperous and lay at the feet of the Himalayan range. Shortly after Siddhartha's birth, his mother died, leaving him to be reared by a maternal aunt, Mahaprajapati. His education consisted in learning the manly arts of the day, plus the ethics and traditions central to his clan. No evidence exists to support that he could read or write. While a child, he did experience a "mystical" event of purity, peace, and intense bliss. He would never forget this. He enjoyed all the luxuries that his father, Suddhodana, could afford, who placed three palaces at his son's disposal: one for the summer, one for winter, and one for the rainy season. The youth rarely left the confines of his palaces and their pools of lotus blossoms that adorned each residence. He was married and had a son. But he was unhappy. The noble-born young prince was tormented by the problem of existence, obsessed with the human condition that was subject to birth, old age, disease, and death. In accordance with the time-honored traditions of his era, he donned a mendicant's robe and left home. He studied under several renowned Hindu sages of the time, whose doctrines were based on Upanishadic wisdom. He apparently experienced the states of consciousness that these sages espoused, but their states of "superconsciousness" only deepened his depression and quickened his search for the truth. Once more he journeyed on, settling down in a location called Uruvela. For the next six years he practiced the most austere self-mortification regimen imaginable. No enlightenment, however, accompanied his deprivations. Thus he abandoned them and engaged in a year of indulgence. His five closest friends, who had been drawn to him across the past six years, left him in disgust. Undeterred by their departure, Siddhartha sat in a knot of grass beneath a *peepul* tree (or fig tree), and resolved that he would not stir until he had experienced supreme enlightenment. Passing through several watches, he transcended the mental states that hold one back, recollected his former births (or past reincarnations), envisioned in his mind the process by means of which good and bad karmic activity impacts lives, and letting go of prejudices for or against existence, as well as all forms of speculation, he "realized the ineffable Truth and saw in its light the contingent and conditioned character of all mundane things whatsoever."[2]

1. Sangharakshita, *The Three Jewels*, Garden City, 1970, pp. 44–46.
2. Ibid., p. 14.

Other Historical Figures and Movements and Their Impact on Mankind

It took several weeks for the now "awakened one" to assimilate his experience. Once he did, he resolved to share it out of a sense of compassion for the rest of humankind. He sought and found his five former friends. They were residing in the Deer Park near Benares, and, although they were reluctant at first to embrace his experience, ultimately they accepted his new ideas. While there in the Park, he shared with his friends his Middle Way, the Four Noble Truths, and the Noble Eightfold Path. Succinctly put, the Middle Way avoids the extremes of mortification and indulgence; the Four Noble Truths are: 1) life is filled with suffering, 2) suffering is caused by craving, 3) extinguishing craving should eliminate suffering, 4) which will occur if the Eightfold Path is followed.

Converts gathered about the Buddha; the idea of the sangha, or order, or community, came into being. Soon the three refuges fell into place: "I take refuge in the Buddha, refuge in the Dharma, and refuge in the order." By the time Siddhartha's group made it to Rajagara, many arahants (bhikkhus, or monks) had joined the order, along with King Bimbisara, who gave the order one of his royal parks: the Bamboo Grove. Gradually, Siddhartha's influence became ubiquitous. Wealthy and princely classes welcomed his presence and ideas. His wanderings brought him into contact with many classes: ascetics, peasants, artisans, shop-keepers, even robbers, along with the young and the old, the rich and the poor, women, outcasts, and untouchables. Sangharakshita describes him as approachable, fearless, energetic, gracious, and accepting of all. The newly Awakened One denounced the then current Hindu practice of class distinctions with its disdain for untouchables. All were capable of experiencing enlightenment. His father, cousins, and own son, Rahula, became his followers. Toward the end of his life, his cousin, Devadatta, sought to betray him and have the Buddha assassinated, but Devadatta's attempt failed. His other cousin, Ananda, became his most beloved disciple.

The Buddha fell ill during a rainy season retreat near the village of Beluva. Knowing that he was dying, he continued to teach, encouraging his followers to embrace the dharma (his teachings) and become lights unto themselves. Only they could devote themselves to their own spiritual growth. No one else could do that for them. He refused to name a successor. The Buddha rallied long enough to make it to the village of Kusinara. His last meal consisted of mushrooms, which caused him great discomfort. His lasts words were: "Behold now, brethren, I exhort you, saying, 'Impermanent are all component things. With mindfulness strive on.'"[3] He was 80 years old when he died in the year 483 BC, as far as his death date can be determined.

From a narrative perspective, dissimilarities between himself and Jesus loom obvious. The Buddha was born of royalty, enjoyed luxury, married, had a son, practiced a dietary regimen that would have brought smiles to Jesus' face, moved freely among the rich and powerful, the religious and autocratic, managed to avoid alienating the ruling classes, was a recipient of generous benefactors, and had a place to "lay his head" in the rainy seasons. Above all, he lived, like Socrates, to a ripe old age and died in the company of his beloved friends. He never experienced their abandonment, except at the start. A relaxed sense of tranquility seems to guard his coming and going, although he had his moments of controversy and confrontation. He died from an illness, not on a cross as a criminal. His body was burned and his ashes committed to urns, which stupas across Asia boast of housing. He slipped into the memory of a nation, a culture that came to revere him and quarreled over his beingness and dharma. The Mahayana School elevated him to the status of a Boddhisattva, an enlightened one, who postpones his entrance into nirvana, until all sentient creatures are enlightened themselves. The Theravada School preserved his memory as a man, like any other man, who came to enlightenment on his own, and whose pathway demands the same of his followers.

Nonetheless, similarities of personal integrity abound. Their sayings, especially, create a fascinating bond between the two. This is true in spite of their philosophical differences. The Buddha perceives all sentient entities as interrelated and continuations of past karmic action and influencers of future beings and actions. As "selves," individuals are more than conscious egos in isolation from everything else. In other words, a person is always more than the "conditioned states" that comprise one's physiology or consciousness. With Jesus he taught that to lose the self is to gain the self at its truest level. The Buddha also emphasized an enlightenment of "seeing things as they are," of not being deceived about a self-conscious future life, or deluded about self-responsibility. You are your own master. You alone can become enlightened for yourself. There are no gods in the universe who are going to save you. It is an illusion to think so. That veil of assumption must come down.

Unlike the Buddha, the historical Jesus believed very much in the presence of God, in a personal God, or the Eternal Now, who encounters men and women in personal terms. All lives are lived under his solicitous concern. God's sense of righteousness, his desired kingdom, or "imperial

---

3. Ibid., p. 24.

rule," transcends all class, gender, racial, geographic, political, and religious bounds. Jesus meant to woo God's children toward fairness, justice, and love, not in some distant age to come, but now.

Having said this, the two historical figures addressed many similar problems. Each in his own way was concerned about inclusivity, detachment, finding one's "true" or "higher self," authentic forms of renunciation, seeking a right path, displaying compassion, emphasizing life's brevity or impermanence, encouraging a life of integrity free from disabling vices, pointing the way to a liberation filled with hope and healing, and enjoining a commensality of all (the bhikkhus around their begging bowls; Jesus' disciples about their tables and shared loaves). Equally, they spoke in memorable aphorisms and engaging parables, often referring to numerous common images, such as birds, fish, flowers, mustard seeds, hidden treasure, pearls, tares, and light. All of this may be found in the Buddha's *Dhammapada* and in Jesus' collected sayings in Q, the *Gospel of Thomas*, and in Luke and Matthew. Perhaps a few examples may be cited.

1. *Each saw the self as belonging to a higher order* that alone can set it free and fulfill one's existence. Each disciple must seek, find, and accept this order on one's own. "Whoever seeks to save his life will lose it, and whoever loses his life. . . . will find it" (Luke 17: 33; Q, the *Gospel of Thomas*). "Even one's self is not one's own."[4]

2. *Each taught to overcome evil with good*: "Hatreds do not ever cease . . . by hating, but by not hating: this is an eternal truth"; "overcome evil by good."[5] "Love your enemies and pray for those who persecute you" (Matt 5:44).

3. *Each taught to examine oneself before faulting others*: "Do not look at the faults of others; . . . observe what you yourself have done and not done."[6] "Why do you see the speck in your neighbor's eye, but do not notice the log in your own eye?" (Luke 6:41; Q, *Thom* 26).

4. *Each knew the way he recommended was not easy*: "Few are the people who reach the Beyond; the others run along this Shore."[7] "For the gate is wide and the road is easy that leads to destruction" (Matt 7:13).

4. T. Cleary, *Dhammapada*, New York, 1995, p. 25.
5. Ibid., pp. 8 and 77.
6. Ibid., p. 21.
7. Ibid., p. 32.

5. *Each understood the brevity of life*: "others do not know we must pass away; but for those who know this, contention thereby ceases."[8] "But God said to him, 'You fool! This very night your life is being demanded of you'" (Luke 12:20).

6. *Each prized the influence an individual can make*: "Good people shine from afar, like the snowy mountains."[9] "You are the light of the world. A city built on a hill cannot be hid" (Matt 5:14; *Thom* 32).

7. *Each knew that life's corrupting influences are fatal for self and society*. "Just as rust eats away the iron from which it is produced, so do their own deeds lead the overindulgent into a miserable state."[10] "Do not store up for yourselves treasures on earth, where moth and rust consume . . . ; but store up for yourselves treasures in heaven" (Matt 6:19).

Both Jesus and the Buddha were prophetic sages of their time. Both challenged their respective cultures with new perceptions, new depths of self-awareness, new concepts of justice and fairness, and that sense of belonging to *Life* that fulfills the restlessness all human beings experience. They remind the world that human beings are not their own, but belong to each other, and are linked to each other's highest good, now, as well as in the future. No dogma can replace, nor needs to, this profound and simple truth about the human condition, which each man drew from the well of himself in openness to Life's mystery and wonder.

Lao Tzu (604–? BC)

The historical vagaries that surround the life of Lao Tzu are even more challenging than those that frustrate Jesus or Buddhist studies. Many scholars doubt that Lao Tzu existed. His name can mean, simply, "Old boy." Tradition asserts that he was the author of the *Tao Te Ching* and lived in the State of Ch'u in sixth-century China, BC. According to D. C. Lau, this tradition is located in the *Records of the Historian* and was written at the beginning of the first century BC by Ssu-ma Ch'ien.[11] Ch'ien's history purports that Lao Tzu was a native of a hamlet in the Li village of Hu Hsien. His family's name was Li and his first name Erh, though he was also called Tan. He was the curator in charge of the archives in the state of

---

8. Ibid., p. 9.
9. Ibid., p. 98.
10. Ibid., p. 81.
11. D. C. Lau, *Lao Tzu: Tao Te Ching*, Baltimore, 1963, p. 8.

Chou. Confucius (551–479 BC) is reported to have journeyed to Chou to be instructed by Lao Tzu on the subject of "rites." Ch'ien's work records the infamous rebuff Confucius received. Said Lao Tzu:

> "What you are talking about concerns merely the words left by people who have rotted along with their bones. . . . Rid yourself of your arrogance and your lustfulness, your ingratiating manners and your excessive ambition. These are all detrimental to your person. This is all I have to say to you."[12]

Supposedly, Confucius confided to his disciples, who were waiting outside: "the dragon's ascent into heaven on the wind and the clouds is something which is beyond my knowledge. Today I have seen Lao Tzu who is perhaps like a dragon."

Ch'ien's history attributes the *Tao Te Ching* to Lao Tzu and maintains that he cultivated its way and virtue in his own life, aiming at "self-effacement." He remained in Chou until he witnessed the province's decline, upon which he departed. As he reached the Pass, its keeper purportedly requested: "Could you write a book for my sake?" Lao Tzu complied, thus creating a volume in two parts, in which he explained "the way and its virtue," which is what *Tao Te Ching* means. Ch'ien describes Lao Tzu as "a gentleman who lived in retirement" and reached a venerable age of over a hundred. He had at least one son who served as an army general in the state of Wie and other notable grand- and great-grandsons whose own descendants played significant roles in Chinese life. Particularly insightful, is Ch'ien's preservation of Lao Tzu's contemporaries' assessments: "Li Erh 'does nothing and the people are transformed of their own accord'; 'remains limpid and still and the people are rectified of themselves.'"[13]

Lau acknowledges that very little is known about Lao Tzu, or, indeed, can be. He suggests that Lao Tzu "was not a historical personage at all."[14] During Confucius's time, there were numerous hermits and collections of hermitic sayings and literature. These works were anthologies of ancient as well as current wisdom. They were the works of editors more than compositions by specific authors. Whatever the case, the philosophy of the *Tao Te Ching* came to represent a masterpiece of wisdom belonging to China's Golden Age.

What is remarkable is that the subtle philosophy that ripples through it is not dissimilar to aspects of the historical Jesus' own perceptions and

12. Ibid.
13. Ibid., p. 10.
14. Ibid., p. 11.

attitudes. For Jesus, the kingdom of God is present, like the Tao, all around. "Ask and it will be given you; seek and you will find, knock and it will be opened unto you" (Q, the *Gospel of Thomas*, Matt). Jesus does not give that kingdom another name. It requires no other name. "Seek first God's kingdom and his righteousness and" (food, clothing, drink) "will be given you as well" (Matt 6:33). Nor does the kingdom have to be taken by storm. "But when you pray, go into your room and shut the door and pray to your Father who is in secret; and your Father who sees in secret will reward you" (Matt 6:6).

Likewise, for Lao Tzu, the Tao requires no other name. What other name needs be given to fathom the mystery of life that is manifest in the secret, other than that nameless name and its invitation to human openness?

> The way that can be spoken of
> Is not the constant way.

Lau argues that the nameless is not so bad a name for that elusive power that has brought the world into existence and that sustains it. It precedes the universe and permeates the universe and is there for all to experience. "It" is not even a name either. For the Taoist, there is nothing shocking about acknowledging that the Tao is unknowable. "There is no reason for us to assume that the totally real is totally knowable, particularly when the real is thought of as transcendent."[15] Yet, living in accordance with the Tao issues in wholeness for both individuals and states.

> When the way prevails in the empire,
> Fleet-footed horses are relegated to plowing the fields;
> When the way does not prevail in the empire,
> War horses breed on the border.[16]

Jesus' own view of Nature embraced nuances of the Taoist natural order. "Behold, the lilies of the field, how they grow; they neither toil nor spin, yet I tell you, even Solomon in all his glory was not clothed like one of these. But if God so clothes the grass of the field, which is alive today and tomorrow is thrown into the oven, will he not much more clothe you—you of little faith" (Matt 6:28–30), Q, the *Gospel of Thomas*)? Like Lao Tzu, Jesus also extended his thoughts to politics. "Render unto Caesar the things that are Caesar's and unto to God the things that are God's" (Matt 22:21, *Thom* 100).

15. Ibid., p. 20.
16. Ibid., p. 107.

That a generation of Christians, living somewhere in Asia Minor toward the middle of the second century AD thought of Jesus as an embodiment of their own culture's Tao comes as no surprise. Their term was Logos. "In the beginning was the Logos, and the Logos was with God, and the Logos was God" (John 1:1). They saw him as the Way. "I am the way and the truth and the life" (John 14:6). At this point, the historical Jesus had become the transparent symbol of God, just as the Tao remained the transparent mystery of the East. Both are known in the ego's encounter with that nameless reality that underlies, permeates, and nudges the essence of our human inquisitiveness. This reality is inescapable, as the world's spiritual teachers witness. At the very least, Jesus and Lao Tzu experienced this reality.

Black Elk

The American continent is no stranger to historical persons who have also experienced the Tao, Logos, or Eternal Now. The Oglala Sioux holy man, Black Elk, has spurred admiration of his own spiritual insight and depth of sacred wisdom. Now revered as a phenomenal conduit of sacred dreams and visions, his story, as preserved in John Neihardt's *Black Elk Speaks*, has spoken to thousands of secular-minded men and women and quickened their own hunger for inner wholeness and life. The sheer magic of Black Elk's humility, visions, and imaginative recollection of his people's life on the Plains, has endeared him to an entire generation of new seekers. Neihardt's book presents Black Elk as historically and as accurately as the author knew how. In his "Preface," Neihardt's concern to portray the holy man just as he was comes through with haunting clarity. Neihardt felt the Oglala's "supernormal powers," he tells us, from the moment he met him. Sitting on the ground in front of his log cabin, Black Elk perceived the reason why Neihardt had come, and, speaking through an interpreter, assured him: "I can feel in this man beside me the strong desire to know the things of the Other World. He has been sent to learn what I know, and I will teach him."[17] From that instant on, the reader is caught up in a perception of reality that inspires, informs, and illumines one's heart and mind. What it means to live and suffer, to dream and die, to gain and lose, to be human and part of the earth and sky, enfolds the seeker in a spiritual balm that renews the mind and soul.

When Neihardt first met Black Elk, the latter was living within the confines of the Pine Ridge Indian Reservation in South Dakota. It was in

---

17. Neihardt, *Black Elk Speaks*, Lincoln, Nebraska, p. xxvii.

August of 1930 and Neihardt had come to interview the old Indian about the dance movements of the 1880s and 90s. His visits quickly took on a new dimension: the spiritual view of the Plains Indians and their transcendent truths. During the process, Neihardt not only learned the details of Black Elk's life, but he learned about the universal symbols that nurtured the Plains People. These he found to be as profound and uplifting as the time-accepted principles basic to Christianity and Buddhism.

Black Elk was born in December of 1863 on the Little Powder River in present-day Wyoming. He was a second cousin of Crazy Horse. His father, also named Black Elk, had been wounded at the Fetterman Massacre in 1866 and limped until his death in 1890. As a child, Black Elk grew up in the knowledge that the Wasichu (white men) were invading his country and filling it with lies and greed. His band, under the leadership of Red Cloud and Crazy Horse, engaged the Whites in several skirmishes, which succeeded momentarily in keeping the Whites at bay. For the excitable boy, it was a time of great joy, of nomadic wanderings in search of bison, a time of learning the traditional ways of the Plains Indians.

At the age of nine, he experienced a vision (whether a dream, a fever-driven hallucination, or out-of-body experience no one can tell) that would change his life. From time to time he kept hearing voices, mainly when he was alone. They were the voices of his "Grandfathers." Like the boy Samuel's experience of old (1 Sam 3:4), they would call to him. "Hurry, come!" But he hadn't the faintest notion what to make of them. During a debilitating illness (a paralysis of his legs), as he stepped outside his teepee, a small, white cloud swept down and bore him away to the realm of the Six Great Grandfathers. Each of the Grandfathers spoke in turn, granting the boy special gifts. They represented the cardinal points of the compass and zenith and nadir, or sky and earth. Their gifts included the powers to make alive and destroy, to heal and make well, to bring peace and save his people. All six figures warn him of the desolation to come. All six embolden him with courage. He is shown the "red road" as well as the "black," the former good, the latter filled with sorrow and evil. His people are to choose the "red." Symbols of apocalyptic horses, trees, the peace pipe, eagle, birds, lightning, flames, the rising star, the rainbow, the *axis mundi* of the "tall rock mountain at the center," and above all, the sacred circle, accompany his prolonged vision. Like Isaiah and Daniel in their time, he has been called to be a holy man, a prophet of sorts, to save his people. At last, the cloud descends, and Black Elk returns to his family and wakes up. His heart is heavy with sadness, for what he knows he can't communicate but must keep to himself.

Black Elk took part in the "rubbing out" of Custer and escaped to Canada with Sitting Bull's group. He went on to star in Buffalo Bill's famous Road Shows, even touring Europe with the wily frontiersman. He returned home, only to witness the tragedy of Wounded Knee. His retelling of the story plunges the reader into one of the greatest heartbreaks recorded in American history. Black Elk told Neihardt that the scene of the dead and the dying, heaped in a pile of frozen blood and snow, made him wish that he had died that day.

We do not know if Jesus saw visions. Paul apparently did. The historical Jesus did seek solitude. Solitude provides ground for self-reflection, meditation, for the psychosphere's plunge into one's depth and the depths of Being. There is no substitute for self-examination and the opportunity to listen to the voice of the subconscious, or Jung's realm of the unconscious. It houses both the matrix and vortex of past and future visions. When Jesus entered into the "secret place" to pray, we must conclude that either the voice of Transcendence spoke to him, or that he listened in silence to the "Grandfathers" within himself. The same happened to Siddhartha under his tree, and Mohammed in his cave at Mt. Sira.

Tradition added to Q and to Mark's narratives the words: "Let him who has ears to ear, hear what the Spirit is saying." It is this voice of the Spirit, I believe, that empowered Jesus, that informed him, and inspired him to speak and act with the courage he did. He drew it from within himself, from his ancient heritage, and from the Ground of Being that forced him to seek his own Father. He remodeled all of it as a message for his time. He became a conduit of the holy, in whom his people felt the presence of God, who reached out to them through Jesus' hands to embrace and heal them. Through his words they heard the Word, the living word of God. Just to touch the hem of his garment filled them with hope and joy. Just as Neihardt sensed the presence of a "holy other" in the seated figure of Black Elk, so Jesus' era experienced the same in his presence.

Kabbalah

Daniel Matt, a specialist in Jewish Studies and translator of the *Zohar*, explains that Kabbalah has to do with Jewish tradition and spontaneous wisdom. It is a mystical movement drawing upon the Hebrew Bible, rabbinic literature, and, especially, the teachings of the *Zohar*. In Kabbalah, the rabbanic idea of *shekinah* (see Isa 6:3), the glory or presence of God, symbolizes the immanence of God, but in feminine terms. This feminine side of the Divine has gone out from God and longs for reunification with the masculine half of God, represented by the Torah and Talmud.[18]

At some point in Palestine, between the third and sixth centuries, a text entitled *Sefer Yetserah* (The Book of Creation), appeared, in which its author or authors created the concept of the ten *sefirot*. The *sefirot* are numerical qualities, something like Pythagorean principles, through which the universe comes into existence. By the twelfth century, in the region of Provence, these *sefirot* became viewed as divine powers, or divine attributes, representing "stages of God's inner life," or "aspects of the divine personality."

In the late thirteenth century, a Jewish mystic by the name of Moses de León added to this tradition by composing his monumental work, *Sefer ha-Zohar* (The Book of Radiance). This "mystical novel" became a masterpiece of esoteric and arcane wisdom. His work treated the Torah as a biography of God's feelings, responses, and activities and explained something of the inner activity of God's feminine and masculine sides.

Of supreme importance, is de León's interpretation of Genesis, chapter 1. Herein he explores the phenomenon of how the *sefirot* emanated from the Infinite mystery of God, or *Ein Sof*. The latter represents the high transcendence of God. Out of *Ein Sof* emanated the chain of ten *sefirot*.

---

18. See Daniel Matt, *The Essential Kabbalah: the Heart of Jewish Mysticism*, Castle Books, New Jersey, 1997, p. 1. All further quotes in this section are from this book.

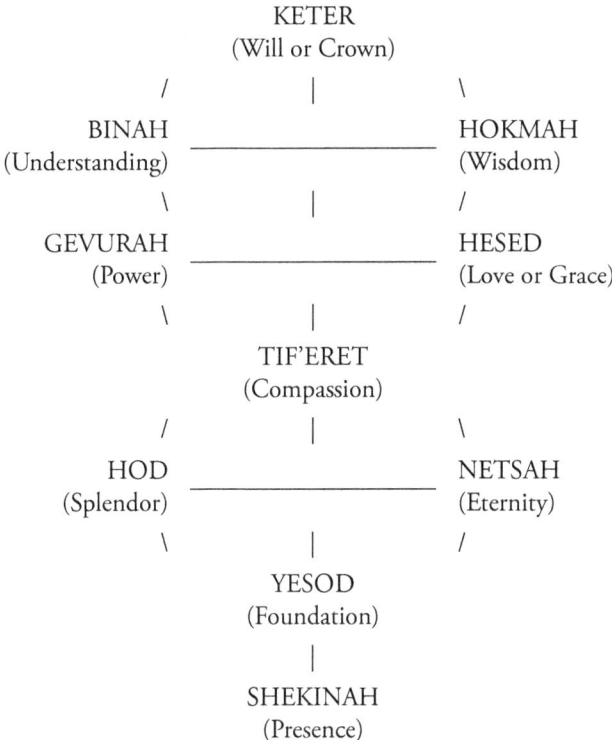

Keter, hokmah, and *binah* represent the divine head of the mystical body of God. *Binah* gives birth to *hesed* and *gevurah,* symbolizing the right and left arms of God. Both Love and Power, or Grace and Judgment, are essential for creating *tif'eret,* or Compassion, also known as the Blessed Holy One. Eternity and Splendor form the right and left legs of God, respectively. The right side of the torso is viewed as feminine and the left as masculine. *Yesod* represents the procreative forces at work in the universe and is also known as *tsaddiq,* the Righteous One. The Righteous One becomes the channel through which *shekinah* ascends toward reunification with God. Such a movement also constitutes the focal point of kabbalism's religious life: reuniting *shekinah* with *tif'eret.* This aim will also play a vital role in the religious hopes and activities of the Hasidic movement.

What all this seems to suggest for Kabbalah is that the essence of divinity, the primordial *Ein Sof,* exists in everything. Nothing that exists enjoys its beingness apart from *Ein Sof.* As Matt explains *Ein Sof*:

> God is everything that exists, though everything that exists is not God. It is present in everything and everything comes into being from it. Nothing is devoid of its divinity. Everything is within it; it is within everything and outside of everything. There is nothing but it.[19]

At first glance, this phenomenon may appear pantheistic. But one must remember that the six days of creation are all pronounced "good," and all six are the product of Elohim's word, God's *dabar*, speech, or thought propelled into action. If not taken literally, this kabbalistic analysis of creation is similar to Augustine's position that everything that God created he created good. Thus nothing can exist that is not, of itself, "good," the embodiment of God's noetic ideal.

To interpret the post-Easter Christ as the manifestation of God, the hidden *Ein Sof*, or the very logos of God become flesh, is theologically akin to the medieval Jewish view of *shekinah's* longing for reunion with her Ground of Being—God, only in reverse, that is, in Christianity the movement is from above to below. In Kabbalah, the original Neo-Platonic descent of the *sefirot* provides a way for a human *ascent* through the mystical chain of being, which promises redemption and human renewal. This theology from below to above, however, is balanced in Christianity in the image of the Cross. For in the Cross, the upper and lower are reunited by God's initiative, by God's *descent*, not by mankind's ascent. In the Cross, God fulfills both his righteous power (*gevurah*) through means of God's grace (*hesed* love). As a result, compassion (*tif'eret*) triumphs for mankind's salvation. Harmony and righteousness reunite in the "new being" of man.

Finally, of central significance to kabbalism is the idea of "divine sparks," or "divine shards," introduced about 1572 by Isaac Luria. In Luria's mind, the process of emanation began when *Ein Sof* withdrew from creation, creating a vacuum, pierced by divine light. The raw material or vessels of creation could not contain this brilliant light; they burst, and the light's sparks fell into the shards of material existence. Thus all existing things contain a spark of the divine, which longs to return to God.[20]

Hasidism

Perhaps no contemporary movement of the twentieth century captured the imagination of mankind's spiritual aspirations as profoundly as Martin

19. Ibid., p. 24.
20. Ibid, p. 15.

Buber's commentaries on the Hasidic movement. Buber recognized that many Hasidic communities had emerged across the Jewish landscape and had passed on, but the movement that was inspired by Israel ben Elizer, or the Baal-Shem of the eighteenth century, was an exception. Buber's *Hasidism and Modern Man* and his two-volume work: *Tales of the Hasidim*, opened the world to the movement's magical and mystical piety as few other studies have. The importance of Buber's work lies in the fact that it provides remarkable insight into how the Christian community may interpret its own famous rabbi of the past: Jesus of Nazareth. The life of the Baal-Shem Tov, along with his disciple-rabbis, is hailed by Buber for many of the same reasons that early Christianity became enchanted with the Christ. For the focal point of this movement orbits around men whose sayings, parables, stories, deeds, and miracles remind readers of Jesus' own sayings, stories, and deeds and their powerful impact on one's religious imagination. At least in spirit, Christians are linked to the Hasidim as fellow sojourners, all yearning to experience the presence of the Divine, of the *shekinah*, in this life *now*, and not just in a world to come. Drawing upon the kabbalistic concept of the "divine sparks," Buber explains that the teachings of Hasidism can be summed up in a single sentence: "God can be beheld in each thing and reached through each pure deed."[21] Buber goes on to explain that there is nothing in the world that cannot be used of God to reveal Himself to anyone who seeks Him. Since everything contains a divine spark, anyone at anytime can "uncover and redeem" this spark to experience the presence and peace of God in one's life. By serving God with one's whole life, in all the simple and everyday affairs of life, one finds divine meaning. In so doing, one overcomes the separation between time and eternity, the sacred and the profane, the mundane and the holy. By affirming oneself and the world, and by consecrating both to God, one transforms oneself and the world. This makes every human life unique and every human life of infinite value. This Hasidic form of "letting God in to one's life," as Buber calls it, is identical spiritually to the Christian ideal of "incarnating" the Spirit of Christ in one's life and thought.

Buber's *Tales of the Hasidim* preserves hundreds of stories and legends ascribed to the great rabbis. Two in particular stand out as relevant to this chapter.

The story alluded to as "The Fiftieth Gate" and associated with Rabbi Barukh's school is especially noteworthy. One of the rabbi's disciples had inquired about God's nature and had actually penetrated the subject to the point that doubts and uncertainties finally overwhelmed him. When

---

21. *Hasidism and Modern Man*, Harper Torchbooks, New York, 1958, p. 49.

the rabbi noticed the young scholar's absence from his classroom, he journeyed to his home, slipped unnoticed into his room, and surprised the youth. "I know what is troubling you. You have passed through the fifty gates of reason. Each time you think you have discovered the answer a gate opens, only to confront you with another question. On and on this has gone, until you have forced open the fiftieth gate. There you stare at a question whose answer no one has ever found. If one knew it, there would no longer be freedom of choice." "Alas, must I start over?" asked the young man. "If you turn, you will not be going back. Rather, you will be standing beyond the last gate. You will be standing in faith."[22]

The realization that there is no substitute for faith, for that leap of faith which only an individual can make, and which acknowledges the reality of the mystery of God as the ultimate reality one cannot escape, only this leap leads to the fulfillment of one's moral and spiritual essence. It is similar to Jesus' statement about the grain of wheat that must fall to the earth and die before it can bear fruit (John 12:24), or his saying about losing one's life in order to find it (Mark 8:35).

The second story is attributed to Rabbi Bunam, who used to tell potential followers about Rabbi Eisik of Cracow. The rabbi had suffered poverty for years but endured them with unshaken faith. After having a recurring dream for the third time, a dream that directed him to go to Prague and search for a buried treasure under a bridge in front of the royal palace, he did. Upon his arrival, however, he discovered that the bridge was guarded day and night. Not knowing what to do, he returned to the bridge each morning and lingered until evening. Finally the captain of the guard queried him about his coming and going. The rabbi explained his dream. "Goodness," replied the captain, "so you wore out your shoes coming here! I once had a dream instructing me to go to Cracow, where I would find a treasure buried under the stove of a Jew named Eisik. Imagine that! How many Jews must there be in Cracow by that name? Huh!" The rabbi immediately returned home, dug up the treasure where the captain said it would be, and used the money to build a House of Prayer. "Remember this story," Rabbi Bunam urged his would-be disciples. "There is something you cannot find anywhere in the world, not even in a zaddik's house. Nonetheless, there is a place where you can find it."[23] That place is in one's own soul, like the hidden treasure in Jesus' parable. For Hasidic Judaism, that reality makes everyone unique, unrepeatable, a means to God, in the

---

22. *Tales of the Hasidim*, Vol. 1, p. 92.
23. Ibid, Vol. 2. pp. 245–46, with slight alteration.

place where one is. In the case of the Prodigal Son, the returning youth finds it in his Father's love for a life that was once lost but now is found.

The views of Carl Jung are pertinent, too. I address them, specifically from the viewpoint of myth, in the succeeding chapter, but in Jung's judgment, the *shekinah* is an aspect of those ancient and suggestive powers that formed the foundation for all masculine and feminine deities. He refers to the *shekinah*'s separation from God, or *tif'eret,* as the *"coniunctio oppositorum."* For Jung, the self is a union of masculine (animus) and feminine (anima) principles, or of the conscious and unconscious aspects of the soul. Monotheistic religions achieved psychological unity, whereas in polytheistic religions, anima and animus remained separated. In Jung's mind, kabbalistic influences in Judaism have retained much of this separation. This is especially seen in the Sefirot Tree, where God's justice occupies the position opposite God's mercy.[24] To Judaism's credit, however, the concept of Ein Sof in everything prevents any literal, or theological, separation of God's imminence from his transcendence. There is no psychological disunity or dualism in God. Any dualism, or estrangement, exists in us but can be overcome. This is the earnest conviction of every major religion.

Lastly, there are numerous "sayings" by Buber's rabbis that reverberate with the timeless understanding of the ages, the kind of wisdom that many of Jesus' own insights convey. I list, or rephrase, only a few by way of illustration.

> Struggling with the extraneous is man's fate to "the very hour of his death."[25] (Cf. Matt 7:13)
>
> Pride belongs to God alone.[26] (Cf. Matt 6:9)
>
> There is something precious in everyone, found in no one else.[27] (Cf. Matt 7:9–11)
>
> God is beneficent both to the wicked and the good.[28] (Cf. Matt 5:45)
>
> To accept suffering with love is man's highest task.[29] (Cf. Matt 5:39–41)

---

24. See Jung's *Aion*, Princeton University Press, 1959, pp. 58, 61, 125, and 268.
25. *Tales*, Vol.1, p. 90.
26. Ibid., Vol. 1, p. 100.
27. Ibid,, p. 127.
28. Ibid., p. 174.
29. Ibid., p. 238.

The altar of silence is most pleasing to God.[30] (Cf. Matt 6:6)

God remembers what man forgets (i.e. his good deeds) and forgets what man remembers (his sins, if he repents).[31] (Cf. Matt 25:44)

Prayer is the gateway to God.[32] (Cf. Luke 18:1)

"God dwells wherever man lets him in"—Rabbi of Kotzk.[33] (Cf. John 14:20)

"In order to live, a man must give himself to death."[34] (Cf. Mark 8:35)

The above are but a tiny selection of insights that the Hasidic rabbis gleaned from the joy and pain, the hope and sorrow, of being human. In truth, Jesus' own wisdom sayings are cousins of this timeless method of self-examination, in order to fathom the mystery of life, offer an amenable way, and make sense of life's meaning.

---

30. Ibid., Vol. 2. p. 59.
31. Ibid., p. 219.
32. Ibid., p. 263.
33. Ibid., p. 277.
34. Ibid., p. 291.

3

The Elements of Myth

It is very possible that the historical Jesus' earliest appeal grew out of the social and political agenda he preached and practiced. Crossan's explanations and interpretations of Jesus' memorable parables depict Jesus as a champion of the oppressed and displaced. His was an appeal to the forgotten ranks of "nobodies," of the poor pushed into poverty and destitution. Moved by the systemic powers that crushed and penalized 90% of the Empire's population, his was a call of justice for people on the boundary, for the unclean, degraded, and expendable classes that had nowhere to lay their heads. This Jesus dared to employ magic and meals, therapy and table, in his determination to shatter the disparities that subjugated human beings and brutalized their lives. He was outspoken, dynamic, brash, unafraid, and obviously clever and bright. As Ezra Pound once described Jesus: "No mouse of the scrolls was the Son of Man, but a man o' men was he."

This non-sentimental and non-obsequious picture of Jesus may actually be closer to the real historical Jesus than even its adherents suppose. After all, politics and religion were inseparably united in the Roman Mediterranean Basin, just as in many cases they still are today, worldwide.

Equally, his earliest followers viewed him as having founded a Way. We still encounter this Way as late as the end of the first century, in the writings known as the *Didache*. A good third of the book is dedicated to the "two ways" that the "Twelve Apostles" taught, which the writers of the *Didache* attribute to Jesus. One is called "the way of life," and the other is designated as "the way of death." At the same time, the work speaks very piously and passionately of "the Lord," of Jesus "the Father's child," of the "Christ," and of the Trinity "in the name of the Father and of the Son and of the Holy Spirit,"[1] along with references to "Christians" and the "Church." The document goes on to explain the form in which the

---

1. *Didache*, in V. I, *Early Christian Fathers*, Philadelphia, 1953, p. 174.

Lord's Prayer should be prayed, what fast days should be observed, how baptism and the Eucharist should be celebrated, as well as how the Lord's Day should be spent and Church officers elected. The writers, moreover, agonize over how "prophets" should be treated within the commensality of the Church, while praising God for "the knowledge and faith and immortality which" [God] has "revealed through Jesus."[2]

Within a decade of the *Didache's* appearance, the movement toward cultus expanded extensively. Bishop Ignatius of Antioch's letter *To the Trallians* (AD 107) speaks glowingly of "the Passion of Jesus Christ, who is our Hope, since we shall rise in union with him." The Trallians should continue "in Jesus Christ's way, who for our sakes suffered death that you might believe in his death and so escape dying yourselves." They are to avoid suspect teachings that conflict with the traditions they have received concerning the redemptive power of "Jesus Christ's blood." Finally, he offers them a rule of faith, or credo of his own, by which to measure "heretical" views:

> Be deaf . . . to any talk that ignores Jesus Christ, of David's lineage, of Mary; who was really born, ate, drank; was really persecuted under Pontius Pilate; was really crucified and died, ... He was really raised from the dead, for his Father raised him, just as his Father will raise us who believe on him, through Christ Jesus, apart from whom we have no genuine life.[3]

Whatever else one may conclude, it is clear that Jesus' role in the Church had undergone a thoughtful mental migration. He is no longer simply "a peasant Jewish Cynic." Rather he has become the "Christ" and "revealer" of God's truth and grace. All the elements of a cultus are in place. Jesus has become the symbolic and institutionalized image of God's redemptive activity and will for mankind. The creators of the *Didache* anticipate an apocalyptic end to history. The immediacy of Jesus' Kingdom's message is shifted from the present to preparing oneself for "the fiery trial" that awaits all. The historical Jesus has now become the very person whose identity he refused to claim for himself. As for the good Bishop of Syria, Ignatius of Antioch is on his way to Rome to be martyred for his faith. In his letter *To The Romans,* he begs them not to interfere in his coming martyrdom, as he eagerly looks forward to being "emancipated by Jesus Christ; and united to him," and to rising "to freedom."[4] By now, collec-

---

2. Ibid., p. 175.

3. Ignatius, ibid., pp. 98–100.

4. Ibid., p. 104.

tions of Paul's letters have been gathered across the Roman world and the Gospels of Mark, Luke, Matthew, and Thomas are likely in circulation. The post-Easter Christ has eclipsed the pre-Easter Jesus. I say "Christ," because the Jesus of history belongs to the *category of time*, while the Jesus of faith belongs to the *category of interpretation*. We have clearly moved into the realm of faith, and, yes, of myth, but a myth grounded in the reality of a life "really lived" and "really" transparent with the power of God.

How might myth be defined? As a working definition, I propose the following: *Myth is an objectification of a subliminal need to fathom the mystery of the human condition and to experience it to one's fullest.* It involves both understanding life and one's personal subjectivity; is cognitive and existential. What science cannot satisfy, myth does. *Its source is both the self and that Other, which we name the Ineffable or the Unknown.* It comes to us from both without and from within. It involves response as well as self-examination. In this sense, myth encompasses a dual role. From a religious perspective, it involves a two-way flow: 1) Man's encounter of the Ineffable as a transcendent reality greater than himself and 2) as an *ascending and descending phenomenon within himself*. Myths, in the plural, may focus on origins, God, gods, the beyond, and, above all, one's limitations and unseen fate. But myths primarily seek to address the mystery of the self and its encounter with that *Other*, whether an element of the self or a transcendent reality of its own. We are compelled to "consult" and "retell" myths, in order to assuage the sub-conscious mind's proclivity to put one's existence to the question. Myths are intended to address the psyche's gnawing restlessness that pulsates beneath the calm waters of consciousness and to acknowledge the hidden truth it hungers to share. More than explanations, the psyche seeks wholeness and life. The mind seems willing to settle for answers that the soul views with suspicion. Myth offers that "more," those essential "reasons, which reason knows not," as Pascal put it in his *Pensées*, para. 277.

Joseph Campbell made it his career to explore and examine the phenomenon of myth. He reworked his own definition again and again in an effort to comprehend myth's meaning and power. Writes Campbell: "Myths are clues to the spiritual potentialities of the human life." They enable us to recapture "the inner value," the "rapture that is associated with being alive." They teach us that we can turn inward. They "are magnified dreams," and "manifestations in image form of the energies of the body in conflict with each other." That is what constitutes myth. It is a "manifestation in symbolic images, in metaphorical images, of the energies of the organs of the body in conflict with each other."[5] By "organs ... in conflict," Campbell had the Upanishadic and Vedanta philosophy of Hinduism in mind, namely, that the "self" is more than its "gross body" or even "subtle body of mind-stuff." Rather, it is a higher form of consciousness, in which these *pranas*, or energies, are brought into harmony and fulfillment. He was also drawing on Carl Jung's distinction between the conscious and the unconscious. Both require acknowledgement and balance, and myth has been the age-old means by which the unconscious has been able to sublimate what reason insists alone is true. The unconscious knows better. Myth enables the unconscious to express itself and enrich the self's authentic being. What Campbell, however, seemed to suppress is the possible reality of the Other apart from one's self. I say, "seemed," because I am not totally convinced that he did. But the proclivity is there, as it is in Carl Jung, under whom Campbell studied and with whom he edited several works.

For Paul Tillich, myth enables religion to express theological insight, since myths contain theological concepts that can be made explicit. In general, mythic material is universal and thus consequently lacks the concreteness that is essential for redemptive purposes. This explains why Christianity was initially so successful, because it contained in the historical Jesus of Nazareth that concreteness that fulfills myth, i.e., Christ as the redemptive reality, who was prefigured in the ancient myths of the God-Man stories. Furthermore, the "depth of reason" manifests itself in reason. But under the conditions of human existence (finitude, anxiety, guilt), it has become hidden. Thus, "reason in existence expresses itself in myth and cult," until the anticipated final end. Tillich also argues that under the conditions of human existence, the cognitive function of reason has been separated from the aesthetic function of reason. But truth, beauty, and being are essentially one. The cognitive function expresses itself in philosophy and history, while the aesthetic function preserves its insight in poetry and myth. In Tillich's system, "essential reason" unites these two through the power of the Christian faith and its message. In the Christian "mystery" of "revelation," the power of being overcomes the powers of nonbeing. The result is an ecstatic comprehension of one's life, a standing outside oneself that brings redemption and renewal.[6] Still, only language and symbol have the power to transmit this truth, which explains the presence of mythic elements in the conveying of the Christian message.

5. J. Campbell, *Power of Myth*, New York, 1991, pp. 5, 46.
6. Paul Tillich, Vol. I., *Systematic Theology*, Chicago, 1951, pp. 16, 80–81, 91–92, 110.

The Elements of Myth

Long before either Campbell or Tillich, however, began setting their ideas to writing, the psychoanalyst Carl Jung had already concluded why myths are powerful and instructive for psychoanalysis and religion. He expressed his conviction in the form of his theory about archetypes and dream analysis, which had grown out of his work with neurotic patients. His studies and interpretations of dreams and dream content not only enabled him to assist his patients but also provided insight into the myth-making phenomena that surround religion and culture. The extent to which his insight may be applied to the historical Jesus, however, without skewing Jesus' life or subverting it under psychology, remains problematical. Still, Jung's archetypes and their function definitely shed light as to why a post-Easter Jesus, or Christ of myth, continues to speak to contemporary men and women. In the long run, a historical Jesus, shorn from his mythological mold, not only leads to a diminution of the pre-Easter Jesus, but to the eventual marginalizing of a Christ of faith. No contemporary scholar favors defending dogmas that exclude people from one another, or distort history or historical fact. Yet, paradoxically, to view Jesus through the lens of myth addresses the mystery of the human condition and enables mankind to experience life more fully. And this can be done without compromising the reality of the historical Jesus.

Is it possible to champion the post-Easter Jesus as a relevant and valuable religious figure, without diluting what scholars hypothesize is true about the pre-Easter man? If this is not possible, studies of the historical Jesus risk demoralizing any faith in the "risen Christ" and threaten to erode the Christian faith wherever it seeks to thrive. Some may welcome this final demise of the "tyranny of dogma" and the Christianity it has produced. But any Christianity that rises from the ashes of this development risks losing its mystical and ontological appeal, which would result in a Jesus Movement whose primary *telos* is ethical, communal, and political, without the power to speak to the hidden depths of human existence. To that end, Jung's analytical program renders vital service.

Jung distinguishes between the conscious and the unconscious, and within the latter, between the personal unconscious and the collective unconscious. The collective unconscious is universal. It reveals contents and modes of behavior that are generally the same everywhere and experienced in and by all individuals. Jung labels these contents *archetypes* and identifies them, in part, with Plato's *eideos* (ideas). These archetypes refer to the "archaic," or "primordial types," or "universal images that have existed since the remotest times."[7] In the case of myth, they have been handed

---

7. Carl Jung, *Collected Works*, 9, I. Princeton, 1969, p. 5.

down across millennia. They are part of the collective unconscious. We now encounter them in dreams and visions and in the great trove of myths and fairytales, whose origins defy tracing. For this reason, "myths are first and foremost psychic phenomena that reveal the nature of the soul." They are "symbolic expressions of the inner, unconscious drama of the psyche," which itself becomes accessible to reason or consciousness by way of projecting itself onto the events of Nature.[8] These images have enabled humanity to cope with the unseen in human psyches and have provided the world with rich images that promote order and healing. Their loss has been catastrophic in modern time. For they were meant to overpower, attract, and fascinate human existence. Without them, any individual is less than a whole person.

Jung explores the powerful imagery of numerous archetypes, but three in particular are axial: the shadow, the anima, and the wise old man. The failure to relate to these in a healthy manner results in complexes that block wholesome self-development, or individuation. The relevance of these archetypes to the Christian faith is indisputable. That they might have had a subliminal role in shaping Jesus' followers' views is likely, but any cause and effect relationship would be impossible to prove. It can only be suggested. How do the shadow, the anima, and the wise old man function?

They are aspects of the unconscious, the psyche, that part of the larger self whose existence the conscious self doesn't want to acknowledge. This incomplete conscious self, Jung calls the *persona*. It is the mask we wear to hide our face from the world. Plunging into the self is unpleasant, but at least it constitutes a start. In doing so, one confronts the "personal unconscious," that individualized segment of the collective unconscious, which derives from a person's unique biological and genetic structure. Feelings of helplessness surface as one sinks into the hidden self. This meeting of the deeper self is an encounter with one's *shadow*, that "tight passage" and "narrow door, whose painful constriction no one is spared who goes down to the deep well."[9] Water symbolism abounds at this level as a clue to the phenomenon of the inner self and its needs. It plays a paramount role in Taoism, as well as in cleansing rites.

The *anima*, which means soul in Greek, houses equally dark components. It constitutes the heart of psychic life. As an archetype, it sums up all the statements of the unconscious, of the primitive mind, which has been passed down through evolution. It is always the "a priori element" in human "moods, reactions, impulses, and whatever else is spontaneous in

8. Ibid., p. 6.
9. Ibid., p. 21.

psychic life." It surrounds consciousness at all times but can never be fully integrated. Jung identifies it with the female life force. "Either sex is inhabited by the opposite sex up to a point," depending on the number of male genes a zygote receives. In a man, his smaller number of feminine genes remains unconscious but vital to his psychological wholeness. If his anima is not integrated, these genes create complexes that frustrate his process of individuation. In a woman, it is her *animus* that must be integrated.

For Jung, the anima serves as the doorway into religion, for everything the anima touches "becomes numinous." She unites the paradoxes of the beautiful and the good, as well as good and evil. She represents taboo, mystery, magic, and the dangerous. She appears as the Mother Earth, the Queen of Heaven, the *shekinah* of Kabbalah, and the Holy Bride: the Church. Modern man may no longer encounter his anima as the Mother Goddess, but he certainly will in the reality of his misadventures. For that reason, wisdom is also ascribed to the anima. Behind all her cruelties, "there lies something like a hidden purpose which seems to reflect a superior knowledge of life's laws."[10] Often, the most terrifying and unexpected moments reveal deeper meanings to be grasped by the self about oneself and life. From such chaos, one moves toward order. The biblical creation story hinges on such a myth, as the Spirit moves across the *tehom*, or watery depths, and order comes into existence. She is portrayed as the Serpent in the Garden of Eden and the catalyst behind the painful lessons that the Israelites inferred from that story.

Out of the phenomenon of the anima, the *wise old man* emerges. He is the superior master and teacher. He symbolizes "the pre-existent meaning hidden in the chaos of life. He is the father of the soul, and yet the soul . . . is also his virgin mother."[11] He too combines positive and negative elements. He can be both demonic and yet appear as a savior. He is judge and redeemer. His vital qualities are mirrored in the likes of Hermes, Orpheus, and Lucifer, as well as in the figures of the Angel of the Lord, the Suffering Servant, and Son of God.

The shadow, anima, and wise old man are ancient archetypes. They stand as clues to the inner and hidden life of the psyche. And the extent to which they are grasped and integrated into one's conscious life, to that extent wholeness occurs. That is why religion has played such a vital role in the history of mankind's development.

Martin Buber, however, has voiced philosophical and religious objections to Jung's views. For Buber, Jung's thesis is questionable because of

10. Ibid., p. 31.
11. Ibid., p. 35.

the latter's concept of God. In Buber's mind, Jung subsumes God under psychology. God is merely an extension of the human psyche. God does not exist as a reality in himself. For Buber, this constitutes an overstepping of the boundaries of psychology, presuming the non-existence of God outside human minds. Jung can't know this, nor can anyone else. That is why Buber held so tenaciously to his concept of God as *Thou*, a relational phenomenon we encounter, not only in ourselves, but also in nature and others. In Buber's view, Jung's God of total immanence is too simplistic, and statements about him end up being tautological: God is a psychic element that we meet in the psyche.[12]

What now may be said at this juncture? There are elements of myth that are worth identifying. There are many, but at least eight stand out: 1) cognitive, 2) numinal, 3) ontological, 4) regulative, 5) existential, 6) therapeutic, 7) aesthetic, and 8) aretetical. They are interrelated and form a whole the way an octagon is comprised of triangles, radiating out from a central core, to create a unique, geometric shape.

1) The *cognitive* has to do with one's search for understanding, meaning, and knowledge. Mankind wants to know the truth about human existence, its purpose, if there is one, and the origin of the universe. "Why is there something and not nothing?" is the way philosophers have put it across the centuries. People want to know. Thus questions of how, why, when, and where abound in our vocabulary. Aristotle asked similar questions and sought to know the "cause" or *telos* behind things. He was especially fascinated by change and concluded that there are four casual factors that explain growth, development, or change: a formal, material, agent, and final cause. The formal principle represents a thing's essence or unique being; the material the physical building blocks; the agent the immediate preceding factor (parents are the agent cause of their children); the final cause a thing's purpose, *telos*, end, or highest fulfillment. Many myths display this cognitive element or function, the two creation stories of Genesis 1–3 being prime examples. In them, the Priestly Writers' desire for understanding is combined with the older, Yahwistic myth of Adam and Eve, in order to enable Israel's priests to comprehend their ancestors' origins and, above all, their purpose as a people.

The American philosopher John H. Randall, Jr., however, warns not to take this function literally. For Randall, religious language is symbolic, non-cognitive, and non-representative. Religious language neither provides information about the world nor represents any actual entity in it. Science does that, not religion. It is not the purpose of religious language to offer

12. M. Buber, *The Eclipse of God*, New York, 1952, in passim.

descriptions or explanations about the universe. Rather, religious language has to do with a kind of "know-how," a *savoir-faire*, if you please. It helps mankind "unify" his experiences and provides him with a vision of how to live. Religious symbols reveal this truth without declaring anything about the universe per se.[13] Buber might quarrel with this; nonetheless, Randall's distinctions warrant respect. In his favor, Randall is not subsuming the universe under psychology. Science's response to the universe needs to be what it is, just as a spiritual response requires a language of its own.

So, too, Joseph Campbell and others remind us that the cognitive aspects of myth, of necessity, remain symbolic. To presume that mythical "knowledge" actually presents us with knowledge of God, or grasps the Eternal's Ineffability, or sounds the Great Mystery of Life, would be delusional. Lao Tzu put it wisely: "The way that can be named is not the constant way." As the Lord Krishna explained to Arjuna:

> I am the universal father, mother, granter of all, grandfather, object of knowledge, purifier, holy syllable *Om*, threefold sacred lore. I am the way, sustainer, Lord . . . I am immortality and death; both being and nonbeing am I.[14]

You cannot get more esoteric than that. Or as Yahweh sought to console Isaiah: "For my thoughts are not your thoughts, nor are your ways my ways, says the Lord" (Isa 55:8).

Nevertheless, there is a cognitive element to myth, a desire to know the truth, insofar as the truth can be apprehended by the soul. This truth comes as "revelation," even as a divine gift. It is a form of knowing for those who grasp it, or for those whose inner self receives it. Such is the cognitive import of the Gospel of John when its author states of the *Logos*: "I am the way, and the truth, and the life. . . . If you know me, you will know my Father also" (John 14:6–7). This is the "knowledge" that brings "unity" and "vision" to life and illuminates mankind with a commensurate *savoir-faire*.

2) The *numinal* refers to the mystical aurora that myth encapsulates, to the *mysterium tremendum* identified by Rudolf Otto in *The Idea of the Holy*. It attracts and terrifies, fascinates and repels. One thinks of Odysseus's voyage passed the island of the Sirens. Their song was known to anesthetize the stoutest hearts and to have lulled a thousand sailors to their deaths, as their bright bones witnessed on the island's beach. The

---

13. See Randall, *Role of Knowledge in Western Religion*, chap. 4, in passim.

14. See *Bhagavad-Gita*, in van Voorst, *Anthology of World Scriptures*, Belmont, Calif., 2000, p. 57.

glow from this rotting heap could be seen from the decks of Odysseus' vessel. He warned his men to plug their ears with wax. However, he himself "had to" hear their cry. Lashed to the central mast, while his men cowered in the ship's hull, Odysseus listened to the enchantresses' call. Of course, the *locus classicus* in the Old Testament is the burning bush, before which Moses prostrates. Isaiah's vision of the seraphim in the Temple also qualifies: "Holy, Holy, Holy is the Lord of Hosts" (Isa 6:3).

I use the term "numinal." I prefer it to Otto's "numinous." In Latin, *numen* means "inspiration," or "divine majesty." *Numen* is singular; its plural is *numina*. Therefore the numinal suggests a plurality of experiences that escape exact definition. These experiences one feels in the presence of the Unknown, the Ineffable, and even Nature, as the myths pertaining to the Greek goddesses of flora and fauna attest.[15]

3) The *ontological* has to do with being, reality, the universe around us, with the here and the now itself. *Ontos* means "being." Myths deal with being, with beingness and the Ground of Being. What does it mean *to be*? In particular, what is being's essence? Plato offered a two-substance theory, which in turn influenced the Apostle Paul's contrast between the spirit and the flesh. "Set your mind on things that are above, not on things that are on earth" (Col 3:2). This is why Crossan prefers reading the Gospels first, before turning to Paul, or why Paul's Christ must be read in the light of the Gospels' pre-Easter, historical Jesus. Then Paul's Christ can be interpreted correctly, or, at least, "differently," as Crossan puts it.

Myths, then, are not merely "fairy-tales," though fairies might appear in them, along with ogres, nymphs, and trolls. Myths have to do with mankind's encounter with LIFE, with reality, Nature, the *numinal*. Not something distant, fictitious, contrived, unreal, or purely of the self. This explains their power and appeal. They make sense to us and assist us to acknowledge our awareness of life's problems, of levels of self and being, which other resources seem to neglect.

One might ask about Jung's archetypes. Where do they fit in, if they do? They are ontological insofar as they enable the self to acknowledge the hidden dimensions of one's being and to integrate them into one's personality. Cutting across this spectrum is a reminder of Campbell's. He notes that there are two types of mythology. One form addresses the "motivating power" and "value system" that operates in human beings and in the universe. It can testify to a personal or impersonal force, whether Taoist, Hindu, and Buddhist, or Christian, Jewish, and Moslem. The second inspires societies, groups, cultures. In his view, biblical myth mirrors the

---

15. See B. Farley, *Son of the Morning Sky*, Lanham, Maryland, 1999, p. 3.

second type, inasmuch as the Bible condemns Nature and pronounces it fallen. God stands above nature as its creator; God must never be confused with nature, or its powers, as the Egyptians and Mesopotamians did.

Alfred North Whitehead, however, warns against what he calls "extreme" views. In his judgment, Eastern concepts that perceive the universe to reveal an impersonal order, to which the world conforms, express the "extreme doctrine of immanence," while the "Semitic concept of a definite personal individual entity, whose existence is . . . absolute and underivative" and creates all that is derivative, "expresses the extreme doctrine of transcendence."[16] For Whitehead, neither does justice to the reality of the universe in which we live and with which we must bring our lives into harmony. The facts about the universe are not always pleasant. Religion has to do with *life*, with a life in process, to be lived in a universe under going its own processes. Religion and life have to do with "quality" and "quantity." Each contributes to the other's fulfillment. Writes Whitehead: "There is a quality of life which lies always beyond the mere fact of life."[17] In essence, then,

> religion is what the individual does with his own solitariness. It runs through three stages, if it evolves to its final satisfaction. It is the transition from God the void to God the enemy, and from God the enemy to God the companion.[18]

Myth runs the entire gamut of this trinity, thus assisting mankind along life's road, as he makes his transition from stage to stage.

4) The *regulative* function stems from a myth's capacity to provide direction or focus. I borrow the term from Immanuel Kant's *Critique of Pure Reason*. Kant argued that, although all knowledge begins with experience, not all knowledge is derived from experience. The mind presses beyond sensory experience to "unify," or make sense of, the wealth of data that it daily analyzes. Because of the way in which the mind is structured, it can never provide knowledge of *noumena*, or knowledge of things-in-themselves. It can only proffer knowledge of *phenomena*, or things as they appear to us. These structures of the mind legislate, or determine, what can be known. But the mind wills to go beyond phenomena to the root of being, if possible. Indeed, the mind is even aware of ideas that transcend phenomena. Kant calls these "transcendental ideas." They exist because the mind is driven toward unity. It is dissatisfied with knowing simply

---

16. Alfred N. Whitehead, *Religion in the Making*, New York, 1974, p. 66f.
17. Ibid., p. 77.
18. Ibid., p. 16.

bits and pieces. Thus the transcendental ideas, such as God, the Self, and Immortality, sharpen the focus. They guide and "regulate" human potential. They may not constitute being, but they offer a vital service for understanding being. In many ways, Randall's position, with respect to religious language, is actually a restatement of Kant's principles as applied to religion. That myth has regulated or sharpened humankind's sense of direction, or focus for life, lies at the heart of its appeal.

One might also label this fourth element "axial." It is axial, because of its dynamic impact and the way myths employ and interpret watershed events. Past, present, and future take on new meaning, owing to such axial events. The deliverance at the Sea of Reeds is one example. Elijah's contest with the priests of Baal at Mt. Carmel is a second.

5) *Existential.* Myths lose their power only when they cease to grasp one's imagination, or cease to speak to one's subliminal restlessness. So long as they nurture and illumine one's existence, they exercise enormous import. Their stock remains sound, their cash-value unquestioned, their pragmatic worth unassailable. For this reason, William James considered religion one of the greatest forces of good. Yes, it has its neurotic side, its saints and mystics who border on the psychotic, but, principally, religion provides "immediate luminousness . . . philosophical reasonableness, and moral helpfulness."[19] As long as myth's illuminative powers seize you, it possesses existential merit. As long as the Christ of faith uplifts and empowers a believer, the existential element fulfills its function. The same may be said of the value of the historical Jesus for all seven of the scholars whose positions were reviewed.

6) The *therapeutic* value of myth speaks for itself. Aristotle recognized this motif in his analysis of tragedy. Reading great myths, or attending the tragic dramas of the Greek playwrights, led Aristotle to postulate a cathartic value to myths and drama. They produce a cleansing effect on their audiences, because of the human capacity to identify with the hero or heroine in the drama, to suffer vicariously with him or her, and thus experience release from a similar fate. The Last Supper embodies this catharsis, or therapeutic value for the supplicants gathered at the table, or kneeling or standing at Mass. "This is my body, given for you." Or, "*Hoc est corpus meum,*" in Jerome's Bible. Past, present, and future overwhelm the worshiper in this commemoration of Christ's inimitable sacrifice of life. Abounding grace cleanses the supplicant. "Into thy hands Father, I commend my spirit" (Luke 23:46). Indeed, it is finished.

---

19. Wm. James, *Varieties of Religious Experience*, New York, 1961, p. 33.

7) So, too, the *aesthetic* function scarcely requires elaboration. Campbell expresses it with eloquent effectiveness: "I think of mythology as the homeland of the muses, the inspirers of art" and "poetry." "To see life as a poem and yourself participating in a poem is what the myth does for you."[20] Bullfinch ventures the same: "For mythology is the handmaid of literature: and literature is one of the best allies . . . and promoters of happiness."[21] Thereby, he promised to deliver for his readers "the most charming fictions which fancy has ever created." It is this aesthetic value that has been separated from the cognitive and ontological structures of Being that Tillich addressed in Volume I of his *Systematics*. Being, truth, and beauty belong together and together attest to the Ground of Being within and all about us.

8) *Arêté* means "excellence," or "virtue," in Greek. In Aristotle's *Nicomachean Ethics*, arêté plays a major role. Aristotle asks, "What is man's highest arêté?" What is that unique excellence that is accessible to him? The aretetical function of a myth, thus, has to do with the ethical vision it inspires, or the goal it offers mankind. For the Greeks, some goals were more fitting than others, just as they were for the Hebrews, the Israelites, and the Jewish people, whose turbulent hill country of Galilee produced Jesus.

Today's Christian ethicists distinguish between a variety of principled systems. Edward LeRoy Long, Jr. summarized three of these in his *A Survey of Christian Ethics*. Some are *deliberative* in form. They are time-honored *principles* that have enjoyed debate and deliberation over a long period of time. Many of these we find in the Book of Proverbs, as well as scattered here and there among Jesus' parables. They are practical, optimistic, memorable. They represent traditional values. We find them in Paul's lists of virtues, time and again. They are flexible, general, and fitting. Others are *prescriptive*. They adhere to a code, like the Leviticus Code (Lev 17–25), or the Covenant Code (Exod 20–23), or the Deuteronomic Code. They *prescribe* what to do, either apodictically or conditionally. Apodictic lays down unwavering commands; conditional law responds to "if-then" situations. Apodictic law is often expressed in terms of rules and duties. In many respects, New Testament duties tend to be *relational*. They constitute still another way of fashioning legislation. They are guidelines for followers of Jesus to consider. Paul's admonishments of this sort tend to be less apodictic than the rules laid down in the *Didache*. He allows more room for personal choices. And they appear to have grown out of his reflection on what it means to take the post-Easter Jesus' life and death seriously.

20. *Power of Myth*, p. 65.
21. *Bullfinch's Mythology*, New York, p. 3.

Mythical systems spawn virtues indigenous to their culture's worldview. Hinduism's *Code of Manu* prescribes duties for its adherents that are appropriate for each stage of life and, especially, for members of the higher castes. Buddhism's teachings also contain advice suitable for lay people, monks, nuns, and priests, whatever their walk in society. The *Tao Te Ching* and Chuang Tzu's *Inner Chapters* are filled with aphoristic poems and parables, from which each Taoist may infer lessons applicable to one's respective station in life. Jesus' parables of the Kingdom of God, which itself is symbolic of his spiritual vision, are replete with values for hearers to infer. Recall how Mack's *The Lost Gospel: the Book of Q* suggests scores of "aphoristic maxims" and "aphoristic imperatives," which is his way of deducing aretetical elements from the historical Jesus' collected sayings.

In the next two chapters, I hope to focus on some of the major mythological motifs that are associated, first, with the historical Jesus and, second, with the post-Easter Christ. My point being, that beyond the historical Jesus' worldview and the early Church's mythologization of his life, the functions of myth enable Christians and Jesus' admirers to find meaning for themselves and society in reflecting on Jesus' life. In no way does this detract from the Church's perception of the Christ of faith, but rather enriches it. If anything, the two go together. The Church borrowed mythical strands wherever they applied, and it filled them with Hebraic, or Jewish content, drawn from the Old Testament. The two supplement each other, while not replacing one another.

4

Mythical Dimensions in the Life of the Pre-Easter Jesus

Isolating the pre-Easter Jesus from the post-Easter Jesus, or Gospel accounts that celebrate him, constitutes the daunting challenge that those who would reconstruct the life of Jesus must resolve. Nonetheless, as successful as Mack, Borg, and Crossan have been, the framework of the post-Easter Christ remains transparent in depictions of the pre-Easter Jesus. The two figures overlap and interpolate each other. Take the *Gospel of Thomas* for example. Its one-sentence preamble assumes a time lag between the recorded sayings and the "living Jesus," whose words then follow. A sense of the esoteric already hovers about the collection. They come cocooned within a Wisdom Tradition, or the Sophia School, if one may call it that. Readers are not simply ruminating over past sayings. The collector, Didymos Thomas, has invoked the presence of the living Jesus to guide a new generation of disciples. The pre-and Post-Easter Jesuses go hand in hand. To that extent, Crossan is correct in insisting that the "two Jesuses" are *the same person*. It's just that we are dealing with two categorically different ways of preserving this figure, and thus, essentially, a man of history transformed into a figure of faith. Still, the point is that mythological elements, as part of the tradition, both inform and create a framework for presenting the written stories and collected segments, i.e., inferred in Q, and visible in the Evangelists' Gospels, the *Gospel of Thomas*, the *Didache*, and Ignatius's *Letters*.

This fact does not jeopardize the truth about the pre-Easter Jesus' identity, nor detract from the spiritual value of the post-Easter Christ. Recall that *myth has to do with the objectification of one's subliminal need to fathom the mystery of the human condition and to live and fulfill it as wholly as possible*. This dynamic "dual phenomenon," as I perceive it, underlies the attractiveness of the historical Jesus, as well as the Church's re-configuration of him for its time. Moreover, mythological elements embedded in the Christian texts possess as much power to speak to us today as they did to Jesus' earliest followers. To acknowledge this is the path of wisdom. To reject it runs the risk of 1) sinking again into the slough of dogmatic bickering that has defined so many Christian doctrines, or of 2) turning Jesus into an icon for social justice, but whose sayings may or may not have relevance, depending on the political and cultural issues of the day.

A study of Jesus as man and myth has much to commend itself concerning our need for self-understanding and self-fulfillment. What are some of the major mythical dimensions that underlie the pre-Easter Jesus' attractiveness and that address the human condition?

Jesus as the Supreme Archetype

This is Jung's view, found in his chapter: "Christ, A Symbol of the Self," located in his collected works, entitled *Aion*. In truth, his chapter is more about Christ than the pre-Easter Jesus, but Jung's analysis serves as an illuminating example of how Jesus' life may be interpreted as a myth that probes the essence of the self. It is the myth of myths! Jung justifies his fascination with Jesus, or the post-Easter Christ, "because he is still the living myth of our culture."[1] In short, Christ objectifies the archetype of the self, or "exemplifies" it in his own life and death. He "embodies the myth of the Primordial Man, the mystic Adam" of Paul's letters. "He is in us and we are in him," states Jung. "His kingdom is the pearl of great price, the treasure buried in the field, the grain of mustard seed . . . and the heavenly city."[2] Both Christ and his heavenly city are in us.

For Jung, Christ represents the perfect *imago Dei* who never fell. He symbolizes wholeness for mankind, because it is a wholeness that can be regained. At the Fall, the God-image in man was not destroyed; rather, it was corrupted. Thanks to God in Jesus' cross, it can be restored. "The psychological equivalent of this is the integration of the collective unconscious which forms an essential part of the individuation process."[3] In Jung's mind, Paul acknowledges the same when he writes: "Do not be conformed to this world, but be transformed by the renewing of your minds, so that you may discern what is the will of God—what is good and acceptable and perfect" (Rom 12:2). Nevertheless, Jung finds a disparity in Paul that has led Christianity to create a less than "whole" Christ. How? By excluding the dark side of human nature from Jesus' own nature, it has depicted him as perfectly good and without sin. Furthermore, in its wrestling with the

---

1. C. Jung, *Aion*, Princeton, 1969, p. 36.
2. Ibid.
3. Ibid., p. 39.

origin of evil, the Early Fathers placed evil outside God and treated it as an absence of good (Jung sites Irenaeus, Origen, Augustine's works to substantiate his point). This psychological imbalance was solved by turning the Lucifer who wanders the courts of heaven with Yahweh in the Book of Job into Paul's Antichrist, or "man of lawlessness," associated with the End-time. This ontological bifurcation, which pits good against evil, led unhappily to a metaphysical dualism in Christian doctrine. For Jung, the dark side of reality cannot be omitted, if true salvation is to occur. Thus, the traditional figure of Christ must be re-united with the Antichrist, who represents the "shadow of the self." A psychological concept of the self requires an inclusion of the unconscious "as an archetypal quaternity bound together by inner antimonies."[4] By quaternity, Jung means a four-sided image, with eternity and time respectively at the top and bottom of a vertical plane, and good and evil as opposites along the horizontal plane. Mankind is a conjunction of all four of these forces within himself.

The older gods of antiquity represented the struggle between anima and animus in every person. The gods had both a dark and good side. Today, however, "Christ is our nearest analogy of the self and its meaning." But, unfortunately, in Jung's estimate, Christ as he is currently perceived, "corresponds to only one half of the archetype."[5] The Antichrist constitutes the other half. Nonetheless, the tradition that placed the shadow outside the Christ can be corrected by a psychological interpretation. This involves a fresh look at the cross and the two men who were crucified to the left and the right of Jesus. Christ and the Antichrist are both Christian symbols. According to Jung, the tradition of Jesus' execution between the two thieves

> tells us that the progressive development and differentiation of consciousness leads to an ever more menacing awareness of the conflict and involves nothing less than a crucifixion of the ego, its agonizing suspension between irreconcilable opposites.[6]

Insofar as Christ stands as a symbol of the self, Jung suggests that a distinction between "perfection" and "completeness" ought to be drawn. He favors "completeness" over "perfection." When Christ is taken as a symbol of the self, seeking the restoration of its true *imago Dei*, the idea of completeness proves superior to perfection. As Jung explains it, the realization of the self leads to a fundamental conflict between two opposites held

---

4. Ibid., p. 42.
5. Ibid., p. 44.
6. Ibid.

in suspension: the *conscious* on the one hand and the *unconscious* on the other. Jung sites passages from Matthew and Romans to argue his case: "Therefore be perfect as your heavenly Father is perfect" (Matt 5:48); and from Paul's verse: "I find then a law that when I would do good, evil is present with me" (Rom 7:21).

Jung prefers to speak of this as a paradox. Christ as the symbol of the self incorporates what is indescribable and transcendental. Christ's death symbolizes a state of wholeness for the self, but not perfection. The struggle goes on throughout life.

Jung disavows any interest in metaphysics, but he insists that his interpretation is based on sound psychiatric and medical research. In sum he believes:

> Like the related ideas of *atman* and *tao* in the East, the idea of the self is . . . a product of cognition, grounded neither in faith nor on metaphysical speculation but on the experience that under certain conditions the unconscious spontaneously brings forth an archetypal symbol of wholeness. . . . Whenever the archetype of the self predominates, the inevitable psychological consequence is a state of conflict vividly exemplified by the Christian symbol of crucifixion.[7]

Only the final consummation (death) will bring an end to this conflict.

Contrary to Buber's criticism of his work, Jung did not believe that his interpretations compromised or denigrated Christian teachings. They simply enriched them from the perspective of psychotherapy. From Jung's viewpoint, this enrichment awaits all who see the pre-Easter Jesus as a symbol of an *imago Dei* that mirrors their own need for wholeness, and the post-Easter Christ as a promise of a self-fulfillment that can be realized now. In seeing one's life as a combination of ontological and cognitive realities, the process of individuation drives one toward true wholeness with renewed confidence.

Other Important Mythical Symbols

Water and Its Depths

Jesus' travels carried him frequently about the Sea of Galilee. Beyond its reality as a barrier and source of food, as a vista of beauty and flowers, of green hills and cobalt sea, its imagery awakened numerous metaphors in

---

7. Ibid., pp. 69–70.

his mind. Its shoreline served as the amphitheater for his "sermons" and its secret groves his sanctuary for morning prayer. "In the *morning*, while it was still *very dark*, he got up and went out to *a deserted place*, and there he prayed" (Mark 1:35; italics for emphasis). Mark's Gospel sets this prayer near Capernaum. If the shadow was not ontologically part of Jesus, nor the deserted place a corner in his soul, the pre-Easter Jesus was well aware of its presence and the need to cope with it. Perhaps it became his womb for encountering the Ineffable in his heart. In Mark's passage, it is while Jesus is by the sea that he seeks God, who in turn lifts his hidden shadow upward into the conscious light of a greater self. At what point Jesus made his own transition from God the void to God the enemy, and from God the enemy to God the companion, would be intriguing to know.

The Sea of Galilee, as an *axis mundi* and window onto the infinite within, is more than mere metaphor. In the Greek the two words for "sea" and "water" are, respectively, *thalassa* (feminine) and *hydor* (neuter). When applied to the Sea of Galilee, *thalassa* is employed; its waters are *hydor*. In the *Septuagint*, *thalassa* translates the Hebrew word *yam*, i.e., sea, even at the Red Sea; while *hydor* designates the chaotic waters over which God's Spirit stirred in Gen 1:2. The *Septuagint* employs the word *hydor* to describe the waters that engulfed the pursuing Egyptians. I am hesitant to say more, but the background is there.

From both a theological and psychological perspective, mankind is *ontologically* driven to seek wholeness, to rise above his chaos. As the locus of the anima, the *thalassa* stirs with the troubled *hydor* of the unconscious, longing for integration and healing. The sea's reality became a source of Jesus' insight, as well as the geographical location of his Galilean ministry. No doubt its beauty and that of the surrounding hills inspired the aesthetic qualities of Jesus' prose. Its eloquence is preserved throughout Q and in strophes of the *Gospel of Thomas*. "Consider the lilies of the field, how they grow; they neither toil nor spin, yet I tell you, even Solomon in all his glory was not clothed like one of these" (Matt 6:28–29). "Do not fret, from morning to evening and from evening to morning. . . . You're much better than the lilies, which neither card nor spin" (*Thom* 36).

As a symbol, water contains a sea of metaphors for the exploration of the self. It functions as both a cleansing agent and realm of terror. That the motivation for cleansing should come from within provides the surest source of liberation from one's own shadow and restive anima. "Seek and you will find" is embedded in Q and *Thomas*. This "out-of-the-depths cry" for help is grounded in the self and scripture. The Psalms abound with the metaphor. "Out of the depths I cry to thee, O Lord. . . . If thou, O

Lord, shouldst mark iniquities, who could stand?" (Ps 130:1, 3—RSV). "If I take the wings of the morning and settle at the farthest limits of the sea, even there your hand shall lead me" (Ps 139:9–10). Shadow and integration, the dark side and liberation pulsate in these passages. *Ontology* and *cognition*, being and the unconscious, are lifted out of the depths that healing might occur. More than metaphor, we are in the presence of the elemental nuances of the self in its quest to become whole. This is true of one's need to relate to the universe as well as to the self. For the "quality" and the "quantity" of the universe equally impact human existence.

What at first appears to be an esoteric strophe in the *Gospel of Thomas*, on further reflection, becomes a brilliant insight. "When you make the two into one, and when you make the inner like the outer and the outer like the inner, and the upper like the lower, and . . . you make male and female into a single one, . . . then you will enter the Father's domain" (*Thom* 22). Sea imagery has dropped out, but not "the lower and the upper," "the inner and the outer," or the dichotomy of *anima* and *animus*, or Whitehead's "quality" and "quantity." As the Jesus Seminar editors note: "One enters life by recovering one's original self, undivided by the differences between male and female, physical and spiritual," a theme "of unifying opposites . . . well known from later Gnostic texts."[8] A similar saying appears in *Thom* 29: "If the flesh came into being because of the spirit, that is a marvel, but if spirit came into being because of the body, that is a marvel of marvels." The Seminar editors discount this saying as authentic, since it fails to square with the pre-Easter Jesus' willingness to associate with the unclean, outsiders, drunkards, and gluttons, and because it belittles the body and the flesh. It is too ascetic to represent the real Jesus. But from a mythical perspective, more than flesh and body are involved. If the body is the house of the unconscious that becomes integrated with the spirit or the conscious, indeed, that is a marvel, for a more wholesome development of the self has occurred. If that were the case, the saying might well have come from the lips of Jesus. But such an inference falls outside proof.

The extent to which Jesus might have been familiar with Egyptian and Greek myths is beyond knowing. Nonetheless, he grew up in an environment that had been subject to Hellenistic and Asian influences far longer than it had been to its original Jewish roots. In all likelihood, a common knowledge of the Egyptian Isis and Osiris myth and its counterpart among the Greeks, namely, the Demeter rites, had made their way into cosmopolitan Sepphoris and the surrounding Galilean hills. Of course, this conjecture is purely that: conjecture. Still, the parallels between the

---

8. See *The Five Gospels*, San Francisco, 1997, p. 487.

myths and Jesus' sayings about "the inner and the outer" and "the upper and the lower," hint of traces of such lore. No immediate parallels come to mind in either Q or the Synoptics, but Paul's Letter to the Romans echoes with the Greco-Roman world's concept of cosmological structures: "For I am convinced that neither death, nor life, nor angels, nor . . . powers, nor height, nor depth, nor anything else in all creation, will be able to separate us from the love of God in Christ Jesus our Lord" (Rom 8:38–39). Few passages match this vision in terms of the victory of order over chaos, of wholeness over the Void.

Water and *depths* further symbolize the New Testament's "rebirth" motif. They are manifestly central to John the Baptizer's ministry, which, in Crossan's view, Jesus at first embraced. They are especially incorporated in the Johannine community's reflections of John 3:1–10 and 4:7–15.

In the first instance (John 3:1–10), rebirth is a conjunction of "water and Spirit," a movement from "above" to "below." Literally, re-entering the "mother's womb" is impossible and of no avail. Still a "rebirth" is required. "Do not be astonished that I said to you, 'You must be born from above'" (John 3:7). Integrating the upper and the lower is seen by John's Jesus as the work of the Spirit and alone leads to newness of life.

In the second text, the setting occurs by a well. It involves the "gift . . . of living water." The water of John's post-Easter Christ "will become a spring of water gushing up to eternal life" (John 4:14). "You have no bucket and the well is deep," the Samarian woman laments. "If only you knew who were speaking to you," Jesus replies. Suddenly, the woman is jolted. She recognizes who he must be. Thus, the story ends with her pleading for "living water."

Traces of Gnostic preference for the "above" at the expense of the "below," and the superiority of the "Spirit" over "the mother's womb," certainly prevail in chapter 3; nevertheless, the integration of the conscious with the unconscious is instrumental in the process of individuation. The difficulty of this process is correctly reflected in Nicodemus's awareness of "how can these things be?" and in the fact that he comes to Jesus by "night," protected by the shadow of his own darkness, or his anima in Jung's parlance, or "sin" in Paul's parlance, and the fear of its exposure. This is myth at its best, and why it has to do with the mystery of the human condition, to which religious language speaks so powerfully. One is tempted to conclude, therefore, that any depictions of the pre-Easter Jesus that lose sight of this dimension, lose sight of the reason why history ever bothered to record his words or reify him after his death.

Water symbolism also forms part of the Evangelists' stories, in which the pre-Easter Jesus' miracles are framed. The stilling of the storm, the swineherd that drowns in the sea, Jesus walking on the water, and Peter's attempt to do the same all draw from myth's numinous depths. In the first story, the wind and the waves threaten to swamp the disciples' boat, while Jesus himself sleeps quietly. He is at peace—this non-fallen *imago Dei*; they are alarmed, in a state of terror. "We are about to perish!" they shout. "Why are you afraid, you of little faith?" he replies. Then he rebukes the "winds" and the "waves" and a "dead calm" settles over them in a hush. (Matt 8:23–27.) This is a story about mankind, more than it is a metaphor. It forces the reader to look within, where his own storms rage, threatening to swamp the vessel of the self. That storm must be "rebuked," if calm is to be restored.

The second story takes place in the "country of the Gadarenes." In Matthew's account, two demoniacs creep out of their tombs to confront Jesus. As specters of terror and as those who terrify others, they challenge his presence. "Why have you come here to torment us?" they cry. Are they not already tormented enough? Are they not already victims of their own bi-polar disorders? That Matthew has changed Mark's single wretch into two, only compounds the personalities of opposites in conflict. They perceive what he must do, if they are to become whole, and are fearful of the event and its possible outcome. Their "demons," their dark side, their shadow, must be exorcised, however wrenching the cure, or the "crucifixion of their egos." Thus the swine, the unwholesome conflicts in each, are sent plummeting into the sea. The demoniacs are "healed" and herald their story, only to stir the town's anxiety all the more: "Please go away, Thou violent healer!" (Matt 8:28–34).

The third occurrence involves another storm, again, at sea. It follows the Feeding of the Five Thousand. Jesus has gone "up the mountain by himself to pray." It is evening, and he is alone. He has sent his disciples ahead in the boat, to join him "on the other side." But a night squall batters the boat and prevents the disciples from landing. Jesus can see this from the mountain but remains in solitude to pray. After all, has Yahweh not said: "Be still and know that I am God"? Thus, early in the morning, Jesus descends and comes "walking toward them on the sea." Once again, they are "terrified" and cry out in fear: "It's a ghost!" No! No! Something greater than a ghost has come to seek them. Something no less than the *numinal* itself, the holiness that heals! "Take heart, it is I" (Matt 14:22–27). The word for "fear" in Greek is *phobos*. We derive our word "phobia" from it. It can also be translated as "terror," "amazement," and "astonishment." What is the phobia that mankind carries within itself, the "terror" that it knows must be expelled?

The fourth story immediately follows. "Lord, if it is you, command me to come . . . on the water." It is Peter who makes the plea. "Come!" the Master replies. Peter climbs out of his boat and begins to walk toward Jesus. But the wind distracts him, *phobos* grips him, and he begins to sink in the *hydor*. "Save me!" he cries. "O you of little faith, why do you doubt?" Jesus admonishes him (Matt 14:28–31). In the presence of the *numinal*, of the Ineffable within, where the God of one's heart, or the Tao, the Atman, or the Buddha essence, stirs, one knows that one must rise and defy the troubled seas of one's shadow. It is the only way that redemption can occur. One must respond to the saving Voice that commands: "Come!"

At no point in any of these stories do the Jesus Seminar Fellows find any authentic words of Jesus. All four are the invention of Matthew, as he reworks his source: Mark. Nonetheless, the mythic elements embodied in these accounts become treasured as scriptures, in which "the righteousness of God is revealed" (Rom 1:17). In this kind of story telling, myth transcends aphorisms, because it is the vehicle of revelation. As such, it has the power to awaken one's self to the mystery of the human condition, that one may find life, experience it afresh, and fulfill oneself as fully as possible.

Fish Symbolism

In all of Q, the word "fish" appears only once (Matt 7:10; Luke 11:11), in Thomas, twice (3:2; 8:1–2), in the Synoptics, it occurs five times in Mark, six in Matthew, and five in Luke. Most of Matthew and Luke's "fish" references are reworked versions of Mark's narratives concerning the Feedings of the Five and Four Thousand. In every instance, the Greek word *ichthys* is used in either its singular or plural form, to designate fish. The phrase "fishers of men" occurs also, once in Mark and in its reworked setting in Matthew. One of Matthew's *ichthys* usages parallels *Thom* 8; the other is unique to Matthew. Only one of Luke's five stands alone. It is placed at the end of his Gospel, during Jesus' farewell appearance to the eleven.

The phrase "fishers of men" appears to be purely metaphorical and not descriptive of the disciples' *ontological* status, although that might be debatable for some. It probably has more to do with their function than "being." The passage in Matthew 17:27 has to do with catching a fish in order to pay the Temple tax. Scholars doubt that the issue reflects Jesus' time, but rather a later date, when Christians found themselves debating whether to pay taxes to the Romans or not (*Five Gospels*, p. 213). Whatever the setting, Jesus and Paul both advised paying the Romans what belonged to the Romans (Rom 13).

The Q passage (Matt 7:10 and Luke 11:11) is nestled in a cluster of sayings that witnesses to the goodness of God. What father would give his son a snake, if the son were hungry and asked for a fish? Its inclusion in *Thom* 3:1–4 is more complex. By way of paraphrase, if your leaders tell you that the Kingdom God is in the sky, then the birds will precede you. If they claim it's in the sea, then the *fish* will precede you. But God's imperial rule is in neither. Rather, it "is within you and it is outside you. When you know yourselves, then you will be known, and you will understand that you are the children of the living Father." Gnostic self-knowledge can occur only in the depths of one's being. The "fish motif" has been totally "swallowed" by the "sea motif." The editors of the *Five Gospels* go even further by suggesting that there are affinities between the Thomas passage and Bar 3:29–32. Again by way of paraphrase: "Has anyone found wisdom by ascending into heaven, or brought her back from the clouds, or found her by traversing the sea? No! Wisdom is found by one's 'understanding.'"

The Feedings of the Five and Four Thousand unite both mythical and metaphorical themes. The mythical is brought out in the miracle of multiplying the fishes and loaves. These narratives appear to be the work of the Church, in reference to authority issues within it. Crossan views the scenes as attempts to resolve such issues while being faithful to the idea of commensality. Whose role is it to distribute the bread? Just what is it that Church leaders do? None of this debate is viewed to have occurred under Jesus. We see it arise again in Corinth and later in the era of the *Didache*, as to how the Eucharist should be observed and how leaders should be elected. The danger is that the very inclusivity that the pre-Easter Jesus favored may be lost in a too tightly restricted definition of leadership, or even in a development toward a "closed communion."

The "fish and the dragnet" parable in Thomas and Matthew have common nuances, but each interprets it differently. Matthew's setting is eschatological and End-time in interest. The net that has been cast into the sea catches "fish of every kind." Once dragged ashore, the "good" are placed into baskets, while the "bad" are cast out. So it will be at the end time, when the angels come and "separate the *evil* from the *righteous*" and toss the evil into "the furnace of fire" (Matt 13:47–50). The only definition we have of the "good" is "righteous." But this almost seems like a discount of the historical Jesus' plea for inclusivity and a kingdom brokered for outcasts, bandits, prostitutes, thieves, and the poor.

In the case of Thomas (*Thom* 8:1–4), only a splendidly "large fish" is kept; all the "little fish" are cast back into the sea. Gnostic distinctions of who's who and who's better than whom override any eschatological motifs. Hints of a mythic upper and lower are present, and the insignificant "little ones" appear to be persons whose true self remains below the surface. They will never be free of the unconscious, or able to become integrated into consciousness. They simply do not qualify for inclusion in the Sophia School. As in the case of *Thom* 3:1–4, *knowing oneself* is the key to entering God's realm. No pun intended, but at least the "little fish" are spared from becoming "basket cases."

It is only when we look beyond the aphorisms of Q and Thomas and enter the world of the Johannine community that the mythical power of "fish symbolism" points to deeper meanings. John 6:9–11 and 21:5–13 contain the passages in question. This time a different word for "fish" is used: *opsarion*. The writer of John uses the word in 6:9, 11 (Feeding of the Five Thousand); and again in the story beside the sea in 21:9, 10, and 13. *Opsarion* means "cooked provision" in distinction from bread; it can also denote a "dainty dish," or even a "little fish." Here the "little fish" are kept, instead of being cast back into the sea. For Crossan, however, the import of the story lies in its connection with the "bread" that Jesus offers his disciples, along with the "fish." Crossan sees the symbol as a post-resurrection ceremony in which the Church recognized Christ's presence during a now ritualized common meal. Peter has risen to the top in this community. Once again commensality and leadership are kept conjoined. But with the appearance of Mark and Matthew as written sources, the ritual was placed before the resurrection, as well as after it in Luke and John.

The giving of the fish, along with the bread, to the disciples suggests still another motif that John 6 preserves with bold intention. Now the "fish" disappears all together. John 6:25–65 presents the reader with a long commentary on the "food that endures for eternal life." This "food" is equivalent to believing in Christ and is symbolic of the mana that God gave Moses and the Israelites in the desert. It is God's mana, the Christ, who descends from heaven, who truly "gives life to the world." What John's post-Easter Jesus is offering his disciples by the sea is his continued presence that alone guarantees "eternal life" and brings fulfillment to the self. After all, what is eternal life, if it isn't "knowing the only true God, and Jesus" whom God has sent? (John 17:3).

The ontological, existential, therapeutical, and cognitive elements of myth are all present in this story. Only the *numinal* power of the holy, that Other experienced as the Ground of Being, can nurture the shadow within and calm its feverish soul. Though it is an inward encounter, objectified in myth, nonetheless it provides therapy and catharsis sufficient to address the mystery of the human condition. Shared in commensality, while safeguarding one's solitariness, this mana from heaven nurtures and enables one to make that private transition from God the Void to God the Companion.

The Mustard Seed, Tares, Pearl and Hidden Treasure

Crossan's explication of these four metaphors focuses on Jesus' political agenda. They have to do with Jesus' perception of the kingdom of God as "a kingdom of undesirables." The first two (mustard seed and weeds) are meant to stir the political hopes of the landless poor. The parable of the mustard seed—found in the *Gospel of Thomas* 20, Q (Luke 13:18–19; Matt 13:31–32), and Mark 4:30–32—varies slightly in each account. In the first (Thomas), the fallen seed (smallest of all) produces a "great plant." In Q, it is deliberately sown in a garden, becomes a tree, and birds nest in its branches. In the last, it is sown on the ground, becomes the greatest of all shrubs, so the birds of the air are able to nest in its shade. Actually, the mustard plant in Jesus' day was prized for its pungent properties, but because it spread so easily, it was viewed more as a nuisance than as a beneficial shrub. Crossan compares these accounts with their nearest parallel in Ezekiel, where the lofty cedar, not a mustard plant, stands symbolic of God's coming kingdom. His point is this: the kingdom of God is more like the pesky nuisance plant than the lofty cedar. It takes over where it isn't wanted, can grow out of control, and attracts undesirable guests. The landless poor would have understood Jesus' import immediately.[9]

The tares, or unwanted weeds, symbolize every landowner's constant fear. No landowner wants his harvest ruined by weeds. Crossan explains that the weed in question is *zizania,* a darnel plant that, like mustard, can take over the best wheat field and compromise the harvest. Such wheat fields often required large numbers of slaves and peasants to work them. Once again, Jesus' audience would have found rough humor in this parable. Let the weeds grow! Let the rich suffer for all their disdain of the poor!

The pearl and the treasure hidden in the field also prove to be troubling images. Of what use is a pearl of great value unless the merchant can resell it? In the *Gospel of Thomas* (76:1), the merchant has purchased it for himself; in Matthew's story (13:45–46), the merchant simply possesses it but has divested himself of all his other pearls.

---

9. Crossan, *Historical Jesus,* pp. 276–79.

In the parable of the hidden treasure, the finder in the *Gospel of Thomas* (109) has fortuitously lucked up, for the family from whom he purchased it knew nothing of the treasure's existence. Now, the new owner is able to use it to earn money at interest. It seems unfair. In Matthew's version (13:44), the finder covers it up, sells his other possessions, then returns to buy the field. For Crossan, "scandal and impiety" grip both accounts. All this is rather shocking and unsettling, as indeed was Jesus' vision and work.

From the viewpoint of myth, all four metaphors pertain to the self. We are the mustard seed with good and evil potential. What part of the self will take over the garden? What seed will spread out of control? The restive unconscious is always there; the process of individuation, of incorporating life's qualitative and quantitative properties, never ends. It is happening right now! It is in us and before our very eyes!

How long must the hidden shadow, the anima, the "I-told-you-so old wise man," muscle its way into a life, before a person awakens and copes with it?

We are the pearl, the treasure hidden in the field. But how do we integrate the truth about ourselves so that we might LIVE and truly experience life's richest values? These stories force us to fathom the mystery of the human predicament. They appeal to our hidden side to come forth and live. They open us to the possibility of the Other, to God, whom we cannot escape, and who meets us in the irony of the self in its attempt to fathom itself.

5

Parable, Metaphor, and Myth

A PARABLE is a story relying on comparison. It is a literary form that the pre-Easter Jesus used with consummate skill. Modern biblical critics favor focusing on Jesus' parables, because they believe that the parables provide their best access to the historical man, himself. Few scholars or churchmen disagree.

Metaphor is another matter, a much broader literary device, of which the parable is but one example. Similitude, allegory, and fables are frequently employed to convey metaphor. The word is derived from the Greek *metapherein,* which means "to carry," or "bring over." Myth uses metaphor, along with allegory, parabolic symbols, and fables.

Defining metaphor, as distinct from myth, may seem to some an exercise in swallowing camels while choking on gnats. Actually, one does choke on gnats. Nevertheless, I believe that there is an essential difference. I offer the following definition: *metaphor is a literary device by means of which a truth encapsulated in a figure of speech may be used to inspire a person to apply its insight to oneself and society.* It is a concrete representation of an abstract principle or idea. It may consist of a phrase or be no more than a single word in length. Metaphor differs from myth in that the latter has to do with *being,* our own being as well as the Ground of Being. It has to do with one's totality as a human person in response to the mystery of life. It is universal, as are Jung's archetypes, and underlies one's sense of self; whereas metaphor pertains to *application*. If the shoe fits, wear it! The same metaphor may have different meanings for different people. Thus in the parable about the Tares, or Weeds, landowners may infer the need to be vigilant, while their peasant-slaves perceive a glimmer of justice. The mythic character of the parable haunts the beingness of each, while not eroding the multi-applicable possibilities of the parable. Metaphor also appeals to the *imagination*, the mother of dreams and visions, but so, too, does myth.

Borg views the parable as a metaphor with a distinct purpose. They are "invitational forms of speech." Jesus employed them to enable his hearers to "see something they might not otherwise see." They arouse the imagination and inspire, or "invite," one to "transform" his or her life.[1] Paul's preaching about the post-Easter Jesus incorporates this aim. He hopes his converts will be "transformed by the renewing of their minds" (Rom 12:2).

The truth is, myth and metaphor overlap. I separate them only to sharpen the power of the mythical within the Christ story to impact one's being, one's *ontological and unique self*, or that individual that no one else can be! As Paul says, "work out your own salvation with fear and trembling; for it is God who is at work in you" (Phil 2:12).

The Lost Coin, Lost Sheep, and Lost Son

All three are powerful metaphors. From a mythical point of view, all three parables enervate the believer to take courage. Life is not lost. One may feel lost. One may be lost at the moment. But being lost does not have to have the last word.

In her book, *Neurosis and Human Growth*, Karen Horney probed the boundaries of the neurotic manifestations that attest to "lostness" in today's world. Though first published in 1950, her insights remain fundamental to personal growth and healthy self-realization. In all likelihood, the pre-Easter Jesus would have concurred with her. A brief summary of her findings is worth reviewing.

For Horney, modern mankind suffers from a genuine alienation of the self. "Evolutionary constructive forces" lie behind the drive to develop potentialities. But this drive toward self-realization does not require one to impose either an "inner strait jacket" on oneself, or bend to "the whip of inner dictates." "Self knowledge . . . is not an aim in itself, but a means of liberating the forces of spontaneous growth."[2] As a *means,* however, it can unfortunately become an end in itself. If that occurs, then "self-idealization" has replaced "self-realization." A "self-idealized" person succumbs to a search for glory, thus the "energies driving toward self-realization are shifted to the aim of actualizing . . . an idealized self." Often this self results in a quest for a perfection that is beyond one's attainment. Self-deception, in turn, succumbs to ambition. A vindictive spirit slips into the equation, and one strives to outdo, outwit, frustrate, and defeat others. In the process, one becomes indiscriminate and compulsive. Others are to blame for one's own failures. Neurotic claims surface. One feels entitled

---

1. M. Borg, *Meeting Jesus Again for the First Time*, San Francisco, 1994, pp. 70–71.
2. K. Horney, *Neurosis and Human Growth*, New York, 1950, p. 15.

to needs and rights without having to earn them. They, themselves, are never to be questioned, doubted, or criticized. Their arrogance deepens. They forget that "fate can strike at any time with an accident, bad fortune, illness, or death."[3] They feel no need to make preparations for such eventualities, nor do they have any compunction when it comes to offending others. Their response to tragedy is always: "Life is unfair." When fully frustrated by life's realities, their anger may take three forms: 1) suppression, even to the point of psychosomatic illnesses and pains, 2) out-right anger, or 3) self pity. The result of any of these is inertia. This way of relating to the outside world condemns one to repeated inauthenticity.

One may also succumb to, what Horney calls, "the tyranny of the should." This path of striving for self-realization leads to imposing exaggerated claims on one's self. The end is equally catastrophic. Strict notions of honesty, generosity, justice, equanimity, parenthood, relations with others, enjoyment of life, etc., overwhelm one with coercive elements. The end of this approach is anxiety, despair, self-condemnation, and self-destruction.

Her analysis of wasted lives and lost souls is mirrored in Paul Tillich's distinction between "autonomy," "heteronomy," and "theonomy." The self-ruled "autonomous" life of enlightened man works fine, until anxiety, finitude, guilt, and mortality nibble away at one's self-centeredness. Then one knows that he or she requires something more. The "heteronomously" pursued life proves just as empty, as it is drowned by others' dictates and limits. Only a life lived "theonomously," open to God as the Ground of Being, fully answers the questions implicit in the human condition.

Martin Heidegger pursued a similar approach, distinguishing between an "authentic" and an "inauthentic" existence, an authentic life requiring one's own choices and risks of accountability, in spite of finitude, fallenness, and death. Nowhere does Heidegger out-do himself as eloquently as in his *Poetry, Language, Thought*. Basing much of his insight on Holderlin's line: "and what are poets for in a destitute time?" Heidegger explores the meaning of poetry as a form of keeping "the wine-god's holy songs" alive. Mortal man is in search of his soul, totally unaware of his destitute condition, or that God has withdrawn from the world, or that night is falling, and that "the evening of the world's age" is in decline.[4]

Both Horney and Heidegger are indebted to Kierkeggard and Nietzsche, whose principles they cite. But their analysis of a "lost life" contributes quite aptly to the three parables in question.

---

3. Ibid., p. 46.
4. M. Heidegger, *Poetry, Language, Thought*, New York, 1971, pp. 89–92.

Mack considers the lost coin and the lost sheep to belong to Q^2. The Jesus Seminar Fellows attribute the lost coin and the lost son to Luke alone (Luke 15:8–9; 15:11–32). These two parables have no parallels elsewhere in the Gospels. The lost sheep is found in Matt 18:12–14; Luke 15:4–6 (thus Q), and in *Thom* 107:1–3.

The Jesus Seminar scholars think that Luke might have created the lost coin story in imitation of the lost sheep parable, which is definitely part of Q. They note the desperation on the woman's part to "recover a coin of little value."[5] That interest reflects the pre-Easter Jesus who cared for the poor, women, widows, and society's destitute. No soul is unworthy of being recovered. All souls are worth redeeming.

The point of the lost sheep parable is similar. "Jesus goes in quest of things that are lost . . . , which illustrates God's concern for sinners." Thomas' version of the story moves in an entirely different direction from either Matthew or Luke's. In their accounts, the value of any stray is emphasized. God loves all his sheep. But in the *Gospel of Thomas*, it is the "largest" sheep that has gone astray. And, as in the case of the fish caught in the dragnet, it is the "largest" sheep that is prized. The shepherd leaves the "ninety-nine" and looks for this one until he finds it. Then he says: "I love you more than all the others." Once again, Gnostic principles of elitism and rank replace Crossan's criterion of inclusivity. One seems compelled to agree with the Seminar Fellows and Crossan, while acknowledging the historical veracity of the parable.

It is the parable of the lost son that has spoken with the most power to Jesus' followers over the many centuries since Jesus' death. So much of what Horney has written about one's "wasted energies" lunges into life in this story. The youth's arrogance, his refusal to think ahead, his insistence on doing it his own way, his misery, and, finally, his humiliation, all take center stage. He almost comes across as bi-polar. It is his passive-aggressive brother who brings out the other side of a lost life. His life has been subservient to his father's will and to a clean, well-ordered life, but one lived heteronomously instead of gladly. At that point, the parable as metaphor has become universal myth. We are the lost son, the lost sheep, the lost coin. It is part of our existential fallenness, part of Whitehead's "quality and quantity" that underlie all existence. Our health, redemption, and healing lie in our acknowledgment that this is so. The theonomous perspective that Jesus' parable affords symbolically answers the questions implied in the mystery of our human situation. What was lost must be found for healing to occur. Heaven itself remains in limbo until the son's

---

5. *Five Gospels*, p. 355.

"return." "For this son of mine was dead and is alive again; he was lost and is found" (Luke 15:23).

No analysis of these three parables would be complete, however, without a closer look at the Greek word *apollumi*. As the verb "to lose," it carries many meanings. It can mean "to lose one's life" due to death in battle, "to suffer loss," "to perish," or "to be lost," as in the case of the lost sheep and lost son. The editors of the *Theological Dictionary of the New Testament* emphasize its figurative use by the Synoptic writers. The loss of one's soul is of paramount significance, as God values it above all else. In the case of the coin and sheep, a search is immediately launched to recover the asset. The figure of the bending woman, rummaging through all her possessions, and the determined shepherd, searching every glen and craggy outcropping possible, attest to God's concern.

As the editors note, the lost son parable is already pre-figured in Ps 118:176 and Ezek 34:4. One might further add that it is pre-figured in *Tobit*, where, instead of the waiting father looking for his son's return, it is the anxious mother. "She would rush out every day and watch the road her son had taken, and would heed no one. When the sun had set she would go in and mourn and weep all night long." "My child has perished!" she would cry (*Tob* 10:7).

The *Dictionary*'s editors also call attention to the Jewish expression *aber nagisho*: "to trifle away one's life." It is this clue that empowers Jesus' saying that whoever seeks to save his life will lose it, but whoever loses his life will find it (Mark 8:35, Luke 17:33; Matt 10:39). In Jesus' view, whoever finally abandons the effort to secure one's own existence, will save it. For he or she will stop trifling it away. They will entrust it to God. They will say "Yes" to that Ineffable phenomenon (whether personal or otherwise) that we encounter in the mystery of our own existence.

The matter of trifling away one's life is preserved in numerous myths. One thinks of Gilgamesh, sporting with all his kingdom's women, until the region's leaders' cries for justice move the gods to create Enkidu, a worthy co-adventurer for the king. Or, for that matter, Samson, or Jacob's hairy brother, Esau, or the restless Absalom! Enkidu, Samson, and Absalom all meet violent deaths. Sorrow engulfs their memories. "O Absalom, Absalom, my son, Absalom!" Only Esau lives to reach old age. After all, he did receive his father's "blessing," if one can call it that. "Esau lifted up his voice and wept. Then his father Isaac answered him: 'See, away from the fatness of the earth shall your home be, and away from the dew of heaven on high. By your sword you shall live, and you shall serve your brother'" (Gen 27:38–40).

One might add that the three parables concerning the lost coin, sheep, and son (as presented by Luke) are set in a context of "joy in heaven" when that which was lost "is found." This emphasis on Transcendence is central to Luke's Gospel. By interpreting the parables as the Seminar Scholars do, this Transcendence is lost. By focusing on the *Gospel of Thomas*, at the expense of the Synoptics, that Other, that divine mystery that the pre-Easter Jesus equally evokes, disappears in favor of the immanent and the worldly—however noble *sarcophilia* may be.

Inner and Outer, Clean and Unclean

Mark 7:14–15, *Thom* 14:5, and Matt 15:10–11 all preserve a saying that scholars attribute to Jesus. If not authentic, it certainly appears to reflect his view. The context has to do with purity laws governing the washing of hands before eating. Issues of "defilement" are central. Jesus rejects these age-old rules that have established boundaries for separating the Jewish people from pagans, as well as from the "unclean" among themselves. "There is nothing outside a person that by going in can defile, but the things that come out are what defile" (Mark 7:15). Matthew's text is even more vivid. "Do you not see that whatever goes into the mouth enters the stomach, and goes out into the *sewer*? But what comes out of the mouth proceeds from the *heart*, and this is what defiles" (Matt 15:17–18). I have italicized *sewer* and *heart* for emphasis. It certainly sounds like something the pre-Easter Cynic Jesus might have said. As metaphor, it is strikingly powerful. The *Gospel of Thomas's* wording is similar to Mark's. "After all, what goes into your mouth will not defile you; rather, it's what comes out of your mouth that will defile you" (14:5). The Fellows conclude that the historical Jesus either "ignored, or deliberately transgressed" his nation's food laws. He ate with the ritually unclean, and in doing so, violated "powerful taboos."[6]

Another set of sayings in Q and Thomas also pertains to this motif. The "cup" becomes the focal point instead of hands, food, or mouth. "Why do you wash the outside of the cup? Don't you understand that the one who made the inside is also the one who made the outside?" (*Thom* 89:1–2). Matthew broadens the saying: "Woe to you, scribes and Pharisees! . . . For you clean the outside of the cup and of the plate, but inside they are full of greed and self-indulgence . . . First clean the inside of the cup, so that the outside also may become clean" (Matt 23:25–26). Luke concurs more with Thomas' saying. He writes: "You fools! Did not the one who

---

6. Ibid., p. 481.

made the outside make the inside also? So give for alms those things that are within; and see, everything will be clean for you" (Luke 11:40–41). The Seminar Fellows note the vindictive quality of Matthew's account, which is lacking in the *Gospel of Thomas*. Nor does the latter mention the Pharisees. It is simply one of Jesus' observations. Many scholars agree today that Matthew's denunciations of the Pharisees reflects his timeframe, not that of Jesus's.

On a theological level, God has made both the inside and the outside of the "cup." Inside and outside together belong to God. For that reason, mankind is to value both sides of his life: inside and outside, the conscious and the unconscious, the physical and the spiritual, the rational and the moral, as well as the "outside" and "inside" of others. This is why Paul's separation of flesh and spirit borders on a compromise for Crossan. It shatters the Old Testament unity of flesh and spirit, of *athama* and *ru'ah*, which together underlie the human *nephesh*, or soul, and its bond with the transcendent as well as the immanent in one's self and others. In Jesus' mind, one's whole being, whether inner or outer, belongs to God. When this truth is applied to society, then all false borders collapse. When one "gives for alms those things that are within," "from the heart," then clean and unclean go. The excluded become included. There are simply no grounds to justify discrimination. In Crossan's analysis of "inside and outside," Jesus' views offend the authorities because they attack the very ground that supports distinctions among foods, guests, social ranks, salutations, table rituals, cherished taboos, and other hierarchies.[7]

In addition to theological considerations, there are ontological and psychological factors that come into play. This places them within the framework of myth and myth's living contribution to the self. Jung's theory of *extraverted* and *introverted* personalities sheds remarkable insight on the problem. "Inner and outer" are not simply theological phenomena. In their *Primer of Jungian Psychology*, C. S. Hall and V. J. Nordby summarize Jung's position. Based on his theory that the psyche performs four functions: *thinking, feeling, sensation,* and *intuition*, Jung hypothesized that there are eight personality types, clustered around extraversion and introversion. An extraverted person, in his *thinking*, enjoys objectivity and understanding; however in his or her *feelings* (especially true of women), he may subordinate the rational to the emotional. An extravert, *sensation-wise*, prefers facts, workable ideas, and practical solutions; while *intuitively* he looks for new horizons to explore. Often the extravert inwardly is an introvert and must wrestle with despair, depression, arrogance, and hidden

---

7. Crossan, *Historical Jesus*, p. 262.

fears. He may become a bigot, display vanity, or become a thrill-seeker. On the contrary, the introverted type seeks self-understanding in his *thinking* and focuses on his own being; with respect to *feelings*, he prefers to keep them hidden. The introvert favors solitude, quietness, harmony. She may appear as aloof and inaccessible. These same characteristics show up in the introvert's attitude toward *sensation. Intuitively*, the introvert makes the perfect artist, prophet, poet, and dreamer. He or she clings to the world of inspirational images and aesthetic ideals, even to the point of self-destruction. Like the extravert, inwardly the introvert is a repressed extravert. Individuals, of course, vary to the extent that they manifest combined aspects of the eight types. Most people are a healthy, adjusted mix of the lot. But this psychological truth about our selves is a mirror of the ontological as well.

Becoming a whole person is no simple matter. One of the great psychologists of our time, Carl R. Rogers, spent his life enabling people to discover their own path to personal growth. In his book *On Becoming a Person*, he summarized his own experiences and presented his methodology for assisting persons along the process of growth. By being himself and listening to others, without trying "to fix" their lives, he enabled them to discover their limitations and fears and move toward fulfilling their potential. In a segment entitled, "The Person Who Emerges," he noted four major characteristics that accompany this process. 1) The person becomes more aware of his or her own feelings "as they exist . . . at an organic level." Equally, the person becomes aware of the outside world as it actually is, without preconceived blinders. 2) The person "increasingly discovers that his own organism is trustworthy," that it is "a suitable instrument for discovering the most satisfying behavior in each immediate situation." 3) The person comes to feel that the "locus of evaluation lies within himself." Finally, 4) the person becomes "content to be a *process* rather than a *product*."[8] Sounding almost like a Taoist, or Buddhist, he concludes: "It means that a person is a fluid process, not a fixed and static entity; a flowing river of change, not a block of solid material; a continually changing constellation of potentialities, not a fixed quantity of traits."[9]

There is an interesting parallel to Rogers' method in John's Gospel. It appears in association with the lame man by the pool of Bethsaida. Magic, legend, myth, and miracle coincide. "Do you want to be healed?" asks Jesus. Then, for no small length of time, Jesus listens to the man. John tells us that Jesus already knew that the man had been coming to the pool for

---

8. C. Rogers, *On Becoming A Person*, Boston, 1961, pp. 115–22.
9. Ibid., p. 122.

years. Perhaps Jesus saw it in his face, in the dark shadows that flickered about his eyes. Whatever, he let him tell his story: how his friends brought him daily to the basin, how he waited eagerly for the angel to "trouble the waters," how others rushed ahead of him, knocking him aside, as only the first to enter the pool could be healed; and how he lay back again, dejected, resentful, if not angry, comforted only by the ruse of self-pity. "Stand up," Jesus said to him. "Take your mat and walk." "At once the man was made well, and he took up his mat and began to walk" (John 5:2–9). Note the word "began." Becoming whole is a long process. By letting the man express his hopelessness, Jesus enabled him to accept himself, his past and present, and, in doing so, revived the man's courage to trust himself. Yet, without his encounter with Jesus, that personification of the something more we encounter in the hiddenness of our human mystery, he would have remained unchanged by the pool!

With respect to all this, Joseph Campbell reminds his readers that the true locus of religious awakening is nevertheless within.

> What's important is what's happening to you now. . . . The divine lives within you. Our Western religions tend to put the divine outside of the earthly world and in God, in heaven. But the whole sense of the Oriental is that the kingdom of heaven is within you. Who's in heaven? God is. Where's God? God's within you. And what is God? God is a personification of that world-creative energy and mystery which is beyond thinking and beyond naming.[10]

That makes self-encounter also an encounter with that "something more" that Tillich repeatedly names "the Ground of Being."

Hidden and Unveiled

Almost identical in meaning and purpose to "outer and inner" is an aphorism preserved in Mark, Q, *Thomas*, Matthew, and Luke. It has to do with the "hidden and the unveiled." Each tradition uses it to promote its own agenda; still the basic message is the same: "There is nothing hidden that will not be revealed. There is nothing veiled that will not be unveiled. Nothing hidden will escape disclosure; the secreted will be exposed." (See *Thom* 5:2 3, 6:5–6; Mark 4:22; Matt 10:26; Luke 8:17, 12:2.) In Crossan's view, Jesus' "message is something that should be open and obvi-

---

10. J. Campbell, *An Open Life*, Burdett, NY, 1988, p. 64.

ous to all,"[11] for Jesus' emphasis falls on the community and the abolition of distinctions, titles, ranks, and discriminatory practices.

I would also add that the "hidden" refers to more than one's anima or individualized unconscious, but also to the Unknown that lies behind the collective unconscious which we encounter in ourselves. It is this "Unknown" that, for the post-Easter Church, the historical Jesus *made known* in his life, death, and resurrection. In this respect, Jesus' fondness for the "secret" and the "private" witness to the Unknown whom Jesus sought to know, if not reveal. His thrice-repeated phrase: "your Father who sees in secret will reward you" (Matt 6:4, 6, 18) speaks of his own requirement for privacy and a secret place to be alone with God where his personal integrity and spirituality could be renewed. We never escape that dimension of the "hidden."

11. Crossan, *Historical Jesus*, p. 350.

6

Children, Women, Prostitutes, Publicans, and Beggars

SOME OF the most compelling units within the collected sayings of the pre-Easter Jesus are those associated with children, women, prostitutes, publicans, and beggars. In Jesus' day, only the second in this grouping was accorded respect, or viewed as having legal rights. Women at best enjoyed a few. That is not to say that children were not prized or that women were not loved. Their status placed them below men. Prostitutes were viewed as criminals. Publicans were necessary to the Roman ordering of taxes. The *Mishnah* devotes only slight attention to the role, obligations, and status of children, views with critical eye the rights of women, and mulls with ambiguity the role of tax gatherers. The overall subservient status of these groups attests to the harshness of the era. It was not always that way.

Merlin Stone and Riane Eisler remind us that, previous to the rise of warrior cultures, women's rights co-equaled male rights. That was owing to the fact that, until about 2,500 BC, Goddess worship prevailed throughout the Ancient Near East. The role of the Mother Goddess bestowed "rights" on women and attributed virtues and values to them that enhanced their status. But with the coming of the age of conquerors and warlords, land and its conquest called for a new mythical order of gods. Goddesses became subservient in the new myths; feminine values took a drubbing. Women as *partners* became women as *property*; so did their children. This cultural shift is documented in numerous artifacts, pottery designs, fertility figures, legal codes, and new myths. Reverence for the Goddess survived, but she was considered ancillary to the male pantheon of Marduk, El, Baal, Molech, Ra, Zeus, and Yahweh. Stone's *When God Was A Woman* and Eisler's *The Chalice and the Blade* address this shift.

Overthrowing *cultural myth* is hard work. If one views this activity as part of the Cynic Jesus' mission, then much of what he says about children, women, prostitutes, publicans, and even beggars, takes on new light. He was not simply redressing wrongs sustained by these groups but was offering a new order of inclusivity.

Children

The single, yet thrice-fold repeated reference to *children* in the Synoptics is believed to reflect Jesus' attitude, if not his very words: "Let the little children come to me; do not stop them; for it is to such as these that the kingdom of God belongs" (Mark 10:14; Matt 19:14; Luke 18:16). All three point to Jesus' concern for the marginal in society. Mark and Luke append a second saying, immediately following the first: "Truly, I tell you, whoever does not receive the kingdom of God as a little child will never enter it" (Mark 10:15; Luke 18:17). *Thom* 22:1–2 follows suit: "Jesus saw some babies nursing. He said . . . 'These nursing babies are like those who enter the Father's domain.'" The Seminar Fellows consider the initial statement more or less authentic, while noting that the appended statement appears to have its setting in a baptismal ritual of "entrance" into the Christian community. Its "first cousin" is found in John 3:5: "no one can enter the kingdom of God without being born of water and Spirit." In all likelihood, Jesus never established any initiation or baptismal rites. Tradition has stressed the children's innocence and their complete trust in parents and caring adults. We are to be that trusting toward God. This may be so, but Jesus' agenda includes far more. He is endorsing a radical shift in social attitudes altogether, which is "a vision of an alternative reality directly ruled by God."[1] This direct rule by God in the present is the radical element. It rends asunder all previous androcentric and paternal models of ordering society. A new pattern, a new vision, a new world precedent has been offered.

A more revealing pattern as to how children were treated may be found in the *Mishnah*. The references pertain to girls, who apparently serve in menial capacities within the family. The father has sole rights to sell them, if they are under the age of twelve. If they have been seduced or abused, then fines may be leveled, which the father collects (*Ketuboth* 3:8 and *Sotah* 3:8). Equally significant is a rule preserved in *Kiddushin* 4:13: "an unmarried man may not be a teacher of children." In the "children passage" of the Synoptic Gospels, the disciples do their utmost to prevent parents from presenting their children to Jesus for him to bless them. Were they trying to protect him, lest he violate the taboo? Do their actions imply his bachelor status? "No, no!" he says. "Let them come on!" Was he

---

1. *Five Gospels*, p. 89.

married, then, or at least betrothed? If Jesus were married, which permitted him to "teach" or "bless" children, then why did the Gospel writers want to hush this? Many popular theories of the present time conclude that he was married. In *The Jesus Papers*, Michael Baigent argues that Jesus was married to Mary Magdalene, alias the Mary of Bethany; that Lazarus was his brother-in-law; and that the wedding at Cana was actually Jesus' and Mary's. Baigent further hypothesizes that Mary was pregnant at Jesus' death, or that perhaps they had already had a child.[2] But all this is crucial to Baigent's interest in Jesus' blood-line, which necessitated Jesus' marriage to Mary.

Women

Jesus' relation to women is difficult to extract, if limited to Q or Thomas. However, Luke's narratives provide us with intriguing details. Outside of the nativity passages, Luke 10:38–42 proves very informative. Martha has welcomed Jesus into her home and has set about to prepare an evening meal. Her sister, Mary, sits at Jesus' feet, listening, enraptured by his teachings. Martha complains, but Jesus reassures her that Mary's choice deserves her support. What the story implies is that Jesus accepted women as disciples. He included them without apology, while trying not to offend his hostess for her own chosen, traditional path. Whether she was his wife or not is another matter.

Luke 13: 10–17 recounts the story of a crippled woman, who for 18 years had been doubled over (scoliosis?) and unable to stand erect. It is a Sabbath and Jesus is teaching in a synagogue. As soon as Jesus sees her, he summons her to his side, places his hands on her, and heals her. When the president of the synagogue objects, Jesus replies: "Ought not this woman, a *daughter of Abraham*, . . . be set free?" Luke ends the story by stating that: "his opponents were put to shame." His goal was to put his whole race, religion, culture, and its privileged classes "to shame." To put Rome to shame and equally his country's corrupt subservience to Rome to shame! That he succeeded accounts for his arrest and execution. In any event, the story underscores Jesus' acceptance of women.

In fact, Jesus' political vision with respect to gender equality has yet to be realized in many parts of the world. We call such visions "worldviews." They underlie and motivate a civilization's belief system, dreams, laws, art works, edifices, social fabric, and religion. They take on mythic proportions, and when they are lost, nihilism and rootlessness set in.

---

2. Baigent, *The Jesus Papers*, San Francisco, 2000, pp. 107–8, 111–13, 121–23.

It is what Nietzsche foretold in his famous "Mad Man" speech in *Die Froehliche Wissenschaft*. "*Wohin ist Gott? Wir haben ihn getotet—ihr und ich!*" "Where is God? We have killed him—you and I!" Beyond Jesus as a peasant Jewish Cynic, there breaks through the social constraints of his day his vision of a world, lived in concert with the "personification of that world-creative energy and mystery which is beyond thinking and beyond naming."[3] It is this vision of "the living God" that constitutes the heart of Jesus' own spiritual views, which informed and inspired his life and work, and opened him to all classes and genders.

Luke tells us that a number of women formed a support group and followed Jesus and his disciples wherever they went. Writes Luke: "The twelve were with him, as well as some women who had been cured of evil spirits and infirmities: Mary, called Magdalene, from whom seven demons had gone out, and Joanna, the wife of Herod's steward Chuza, and Susanna, and many others who provided for them out of their resources" (Luke 8:2–4). It is interesting that in this passage's parallel in Mark and Matthew, the reference to women is missing. Baigent considers these women married, or else they could not have accompanied the men. Since Mary Magdalene is mentioned, he reasons she must have been Jesus' wife.

Two of Jesus' best known parables, and one less well known, are woven about women: the woman searching for her lost coin, the woman kneading leaven into her flour tray, and the woman carrying meal in a jar. The first two acknowledge a feminine tenacity that refuses to let go. In each case, the kingdom of God is *like a woman* doing these things. She is enrolled in the kingdom's work, searching and finding the lost coin, kneading the transforming leaven into herself, her family, her friends, her world. Her resourcefulness summons the hearer's imitation. The *aretetical* value of these two metaphors takes center stage. The Thomas version of the leaven story expands on the far-reaching effects of her action. "She took a *little* leaven, [hid] it in dough, and made it into *large* loaves of bread" (*Thom* 96:1–2; italics for emphasis).

The less known parable is preserved in the *Gospel of Thomas*. Its ending jolts the hearer. It is not what one expects. Its meaning plummets one into endless depths.

> The Father's imperial rule is like a woman who was carrying a jar full of meal. While she was walking along a distant road, the handle of the jar broke and the meal spilled behind her along the road. She didn't know it; she hadn't noticed a problem. When she

---

3. *Open Life*, p. 64.

reached her house, she put the jar down and discovered that it was empty (97:1–4).

The parable abounds with images. They serve as code words: "jar," "full of meal," "a distant road," "broken handle," "spilled meal," "behind her," "discovered," "problem," "empty." The woman's "homeward journey" forces the reader to examine his or her own personal journey, as one moves from "full to empty," and from the "unnoticed" to a shocking "discovery." The kingdom of God creeps up on one like that. Just when you think you have finally figured life out and have it by the handle, you'd better think twice! You'd better glance over your shoulder before closing the door!

The parable equally shares some haunting parallels with Buddhist and Zen motifs. Two in particular stand out: the concept of *emptiness* and the idea of *suchness*. *Emptiness* carries a double meaning. One has to empty oneself of illusions, of thinking of the self as an isolated, unchanging ego, unrelated and distinct from everything else. No. This is not the case. There is no such ego. We are constantly experiencing change, undergoing transformation due to karmic activity and thought, and we are inseparably related to the world about us. Buddhism refers to this as *anatta* (no-soul), the formal name it assigns this doctrine. It is far better to think of oneself as an element, aspect, or manifestation of the life-giving world soul, than as some kind of independent, unchanging substance, that will go on, unchanged and unchanging, throughout eternity.

The other meaning of *emptiness* has to do with one's outlook and openness to life. If, on the journey, we carry a jar full of preconceptions as to what we should find in advance and how to deal with life's problems, we will suffer disappointment and be bound by our own rigidity. Better to empty ourselves of such notions, to be open to the new, and not be a slave to the past, especially, if we haven't re-examined its suppositions and inferences.

Suchness follows immediately on the heels of emptiness. *Suchness*, or *ta-tha-ta*, simply means, "Look! Look at that! Do you see it? Right there? Look! That's what life is all about! To see things as they are!" Openness to the Ground of Being, to the depth of being, and the mystery and wonder of life, enables one to take a fresh look at life, along with a keener look at oneself, ones neighbors, culture, civilization, and the Ineffable Ground of Being. We are all interconnected, inter-related, bound by a commensality that enervates life again.

A remarkable koan, or poem, from the Zen collection known as the *Mumonkan,* captures this Buddhist truth:

> Gateless is the Great Tao,
> There are thousands of ways to it.
> If you pass through this barrier,
> You may walk freely in the universe.[4]

Or as the noted Zen specialist and Zen master, D. T. Suzuki, was fond of phrasing it: "Empty-handed I go, and behold the spade is in my hand." In many ways, Jesus' parables serve as new "spades" for rethinking culture's values.

Women were not only part of Jesus' retinue, but both Luke and John's passion narratives honor them for their grieving presence at his execution and for coming to his tomb, early in the morning following the Sabbath. They came to care for his body. John's tradition lists those at the cross as "his mother, and his mother's sister, Mary the wife of Clopas, and Mary Magdalene" (John 19:25). Luke refers to a similar role call at the tomb. In John's Gospel, it is Mary Magdalene to whom the "risen Jesus" appears first. Thus while Luke and John's accounts represent tradition, they equally attest to the kind of person that the pre-Easter-Jesus, or peasant-Cynic mold, suggests. However, whether Mary Magdalene was Jesus' wife is beyond their texts' capacity to prove. The truth is, the contemporary assessment of Mary Magdalene as Jesus' wife is based primarily on *The Gospel of Philip* and *The Gospel of Mary*. The former twice identifies Mary as Jesus' "companion," suggesting not merely her status as an apostle, but as his lawful wife. *The Gospel of Mary* portrays her similarly, or at least as someone in whom Jesus confided more closely than in anyone else. The key verses in *The Gospel of Philip* indicate that there were three Marys: his mother, his sister, and Mary of Magdala, his *companion*.[5] Jesus loved this *companion* more than all his other students. He kissed her often on her face, more than all his students, and they said, "Why do you love her more than us?" The savior answered, saying to them, "Why do I not love you like her?"[6] In *The Gospel of Mary*, Peter says to Mary, "Sister, we know that the Savior loved you more than all other women."[7] Then, moments later in indignation, Peter adds: "Are we to turn around and listen to her? Did he choose her over us?" However, coming to her rescue, Levi answers: "if the Savior made her worthy, who are you then for your part to reject her? Assuredly the Savior's knowledge of her is completely reliable. That

---

4. *Zen Comments on the Mumonkan*, New York, 1974, p. 14.
5. *The Gospel of Philip* in *The Gnostic Gospel*, Boston, 2006, p. 267.
6. Ibid., p. 273.
7. Karen King, *The Gospel of Mary*, Santa Rose, Calif., 2003, p.15.

is why he loved her more than us."[8] In *The Chalice and the Blade*, Riane Eisler introduces a term for Jesus' new order. She calls it *gylany*. She bases it on a union of the Greek root word *gyne* for woman and the verb *lyein* for resolving problems. She offers *gylany* in place of the older terms *patriarchy* and *androcracy*. Rather than promoting a male-dominated system that suppressed half of humanity, she views Jesus as having offered a system in which both halves of humanity could resolve issues together.[9] Certainly, Crossan's concept of commensality hints at the same.

Even Paul adopted some of this *galantic* philosophy. "There is no longer Jew or Greek, there is no longer slave or free, there is no longer male and female; for all of you are one in Christ Jesus" (Gal 3:27). Frequently he applauds the work that deaconesses and prophetesses were undertaking wherever they lived. In his Letter to the Romans he lists at least eight female co-workers: Phoebe, Prisca, Mary, Junia, Persis, Rufus's mother, Julia, and Nereus's sister. Phoebe is referred to as a "deacon," Prisca as one who risked her "neck" for Paul, both Mary and Persis as among the Roman community's hardest workers; Junia, as having suffered imprisonment with Paul, for being hailed for her "prominence among the Apostles," and for being "in Christ long" before Paul was. But in other matters, Paul remained fettered to his civilization's androcratic ways. He wanted women to veil themselves during worship, to keep silent in church, and to maintain the dignity expected of them by their husbands and the customs of the time. Some scholars doubt that the 1 Cor 14:33–36 admonition to be "silent" is original with Paul, as it appears to be more of an editorial insertion from 1Tim 2:11–12: "Let a woman learn in silence with full submission. I permit no woman to teach or to have authority over a man; she is to keep silent." Such a rebuff hardly seems compatible with Paul's praise for women in the Romans passage. It falls more into conformity with the *Mishnah's* androcentric limitations: "How does a man differ from a woman?" *He may go with head unbound and rent his garments; she may do neither. He may impose the Nazirite vow on his son; she may not. A man may sell his daughter; the woman may not. A man may give his daughter in betrothal; a woman may not* (*Sotah*, 3:8). It is ironic how the early Church could remember so many of Jesus' sayings yet fail to inculcate them in real life. But, as noted earlier, transforming culture is no easy task. It flows downward from concepts that mirror our highest perceptions and struggles upward from the depths, the anima, the very hiddenness of the mystery of the human condition. The spirit, or élan, that inspired Jesus enabled him to draw from both sources:

8. Ibid., p. 17.
9. R. Eisler, *The Chalice and the Blade*, San Francisco, 1988, p. 105.

the inner and the outer, the outside and the inside, the upper and the lower, male and female, as *Thom* 22:4–6 attests: "When you make the two into one and . . . the inner like the outer and the outer like the inner, and the upper like the lower, and . . . make male and female into a single one . . . then you will enter the Father's domain." Whether Jesus actually said this, we may never know. But its truth is hard to refute.

Prostitutes, Publicans, and Beggars

Jesus' references to *prostitutes* and *publicans* are found only in Q. The two groups' condition, along with society's image of them, evokes a formula response from Jesus. He rises to champion both their openness and their willingness to change. "Truly, I say to you, the tax collectors and the prostitutes [*pornai* in Greek] are going into the kingdom of God ahead of you. For John came to you in the way of righteousness, but you did not believe him, but the tax collectors and the prostitutes [*pornai*] believed him" (Matt 21:31–32). Interestingly enough, in the Lukan version, only tax collectors are mentioned (Luke 7:29–30); the reference to prostitutes has been dropped. However, in Luke's parable of the Prodigal Son (Luke 15:30), the youth is described as having "wasted his substance on *pornon*," a term which can also denote "flute players." The *Gospel of Thomas* preserves no sayings at all on either subject. One assumes that Matthew and Luke derived their aphorisms from Q. Whatever the case, the point is clear enough. John's message advocated justice for the poor, the outcast, the sinful in general. Many of the latter listened, took it to heart, and began the process of changing their lives.

Is it possible that some of Jesus' followers might have been *pornai*? Or, if not openly practitioners of the profession, might they have sought and found refuge among his disciples? Jesus certainly seems to have been kindly disposed toward them. The woman "caught in adultery" (John 8:3–4); the woman by the well (John 4:18); and the "sinner" [*amartolos*] of Luke 7:37–39, who bathes his feet with her tears and dries them with her hair, all attest to Jesus' sympathy for their struggle and condition. He was neither deaf nor blind to their need. It is very likely that *pornai* were part of his band.

As for tax collectors (*telonai*), in the *Mishnah*, a house becomes violated if a tax collector enters and the head of the house "touches" him or his bag. One may even equivocate about one's wealth, so long as one doesn't "swear" as to how little he has. One may not exchange money with a tax collector, if he's conducting his practice, but one may do so later, when the man is at home. Moreover, the tax collector's status, which allows him to seize others' goods, makes him immoral in principle and deed.[10]

In his own treatment of tax gatherers, Crossan compares them to "thieves." They are no better than scum, despised outcasts of society. Yet they are precisely the types Jesus' kingdom dares to reclaim.

Finally, *beggars* receive acknowledgement, too. "Give to everyone who begs from you, and do not refuse anyone who wants to borrow from you" (Matt 5:42). Luke repeats this saying from Q and couples it with the Golden Rule: "Give to everyone who begs from you; and if anyone takes away your goods (tax gatherer), do not ask for them again. Do to others as you would have them do to you" (Luke 6:30–31). As the Seminar Scholars are quick to point out, Matthew's sequence deals with *begging and borrowing*, whereas Luke's topics discuss *begging and robbery*. Luke goes on, however, to encourage a lending practice that anticipates no repayment (Luke 6:34). This injunction renders it similar to *Thom* 95: "If you have money, don't lend it at interest. Rather, give it to someone from whom you won't get it back." This radical edge gives the Christian imperative a totally different *telos* and rationale. "For if you give, expecting something back, how does that make you different from anyone else? And how does it help the poor?" (Luke 6:32–34, paraphrase).

The *Didache* had to wrestle with this problem, too, but its writers decided to apply practical limitations. After all, the world teems with imposters, and the world of the Church is no exception. The *Didache*'s writers quote from either Matthew or Q: "Give to everyone who begs from you, and ask for no return" (1:5). Then it adds a hostile warning: Alas for the man who receives it. If he's truly in need, that's one thing, but if not, he stands self-condemned. He will be imprisoned, his actions investigated, and he will not be released until he has "paid back the last cent." Finally, they quote a proverb by way of justification: "Let your donation sweat in your hands until you know to whom to give it" (1:24–25).

How far the Church had wandered from the spirit and savvy of Jesus! What began on his part as a bold and promising revolution, based on a concept of God and of God's "imperial rule," incarnate and present in the lives of humanity, had fallen into the hands of well-meaning, but circumspect people. Though they lived unobtrusively on the margins of the Roman Empire, in their respective places and way, they were beginning to experience the burdens of leadership and fill the very positions of power that the pre-Easter Jesus—only decades earlier—had challenged and stood on end. His sayings had been collected, recorded, and preserved

---

10. See the *Mishnah*: *Hagigah* 3.6; *Nedarim* 3.4; and *Baba Kama* 10.1–2.

in glowing Gospels, but his Spirit had been institutionalized and was now being "conferred" on deacons, elders, priests, and bishops. True, Bishops Ignatius and Polycarp would die for their faith, just as Peter and Paul and so many more would die in the coming years. But already the long, slow transition toward a new religion, complete with creeds and rituals, robes and distinctions, censors and icons, was emerging more and more each day. What happened is still the catalyst that drives scholars anew to search for the Jesus of history.

7

The Hero as Universal Archetype

In *The Hero with a Thousand Faces*, Joseph Campbell provides various diagrams of the hero archetype. No one mythic hero embodies them all, but the pattern is similar: divine birth or lineage, separation, call to adventure, divine aid or supernatural help, trial and temptations, journey, conflicts, battle-death-dismemberment, return-rescue-resurrection, and, finally, apotheosis.[1] Campbell reviews numerous figures who individualize aspects of this pattern. Basically, they symbolize the life-path that humans must also travel. In so doing, they proffer a form of reassurance, that even mortals can pass this way. They incarnate the age-old drama of life's cycle "from the tomb of the womb to the womb of the tomb."[2]

Jesus' life fits this cycle, as do countless others. The extent to which this archetype influenced Jesus' admirers, or the founders and leaders of the early Church, is beyond our capacity to know. That it did, I believe, is irrefutable. His life conforms to the pattern too neatly.

Who were some of the great heroes and hero-gods who loom in the shadows behind the Gospels? There are at least four worth recalling, the most obvious being Dionysus.

According to Bullfinch's sources (primarily Ovid), Dionysus was the son of Zeus and Semele. Semele was a mortal, the princess of Thebes. Hera, Zeus' wife, became insanely jealous and sought revenge. Disguised as an old nurse, she appeared to Semele and coaxed her to ask Zeus to make love to her in his entire splendor. Semele liked the idea, but first asked her lover if he would grant whatever she wished. He agreed and swore by the river Styx that he would, an oath that not even he could break. Once she revealed her request, Zeus shrank in horror, since he knew what would happen. He dressed in all his grandeur, went into Semele, who immediately perished from the radiance of his glory.

---

1. J. Campbell, *The Hero With a Thousand Faces*, Princeton, 1973, pp. 30, 245.
2. Ibid., p. 12.

Zeus committed his infant son Dionysus to the care of the Nysaean nymphs, who reared him. On becoming a young man, Dionysus discovered how to cultivate grapes and turn them into wine. Hera found out, struck him with madness, and forced him to become a wanderer. In Phyrgia, the goddess Rhea, queen of the universe, healed him. He journeyed on, as far as India. On his return to his native city, Thebes, Pentheus the king, fearful of the new rites Dionysus had established, forbade him to enter. He attempted to have Dionysus arrested, but his Maenads (female devotees drunk with wine) protected him. The king's men managed to capture the ship's captain, Acetes, who tried to warn Pentheus that Dionysus was a god. His story of how he himself recognized the divine countenance of the boy only hardens Pentheus. The latter will hear nothing of it and orders his guards to continue their search. By now, Dionysus and his worshipers, along with his Maenads, crowned with ivy wreaths, have fled to a mountain to participate in their wild rites. Pentheus follows but is mauled to death by the Maenads and by his own mother, who has succumbed to madness during the horrific orgies.

The Greeks not only associated Dionysus with the vine, but also with immortality. It was claimed that he had rescued his own mother from Hades and that later the Titans tore him to pieces at Hera's command. As god of the vine, his branches bore no leaves during the winter and, before spring, had to be pruned. Thus the spring signaled his resurrection, as much as it celebrated Persephone's. At the Eleusinian mysteries, these twin traditions were woven together, and he was hailed as both god of the vine and god of immortality. In her work, *Mythology: Timeless Tales of Gods and Heroes*, Edith Hamilton explains that during these festivals, prisoners were often released from jail, and that the locus for the festivals was not in a field but in the theatre. Here the Greek playwrights competed against each other to present the best possible poems to Dionysus. He was Greece's Suffering Servant, its god of death and resurrection, the surest Comforter of eternal life. They deemed him worthy of the highest honors they knew to bestow.

The Gospels' presentations of Jesus mirror this myth in countless ways. Consider them. There is Jesus' divine/human parentage. Like Dionysus, Jesus was forced to flee from his native home (from Bethlehem to Egypt and back to Nazareth). He endured numerous trials and conflicts. Peter, one of his own, recognized him as a divine son, or at least as the Christ. Jesus was always in journey and established his own vision of God's kingdom. His enemies accused him of being a "glutton and wine bibber." He suffered arrest. He was beaten, was forced to wear a crown of thorns, and was executed. God, however, raised him from the dead. He even spoke of himself as the vine and his followers as the branches. As in the case of the Eleusinian mysteries, a prisoner, Barabbas, was released at his trial. His death and resurrection occurred at the end of winter and the beginning of spring—the first Sunday after the first full moon, following the vernal equinox. A cup of wine was drained in memory of him. To this day, torn pieces of bread are eaten in a rite symbolizing his rent body. The connection begs the question, to say the least.

Jason, Heracles, Odysseus, and Aeneas equally come to mind.

Jason was the son of Aeson, a king of Thessaly, who had surrendered his throne to his brother Pelias, on condition that he hold it for the boy until his son could mature. Once Jason matured, Pelias reneged on the deal and urged Jason to search for the Golden Fleece, which was part of Thessaly's heritage. The Fleece lay in a grove, protected by a sleepless dragon, in far-off Colchis, on the eastern shore of the Black Sea. As the young prince listened, he actually warmed to the idea. It represented challenge at its best. Jason had no trouble recruiting adventurers to join him, among them Heracles, Orpheus, and Theseus. They became known as the Argonauts, named for the shipbuilder who constructed their vessel for the voyage. Once they set sail, danger lurked all about, especially at the infamous gates to the Dardanelles, which they managed to pass. Upon their arrival at the kingdom of Colchis, Jason explained his mission. The king agreed, on condition that Jason would harness two fierce bulls and sow the teeth of a dragon, which Cadmus had killed. He warned Jason, however, that as soon as the teeth should touch the soil, armed men would rise up and attack the sower. With the help of the king's daughter, Medea, who provided him with magical dust, Jason accepted the challenge, yoked the wild bulls, ploughed the field, sowed the teeth, and defeated the armed men. Next, he had to approach the sleepless dragon. Medea's dust worked; the dragon fell asleep, Jason slew it, retrieved the Fleece, and departed Colchis with Medea—before the king realized what had happened.

Upon their return to Thessaly, Jason asked Medea if she could use her charms to prolong the life of his aging father, Aeson. Calling upon all the spirits of the sky, air, earth, and water, she concocted a ghastly brew, which she gave Aeson to drink. Upon drinking it, he became forty years younger. Her arts, however, could be used for evil purposes, which she exacted on Pelias and his daughters. In time Jason fell in love with Creusa, a princess of Corinth, put Medea aside, and married the princess. Enraged, Medea called on the gods for revenge. Creusa died a horrible death; Medea killed her own children, set her palace ablaze, and fled to Athens, where she married King Aegeus. Jason never recovered from the loss of his children, nor apparently faulted himself for Medea's behavior.

Of all the heroes, none could match the strength and virtue of Heracles (Hercules). The poet Pindar would refer to him as a hero and a god, *heros theos*.[3] His twelve exploits mirror the signs of the Zodiac, the number 12 bearing sacral relevance from the most ancient of times. Its significance for dividing the cycle of the constellations, the full moon's appearance within a solar year, and the number's eponymous role in sacred leagues (like the twelve tribes of Israel and equally symbolic of the twelve apostles), are well known.

Heracles was the offspring of Zeus and Alcmena, a mortal mother, married to Amphitryon of Thebes. Zeus' lustful liaisons, especially with mortals, always infuriated Hera. Upon the boy's birth, she placed serpents in his crib, but Heracles seized them in his powerful hands and crushed them. His parents wished nothing but the best for their precocious son and hired the wisest teachers to tutor him. Music was part of the curriculum, but in a fit of anger, he struck his teacher on the head with his lute, causing the man to die. By the age of 18, he had mastered all the arts of war and weaponry and had killed a lion, whose skin he wore about his shoulders and head. He married, had children, and seemed happy, but Hera, once again, decided to disrupt his life. She cursed him with a spell of madness, during which time he killed his wife and children. Utterly distraught, he sought comfort from his father and friend, Theseus, who took him to Athens. Still troubled and in sorrow, Heracles visited the Oracle at Delphi to seek purgation and advice. She recommended that he go to her cousin, Eurystheus, king of Mycenae, and do whatever he urged. Delighted to have Heracles in his service, the king assigned the grieving hero 12 daunting tasks. Eleven had to do with animals, or grotesque monsters, nature at her worst. The penitent and powerful Heracles accomplished each task, one after the other.

His last challenge was to bring the three-headed dog, Ceberus, up from Hades. Accompanied by Athena and Hermes, Heracles made the descent. Hades was willing for the monster to be returned to earth, provided the hero would do it unarmed. Heracles managed to subdue the creature and bring it back. He also released his friend, Theseus, who had been detained earlier during the latter's attempt to carry off Persephone.

Often plagued by fits of madness (attributed to Hera), his bravery was compromised by violent deeds. Under one such spell, he killed a friend, Iphitus. The gods condemned him for this act and required him to serve

---

3. Walter Burkert, *Greek Religion*, Cambridge, Mass., 1977, p. 208.

as a slave of Queen Omaphale for three years. While the queen donned his lion's skin, Heracles was forced to dress and act like a woman, performing womanly chores. In Jungian terms, he had fallen totally into the hands of his *anima*.

Once freed, he remarried and enjoyed a period of peace toward the end of his life. While crossing a river, the Centaur Nessus, who assisted travelers for a fee, sought to run off with Dejanira, Heracles' new wife. Heracles killed him with his bow and arrow. The dying Nessus begged Dejanira to keep a vile of his blood, as a lucky potion that would enhance her husband's love for her. Not long after this, in still another exploit, Heracles took as spoils a maiden who caught his fancy. He requested Dejanira to bring him a white robe to wear at a sacrificial ceremony in honor of the gods for his latest victory. Thinking only to restore his love for her, Dejanira washed the robe in Nessus' blood, hoping the potion would work. Instead, as Heracles put it on, its poison ate into his flesh. So great was his pain, and so imminent his death, he asked his friends to place him on the altar, that he might die there. Moved by the flames that consumed him, as well as the hero's purity of intention, Zeus proposed to the Olympian gods that Heracles be elevated to heaven and granted immortality. They concurred, even Hera, for once the flames immolated his flesh (i.e. Alcmena's part), it seemed only reasonable that his father's essence should return to the celestial halls of Mt. Olympus.

Divine birth, temptation, trials, travel, impossible tasks faithfully performed, his descent into Hades, along with treachery, betrayal, and sacrificial death, constitute a pattern that appears in the Evangelists' own Gospels of Jesus' life. Certainly, Luke was no stranger to the Greco-Roman mythic world. His kerygmatic summaries of Jesus' career reflect haunting similarities of Heracles' career. "I truly understand that *God shows no partiality*, but in every nation anyone who fears him and *does what is right* is acceptable to him. . . . You know how *God anointed* Jesus of Nazareth with the Holy Spirit and *with power*; how he went about *doing good* and healing all. . . . They put him to *death* on a tree; but *God raised him* on the third day" (Acts 10:34–41; italics for emphasis). John's use of the "Book of Signs" awakens curiosity, too. Are his "signs" a faint reminder of Heracles' great wonders? The mind-set was there. It echoed the culture.

The German classicist Walter Burkert best sums up the political and spiritual relevance of Heracles for his age. He became

> an influential spiritual force for two reasons above all. First, he is the prototype of the ruler who by virtue of his divine legitimation acts in an irresistible way for the good of mankind and finds his fulfillment

among the gods; thus Alexander stamped the image of Heracles on his coins. Secondly, he is a model for the common man who may hope that after a life of drudgery . . . he may enter into the company of the gods. Heracles has broken the terror of death.[4]

Or as the Apostle Paul would later express it: "Where, O death, is your victory? Where, O death, is your sting?" (1 Cor 15:55).

I mention Odysseus primarily for two reasons. Foremost, he was admired for his wisdom. Throughout the Trojan War, Homer's *Iliad* praises the warrior for his patience and counsel, as much as for his bravery and prowess. He was the son of Laertes, the ruler of Ithaca, and absolutely one of Athena's favorite mortals. Whenever Hera would try to intervene on the side of the Trojans, Athena would resist her in order to protect Odysseus. Secondly, after Odysseus arrived home, following his long and perilous voyage, he revealed himself only to his son. Then, in the guise of a beggar, he set about, with Telemachus' aid, to cleanse his house of his wife's throng of degenerate paramours. "He came to what was his own, and his own people did not accept him. But to all who received him, . . . he gave power to become children of God. . . . And the word became flesh and lived among us" (John 1:11–12, 14). One has to wonder if John's "Beloved Disciple" isn't an unconscious echo, or unconscious archetype, of Odysseus' Telemachus! "Woman, behold your son; son, behold your mother" (John 19:26–27). Or as Odysseus's old orchard keeper put it: "Dear Master, how we missed you! We thought we'd never see you again. But the gods have brought you home!"[5] "Sir, if you have carried him away, tell me where you have laid him, and I will take him away." The gardener studied her, then spoke: "Mary!" She turned and, recognizing him, reached out to embrace him and replied, "Rabbouni!" (John 20:15–16).

As Joseph Campbell insists, myths come from the heart. Rather than pointing to facts about the world, they point to the mystery that "informs the facts." They enable us to interpret our present moments in terms of our inner life. They are "poems," "renditions of insight," that attest to the miracle, wonder, and marvel of life.[6] For Campbell, the real clue of the adventure motif, which lies at the heart of *The Odyssey*, is not to identify oneself with any of the "powers" we experience along the way. Otherwise, we never "return home," i.e., find our real self. Yogis seek to escape these powers by experiencing ecstasy. But the ultimate aim of the journey is neither escape, nor

---

4. Ibid., p. 211.
5. *The Odyssey*, Bk. 23.
6. *Open Life*, pp. 21–22.

ecstasy for the self. The ultimate aim is to discover "the wisdom and power to serve others."[7] In Campbell's mind, Zeus realized that Odysseus was scarcely ready to return home, especially after his prolonged stint in Troy, where he fought and spilled so much blood. He needed time to heal, time to find himself again, thus Zeus decreed or allowed the many ordeals that Odysseus had to experience, in order to reshape his character before returning home. In essence, *The Odyssey* is an archetype of every human being's own journey, especially of one's inward journey.

Drawing on Jungian psychology and Hindu philosophy, Campbell surmises: "The inward journeys of the mythological hero, the shaman, the mystic, the schizophrenic are in principle the same; and when the return . . . occurs it is experienced as a rebirth," of an ego no longer bound by its own time and space. "It is now known to be but a reflex of a larger self," whose function is to "carry the energies of an archetypal instinct system into fruitful play" in contemporary life. As a result, no one has to be afraid of nature or of society anymore, because one's reborn ego is now in harmony with this larger self.[8] Jesus put the same truth to Nicodemus, when he said, "You must be born again." It would constitute a long journey, as Jesus knew. John records that it was Nicodemus who helped Joseph of Arimathea prepare Jesus' body for burial. He, who had first come to Jesus by night, "came, bringing a mixture of myrrh and aloes, weighing about a hundred pounds" (John 19:39).

The Old Testament has an equal supply of heroes and heroines. Enoch and Elijah both ascended into heaven, the latter in a fiery chariot. Abraham, Sarah, Jacob, Joseph, Moses, Joshua, Samson, Deborah, Ruth, David, and Esther—all qualify. The pattern of struggle, trial, journey, accomplishment, betrayal, and death is part of everyone's experience in one form or another. In the case of heroes, their achievements are aggrandized, as memory elevates them to tribal and national prominence. They become the standard by which others measure themselves. Such was Lincoln in a time of discord; he becomes the mark by which every president measures himself.

The Greeks honored the memory of failed and fallen heroes, as well as men of potential marred by inner conflicts and character flaws. Icarus, Phaeton, Theseus, and Achilles come to mind. In the Old Testament, it is Esau, Samson, Saul, Absalom, and Adonijah who vie for this distinction.

Icarus was the son of Daedalus. The latter was the architect of the famed labyrinth of Crete, which held the fierce Minotaur. Following Theseus' slaying of the Minotaur and his escape with the king's daughter,

---

7. J. Campbell, *Myths to Live By*, New York, 1972, p. 234.
8. Ibid., p. 237.

Minos of Crete had Daedalus imprisoned in his own labyrinth, along with his son Icarus. Daedalus fashioned wings for himself and Icarus, and the two flew out. Daedalus warned his son, however, not to fly too high, as the wax on the wings would melt, if he flew too close to the sun. Out over the sea they flew, but the young Icarus kept soaring higher and higher. Daedalus pleaded with him to come back, but Icarus paid no heed. Finally, the wax melted and the wings fell off. Down dropped the boy, never to be seen again. He is not the first youth to disobey his parents, or ignore their pleas. Nor is he the sole human who would ascend to heaven, to find and converse with God. He represents everyman who wishes the same. But God, or the mystery that underlies and is the Ground of Being, or the *Logos* become flesh, dwells in light, unapproachable. "It is he alone who has immortality and dwells in unapproachable light, whom no one has ever seen or can see" (I Tim. 6:16). Yet, what the ancient world longed to behold, Christianity proclaims has come to pass. "He who has seen me has seen the Father" (John 14:9). Here we have myth answering myth, a poetic vision superceded by the highest anthem of all.

Phaeton's story is matched in beauty only by Jesus' parable of the Good Samaritan. Phaeton, doubting his divine birth, went eastward to visit his father's throne. Apollo, the sun, who drives his chariot daily across the sky, assured the youth that he was his father. The boy asks one favor only. Apollo, in his paternal kindness, is only too willing to grant it. Since the gods cannot break a promise, he is shocked and saddened when he learns that Phaeton wants to drive his chariot, just once. Apollo pleads with the boy; he is too young, too inexperienced, to handle the powerful steeds who pull the chariot. Nor does he know the arc that must be followed, nor the dangers along the way. Phaeton insists, Apollo relinquishes, up go the gates, out burst the horses, and sadly the father places the reins in his son's hands. With a shocking lurch, the steeds bolt upward. From then on, Phaeton's ride mounts upward, sideways, downward, crazily on its fatal path across the sky. Disaster after disaster occurs, plaguing the earth, sea, and sky. Finally, Zeus, begged by the Earth, must do something. Thus he hurls a mighty thunderbolt toward the lad, and down, down falls the boy into the sea.

There are limits to what mankind can know and do. Ironically, however, there are potentials that mankind equally fails to realize. First, what are the limits? As the Apostle Paul acknowledged: "Who will ascend into heaven, that is, to bring Christ down? Or who will descend into the Abyss, . . . to bring Christ up" (Rom 10:6–7). In Paul's theological-cosmological view, God must come down. Mankind cannot ascend. A self-emptying is required to receive the divine descent, whose power alone can transform life. For though Christ was "in the form of God" (*en morphé theou*), he "did not regard equality with God as something to be exploited, but emptied himself . . . and humbled himself and became obedient to the point of death" (Phil 2:6–8). Yet, Paul was also aware of that "larger self," which Campbell emphasizes, and to which oriental spirituality aspires. "Do not lie to one another, seeing that you have stripped off the old self with its practices and have clothed yourselves with the *new self*, which is being renewed in knowledge according to the *image (eikona) of its creator*. In that renewal there is no longer Greek and Jew, . . . slave and free; but *Christ is all* and *in all!*" (Col 3:11; italics for emphasis). The divine is already present in human life. The kingdom of God is that close. The inner Christ, the all in all, the *panta kai en pasin Christos* is immanent and imminently in everyone. As a Hindu friend once told me, "The hardest thing to realize is that you are God."

Achilles is remembered for his wrath, his *orgé* in Greek: anger, fury, indignation, mental bent, or destructive impulse. Even Homer winces from the spiteful way in which Achilles slew Priam's son, mistreated his body, and humbled his father. Such disrespect could not go unpunished.

Nor could the Greeks forget the brave Theseus. He risked his life to save the Athenian youth, whom his father was required to send to King Minos to sacrifice to the Minotaur. With Ariadne's help, Theseus slew the monster and led the party to freedom. But after he and Ariadne escaped, he betrayed her and left her stranded on the Island of Naxos. Even worse, as he approached home, he forgot to change the sails from black to white, signaling his victory over the Minotaur. Upon seeing the black sails, his father, Aegeus, king of Athens, assuming the worst, fell upon his own sword.

That Jesus might have known any of these myths is beyond any level of evidence currently known to scholars. No aphorisms or parables in Q point to such knowledge. But the *Gospel of Thomas* preserves sayings concerning two and one and two becoming one that reflect a knowledge of Plato's androgynous primal man, or something of the *shekinah-tif'eret* split. The "primal man" story appears early in Plato's *Symposium*. According to the myth, primal man was a unit of male and female forces. Actually, "he" was three in number: "there was man, woman, and the union of the two." Just as the sun, moon, and earth are three, so was this androgynous creature. His power and terrible countenance was such that the gods became fearful of him, or, of "them," as Plato refers to this tri-natured human. Should Zeus destroy them or not? Zeus concluded that he would separate them. He assigned Apollo the task of achieving this and of smoothing out the wrinkles.

As a result, the two separated halves began to wander about, longing for each other and their original nature. They hungered to reunite, "making one of two." This yearning for reunification implies more than mere amorous affection. Rather, it is a deep desire, of which even the "soul . . . cannot tell." Men and women are driven to seek one another, to fulfill the gap of their lost original state. Thus being two, they long to become one.

The Yahwistic account of man's creation in Genesis also echoes this myth with its buried archetypal and primal desire. The removal of the man's rib to create woman and its ending clearly attests to the collective unconscious at work. "Therefore the two shall become one flesh" (Gen 2:24). Jesus knows of this ancient archetype as well, for he repeats the story, along with its injunction. "Have you not read that the one who made them at the beginning 'made them male and female,' and said, 'For this reason a man shall leave his father and mother and be joined to his wife and the two shall become one flesh'? So they are no longer two, but one flesh. Therefore what God has joined together, let no one separate" (Matt 19:4–6).

The *Gospel of Thomas*, however, appears to have been more influenced by the Platonic myth than the Synoptic Gospels. *Thom* 4:3, 11:4, 22:4–7, 23:1–2, and 106:1 touch recurringly on the division of the one into two and the desire for wholeness again. "On the day when you were one, you became two. But when you become two, what will you do?" (11:4). "And when you make male and female into a single one, so that the male will not be male nor the female be female . . . then you will enter the Father's domain" (22:5–6). "When you make the two into one; you will become children of Adam" (106:1). The Jesus Seminar Fellows are confident that the historical Jesus never espoused any of these views. But if they do not belong to the category of history, they belong to the category of faith. They witness to mankind and Gnostic Christianity's longing for reunification with the divine, for that union with the "larger self" that brings peace, inspires hope, and fosters a sense of immortality in which one's finitude may rest. "Whoever believes in me, though he die, yet shall he live, and whoever lives and believes in me shall never die" (John 11:25–26).

8

Archetypes of the East

THE EAST, too, is aware of separation, alienation, suffering, and the need for reunification. Its path has generally taken the way of renunciation. The lore of the Upanishads, the epic story of the Lord Krishna and his servant Arjuna, the life of the historical Buddha, and the concept of the Bodhisattva all address the reality of these motifs.

Upanishads

As readers of Hindu scriptures know, the *Chandogya Upanishads* contain the most oft-quoted text that reveals the truth about the self and the universe. That truth is known as THAT THOU ART (VI. vii. 7).

First, a quote from two earlier passages will help:

> Now, the light which shines above this heaven, above all the worlds, above everything, in the highest worlds not excelled by any other worlds, that is the same light which is within man. . . . One should worship as Brahman that inner light which is seen and heard (III. xiii. 7–8).

> All this is Brahman. From It the universe comes forth, into It the universe merges, and in It the universe breathes. Therefore a man should meditate on Brahman with a calm mind (III. xiv. 1).

As Nikhilananda, the translator, explains: "the universe, at all periods of time, remains one with Brahman. It can never exist apart from Brahman. The universe is Brahman Itself."[1]

Now, we come to the *textus classicus*. Udalaka is speaking to his son, Shvetuketu: "Now that which is the subtle essence—in all that exists has itself. That is the true. That is the Self. That thou art, Shvetuketu" (VI. vii. 7; xi. 3; xii. 3; and xiv. 3).

No text could make it clearer. We are one, already, with the universe. It is in us and we are in it. To become aware of this truth, of this

---

1. Nikhilananda, *The Upanishads*, p. 299.

fact, opens that gateless gate that the *Mumonkan* celebrates, that Taoism knows as the name that cannot be named, and Buddhism cherishes as the Buddha-essence. To *accept* ourselves as manifestations of this mystery and to *experience* it in ourselves and in others, is what constitutes enlightenment. Illusions fall away after that. *Samsara*, or release from the wheel of rebirth, occurs. *Moksha*, the essence of liberation, is gained. *Ananda*, or bliss, accompanies the salvific experience.

However distant in time the Johannine writer may have been from the pre-Easter Jesus, he saw the post-Easter Christ as the full embodiment of the *Logos*, the world Brahman, if you will, the great I AM. Furthermore, John understood that he, too, that his own life, was hidden in Christ's, much as Udalaka was trying to explain the immanence of Brahman to his son. As Jesus said to his own: "The Spirit of truth abides with you, and . . . [is] in you. . . . Because I live, you also will live. On that day [when the Advocate comes] you will know that I am in my Father and you in me, and I in you" (John 14:17–20). As Campbell adds in a passage of his own: "the ultimate mystical experience is of one's identity with the divine power . . . . That divinity which you seek outside, and which you first become aware of because you recognize it outside, is actually your inmost being."[2] Or as Epictetus explained it for his Stoic friends:

> But you are a principal work, a fragment of God Himself, you have in your self a part of Him. . . . You bear God within you. . . . O slow to understand your nature, and estranged from God.[3]

Krishna and Arjuna

David Noss explains the Way of Devotion as India's response to the inroads of Buddhism on the former's ancient culture. Prior to the Buddha's emergence, Indian spiritualists and members of its Brahmin caste had adopted what scholars call the Way of Works and the Way of Knowledge. The wisdom of the Upanishads, as seen in the quotes from the *Chandogya* texts above, reflects the Way of Knowledge. By knowledge and meditation, one can experience the indwelling Brahmanic reality. The Way of Works refers to the ancient rites that the Indo-Aryan invaders brought when they migrated into India around 2,500 BC. Both these Ways required a form of discipline and ascetic austerities beyond the common man's time, tastes, interest, and spiritual needs. Thus the Way of Devotion evolved to

---

2. *Open Life*, p. 85.
3. *Discourses*, in *The Stoic and Epicurean Philosophers*, New York, 1940, p. 294.

Archetypes of the East

meet these needs. A movement whose advocates favored *bhakti* or devotion opposed the non-dualistic philosophy of the former two Ways. In their mind, such a strict monistic interpretation of the world and the self failed to do justice to the facts of life as ordinary human beings encounter them. Emphasis shifted from union with Brahman to devotion to Vishnu, or Shiva, or Ishvara, as *personal* and *living* manifestations of the divine principle. One could focus one's heart on these deities, pray to them, and experience their grace and love in return. The highest expression of this Way found its literary home in the *Bhagavad Gita,* or Song of the Blessed Lord. In this epic poem, the Lord Krishna, an incarnation of Vishnu, rides on the chariot with Arjuna, as the young prince's horses lunge into battle against members of his own extended family. Though all three Ways are acknowledged as legitimate paths to Brahman, Krishna extols the way of *bhakti* over the others.[4] At the opening of the Song, Arjuna's grief surfaces, because of the carnage that will soon ensue. But Krishna consoles him with these words:

> Never have I not existed, nor you, nor these kings; and never in the future shall we cease to exist. . . . He who thinks this self a killer and he who thinks it killed, both fail to understand; it does not kill, nor is it killed. It is not born, it does not die; having been it will never not be; unborn, enduring, constant, and primordial, it is not killed when the body is killed. . . . I am the universal father . . . . I am the way, sustainer, lord. . . . Men who worship me, thinking solely of me, always disciplined, win the reward I secure.[5]

Though the monistic philosophy of eternal union with the divine is endorsed, it has been softened by the personal appearance of Vishnu's descent (*avatar*) as the Lord Krishna.

One cannot read these lines without thinking of John's *Logos* become flesh. In his Christian text, we have God's own descent as Jesus of Nazareth. Here we meet the ineffable mystery and Ground of Being, stepping onto the stage of human existence, and revealing himself as the way, the truth, and the life. To accept, know, and worship him—the great I Am—is to experience life, now, in all its abundance. It is to know that we are not alone, that the outside and the inside have been united. This is the way that the universe is. THAT THOU ART! It is OK to accept yourself as a manifestation of the mystery that throbs throughout the universe and

---

4. D. Noss, *A History of the World's Religions,* Upper Saddle River, NJ, 1999, pp. 112–18.

5. Van Voorst, Chaps. 2 and 9 of the *Gita,* pp. 55–58.

pulsates in yourself. John certainly saw the Christ as indwelling and empowering his own being. He had become one with the peace that passes all understanding. That divinity which he had sought outside, he realized was of *his own inmost essence.*

Siddhartha Gautama

In an earlier chapter I provided something of an outline of the life of the historical Buddha. As much as anyone, the life of Prince Gautama conforms to the heroic pattern that the principal Western classical heroes embody. His life is associated with a royal birth, if not a divine one, seeing that on the threshold of his supreme enlightenment he elected to descend into his mother Mayadeva's womb and be born on behalf of all mankind. There followed his childhood, his life in the palace, the legend of the four passing sights, his departure, search for the truth, travels, trials, enlightenment experience, call of disciples, and years of teaching and wandering, before his death.

In a magnificent and perceptive chapter, entitled "The Legends," Sangharakshita discusses the three current trends among contemporary Buddhists with respect to the "facts" about the historical Buddha. The first group dismisses legends, insofar as they exaggerate and misrepresent what actually happened. The second group deletes materials which conflict with scientific findings; while the third rejects stories and episodes that are purely symbolic. If all this sounds familiar, modern biblical criticism operates in much the same way. But Sangharakshita, though appreciative of these efforts, argues that in doing so, the "symbolical biography of the Buddha" is lost, and with it, the psychological insights that encourage followers to become like the Buddha, and seek their own enlightenment.[6] In all likelihood, in Sangharakshita's judgment, the Buddha's compilers, drawing upon what oral sources they had, objectified the psychological insights of the Buddha and then projected them back into episodes. To delete these episodes as non-historical is to devalue the great truths of human existence that the Buddha story conveys. This assessment applies, in part, to today's biblical scholars who want to free the pre-Easter Jesus from "the tyranny of dogma." But, to what greater "tyranny" are they relegating his followers, when they dismiss the mythical framework that has preserved his sayings so inviolate?

For Sangharakshita, the truths preserved in the Legend of the Four Passing Sights is that old age, disease, renunciation, and death will come

---

6. *The Three Jewels*, p. 30.

to all. "As I reflected on that," says the Buddha, "all my elation of youth disappeared."⁷ The same is true of the great trial prior to the Buddha's enlightenment. All the forces of lust, hate, and fear assailed the Buddha, but he remained firm. This too is an objectification of mankind's psychological experience, as Jesus' own Temptation Legend attests. As Dostoevsky so powerfully objectified the temptations in *The Brothers Karamazov*, so mankind is forever tempted to settle for mystery, miracle, and authority, in place of the genuine freedom the Christ offers. So too does truth pertain to the serpent story, associated with the Buddha's post-awakening Enlightenment. For seven days and nights, a great storm broke over the area near the Bodhi tree, under which the Buddha rested. Suddenly, the serpent king, Mucalinda, slithered out of the forest, wrapped its coils about Siddhartha and spread its hood over him, to protect him from the heavy rains. Then, when the storm ceased, the serpent appeared as a sixteen year-old boy and saluted him. What is one to make of this? Sangharakshita asks. His answer is purely Jungian. The serpent king represents the coiled energies of the *kundalini*: that spiritual force that accompanies seated, yoga meditation, and which, as it rises along the nervous system, triggers the occult sensations of peace, bliss, assurance, and repose. The serpent also symbolizes the realm of the deep, where countless treasures lie awaiting discovery. This realm of the deep, with its splendid treasures, or *nagas*, "represents the up surging energies of the unconscious . . . in the positive creative aspect which makes available to the conscious mind treasures of beauty, insight and understanding it did not dream it possessed."⁸

As one can deduce, a study of the historical Buddha, minus its mythical context, diminishes the overall Buddhist experience of Enlightenment. In Sangharakshita's view, the mystical and magical episodes that surround the Buddha's Enlightenment enhance a Buddhist's own Awakening, rather than detract from it. It is very likely that the same holds true for Jesus' contemporary followers. Eliminate the post-Easter beliefs, or the post-Easter Christ, and what we have left are disconnected aphorisms, spoken by a Jewish Cynic, whose love of people and personal belief system cost him his life.

The pre-Easter Jesus of the Gospels was executed on a tree. In Paul's interpretation of that event, the righteousness of God was made visible, and all mankind was set free from sin and death. Siddhartha Gautama is also associated with a tree. He deliberately sat under it, determined not to rise until he understood human existence and the nature of its suffering.

7. Ibid.
8. Ibid., p. 32.

When he finally "woke up" and saw things as they are, he became the Buddha, the Awakened One, for all who might follow him. The objectification of psychological needs and experiences onto such figures as Jesus and the Buddha, frees human existence from its rounds of self-doubt and human bondage. This is implicit in the actions and writings of the post-Easter Church, as well as in the works of those who complied the Buddhist scriptures. Otherwise we are captives of our own individualism, in bondage to a solipsism that isolates us, not only from the depths of the self, but from one another, the universe, and the Ground of Being.

The Bodhisattva

The general definition of a Bodhisattva is: *someone who deserves Nirvana, or becomes very close to attaining Buddha-essence, but postpones the final stage in order to help others*. Often such a "person" is looked upon as a reincarnation of the spirit of the compassionate Buddha. The Dalai Lama is deemed such a person. The concept is very old and grew out of the Mahayana School in opposition to the Theravada School. The latter emphasizes a monk, or arahant, achieving Enlightenment on his own. With no god to pray to, the arahant strives to become enlightened by himself. He may live in a community of others, but he seeks awakening, *moksha*, "self-extinction," or "emptiness" alone, on his own. The Mahayana School found this approach too severe. In time, their ideal became, not the arahant seeking his own salvation, but a bodhisattva, dedicated to the attainment of wisdom for others. As Christian Humphreys explains: "It is noble to work for all rather than for oneself. All deeds, . . . good or ill, help or harm all other beings, and deliberate acts of good-will help all living things toward enlightenment."[9] We live for others and not just ourselves.

Sangharakshita, however, provides the best explanation. The Buddha of the Mahayana School became not just a historical person, but also "the embodiment of the highest and most universal ideal of spiritual life." Across time, many followers emulated this "embodiment." In doing so, at death, they became celestial figures of a vast realm of spiritual entities. This universal family "comprises all those who, moved by the sufferings of others, dedicate themselves to the attainment of the highest spiritual good not for the sake of their own salvation only but in order that they may be able to benefit all sentient beings. A great soul of this type is technically called a *bodhisattva*."[10] These figures reside in various Buddha-lands and

---

9. C. Humphries, *Buddhism*, p. 160.
10. *The Three Jewels*, p. 160.

are available to assist those who call on them. In the New Testament, the risen Jesus, or the Advocate, or God's own Spirit, is the equivalent form of a bodhisattva. Roman Catholicism has carried this further in its doctrine of the veneration of saints. It is not out of order at all. As a metaphor, the bodhisattva is anyone who *incarnates* the grace of God. As in Hasidism, he is the zaddik who "lets God in."

If I may be allowed a personal footnote, years ago, when first studying Eastern religions, I dreamed one night that I was seated on a diaz. My legs were folded in the lotus position, my back and neck erect, as the yoga posture requires, and my mind clear and "empty." Suddenly, I was seized by a great calm, a spiritual bliss so powerful, that I felt absorbed into the Ground of Being. While still enraptured in this ecstatic state, a serene and omniscient voice spoke: *"Sir, That Thou Art!"* You are this center within yourself. It is within you. The experience was so intense, that when I awoke, I still felt at one with the divine inner essence.

Not long afterwards, following several months of Buddhist studies, I had a similar dream. Again, I was seated in meditation. Someone was approaching me. It was the Dalai Lama. I easily recognized him by his dark red robe, yellow scarf, shaven head, western glasses, and his huge, congenial smile. "What do you want?" he asked. Somewhat shocked, I had to think for a few minutes. Then, in typical Western fashion, I replied: "Truth, goodness, and beauty." The Dalai Lama studied me for a moment, held out his hands, and said: "Receive them, for they are already yours."

Even I smile. I had been translating too much Calvin. I needed that compensatory peace that only dreams can bring. Still, if the experience of *oneness* had not been so intense, I might have forgotten the dreams, or viewed them as little more than too much overindulgence in late night reading. But at a psychological level, similar to Jung's collective unconscious, I experienced a "reality," a depth within myself that energized and renewed my mind and spirit. I still remember them, especially when I ponder Whitehead's inimitable lines, about the transition from "God the Void to God the enemy, and from God the enemy to God the companion."

9

Nativity, Transfiguration, and the Cross

The Birth Narratives

Like many New Testament scholars before him, Bornkamm found the birth narratives of Matthew and Luke unacceptable from a historian's point of view. They were "too overgrown" with legends and "messianic conceptions" to warrant historical review. At best they were reflections of Jesus' mission and purpose in the eyes of his later followers.[1]

Marcus Borg takes a similar position but is much more positive. They are not historical reports. Nevertheless, they are filled with symbolic affirmation. For Borg, both Matthew and Luke affirm that Jesus' birth was "of God," or "of the Spirit." Both emphasize the "ancient theme of light"—Matthew with his shining star and Luke with the "Glory of the Lord" filling the night sky with singing angels. The Church's decision to celebrate Jesus' birth in connection with the winter solstice builds on the same theme. Light has come into human darkness, bringing hope to mankind once again.[2]

Crossan offers a slightly more contextual view. Neither Matthew nor Luke's birth narratives provide any "biographical information" of a historical nature. Both the "virginal conceptions" and setting at Bethlehem have more to do with historicizing prophecy than with supplying any real historical information. Matthew's account fulfills Isa 7:14 and Mic 5:2; while Luke's passage concerning Augustus's decree in the time of Quirinius is simply inaccurate. Crossan supplies three reasons why this is so. First, Augustus never ordered any such worldwide census during his emperorship. Second, Quirinius's census occurred a decade after Jesus' birth. Third, even if Augustus had ordered such a census, it would have been taken at one's place of work,

---

1. Bornkamm, pp. 53, 173.
2. Borg, p. 24.

not at one's ancestral home.[3] Both Matthew and Luke were interested in "historicizing prophecy," not in offering historical detail.

Of further interest, the Jesus Seminar Fellows provide no commentary whatsoever with respect to the Matthean account, nor do they accompany Luke's birth stories with helpful comments. With almost all other passages in *The Five Gospels*, they do this. Their silence at this point is ominous. One must conclude that in their estimation, both units are the creation of the writers themselves.

The above views should not strike anyone as unusual. Our world no longer believes in the direct divine interaction between heaven and earth as these narratives portray it. We are purely in the realm of legend at best. In the mind of many contemporary scholars, we have moved from the category of history to the category of a one-way myth, from man to God, but not from God to man. Perhaps this is too harsh an assessment of the Seminar's many good works, but one hates to lose what Sangharakshita has called, the value of the "spiritual biography." From that perspective, Jesus remains the central figure, but now from the viewpoint of a two-way myth. And this is not wrong, or mistaken. It is the framework that makes possible the meaning of the post-Easter Jesus while conveying his universal value.

The birth narratives, foremost, confirm Jesus as the long-awaited Messiah, the Son of the Most High, the Davidic offspring of whom Nathan assured David: "The Lord will make you a house. . . . I will be a father to [your son] and he shall be a son to me. . . . Your house and your kingdom shall be made sure forever before me" (2 Sam 7:11, 14, 16). This is a prime example of what Crossan means by historicizing prophecy.

Far more, however, is involved. Few passages convey the spiritual depth of Mary's conception as Gabriel's message to the Virgin. "The Holy Spirit will come upon you, and the power of the Most High will overshadow you; therefore the child to be born will be holy; he will be called Son of God" (Luke 1:35). If we keep in mind the dual purpose of myth, what we actually encounter in this story is (1) *our own re-birth* (2) in *response* to the mystery of our human condition. It is we who need the Holy Spirit, who need to experience the power of the Most High overshadowing us. We are the *child* to be born from the *holy womb* of this union with the Other. We are each individually sons of God, daughters of the Most High. What this story hallows is our wholeness again, thanks to this rebirth. It is filled with *ontological* and *numinal* aspects of myth. It may not convey information about the universe "out there," but the encounter awakens depths we had not thought possible within ourselves. What happened to the Christ can

---

3. Crossan, *Historical Jesus*, pp. 371–72.

happen to us. The "shadow" side of our unconscious is raised to consciousness, and we are made one with the universe and its ineffable otherness again. Phillips Brooks captured it as aesthetically as anyone:

> O holy Child of Bethlehem, Descend to us, we pray;
> Cast out our sin, and enter in, Be born in us today.
> We hear the Christmas angels, The great glad tidings tell;
> O come to us, abide with us, Our Lord Emmanuel.[4]

In *The Masks of God*, Campbell refers to the symbolism of the "Christmas Crib," inspired by Luke's manger scene. Drawing upon Meister Eckhart's wisdom, he explains that the *Crib* is our own heart wherein we cultivate our awakened spirituality. As Eckhart explained to his congregation:

> It is more worth to God his being brought forth spiritually in the individual virgin or good soul than that he was born of Mary bodily. . . . He is not content until he brings his Son to birth in us.[5]

In still another work, *Thou Art That*, Campbell argues that the real meaning of Jesus' birth hinges on the question of fatherhood. Who is one's true father? As Jesus said to Nicodemus, unless you are born from above, you cannot enter the kingdom of heaven.

The archetype of the Virgin, who brings forth new life, wholesome and clean, is ancient, as we have seen in Ovid's account of Phaeton, Dionysus, Heracles, and others. It was not new to Luke. He took that familiar archetype of the innocent maiden and her divine offspring, fathered by the Holy Spirit in his account, and reworked it to create the spiritual background against which he could portray the power of the post-Easter Christ to transform life. His birth narrative may not represent "history," as biblical scholars define it. Its allusions to Hannah (i.e., Samuel's mother's prayer woven into in Mary's *Magnificat*); its depiction of a frightened girl, pale with awe; or birth of the baby boy in a manger-stable; or field of shepherds, who stare agog into a glowing night of shimmering stars, may constitute nothing *cognitive* or *representative* about the universe, but his story touches us. Its *existential* import nudges our being. Our encounter with the story sheds light on us and opens us to a *savoir-faire* concerning our own essential being. That is its glory and truth, which transcends time and history, while enriching the lives it touches.

---

4. Phillips Brook, *The Hymnbook*, Presbyterian Church in the United States: Richmond, VA., 1955, p. 157

5. *Masks of God*, p. 156.

The Transfiguration

The transfiguration motif also borrows from the collective unconscious. Score after score of mythological creatures undergo metamorphosis in the classical world. Zeus can take on any form or shape he wills, so too Hera and the countless other gods and goddesses. Daphne was Apollo's first true love. Like Artemis (Diana), she wished to remain unmarried. But Apollo pursed her. She was simply too beautiful. That she should deny him his wish was irreconcilable with his position as a god. But Daphne's heart belonged to the woodlands, not to men. As he drew closer in his pursuit, she prayed to her father, the river god, Peneus, "Help! Please help me!" At once her limbs grew stiff, her torso thickened, her hair turned into a tangle of leaves. Saddened, Apollo ran his hands across her breasts and felt her flesh tremble beneath the hoary bark. But it was all in vain. She had become a laurel tree.

The story of Pyramus and Thisbe is equally sad, if not overtly maudlin. But the metamorphosis involved is transferred to a tree, the mulberry. The two lovers agreed to meet at a fountain near a white mulberry. Thisbe arrived first, heard a lioness in the brush and ran away. In doing so, she left her veil behind. The animal emerged, sniffed it with its bloody maw, and ripped it to shreds. When Pyramus came upon the scene, he reasoned the worst and slew himself. Soon afterward, Thisbe returned, held her dying lover in her arms, then fell on his sword as well. Consequently, to this day, the fruit and flowers of the mulberry are no longer white but a purplish red.

Hera and Athena were the masters of deception, and story after story pertains to them. Nor were Zeus or Hermes to be outdone. As late as Paul's time, these two were still implanted in the common person's mind. According to Acts 14:12, the inhabitants of Lystra thought that Paul and Barnabas were Hermes and Zeus in disguise. "The gods have come down to us in human form," the people shouted. They even brought oxen and garlands to the city gates to honor the two gods.

The Transfiguration story is preserved in all three Synoptic Gospels: Mark 9:2–13; Matt 17:1–8; and Luke 9:28–36. The Seminar Fellows ascribe the story principally to Mark; afterwards Matthew and Luke incorporated it into their accounts. In the Fellows' estimation, it is purely a work of Christian fiction, "a Christian fabrication."[6] This is owing to the fact that the story draws heavily on prophecy in order to interpret John as the anticipated Elijah and Jesus as God's anointed one (Mal 4:5 and Ps 2:2–7). Moses represents the highest possible authority. His presence

---

6. *The Five Gospels*, pp. 81–82.

Nativity, Transfiguration, and the Cross

attests to Jesus' personage and mission as enjoying God's fullest accord. The Scholars are no doubt right in rejecting the story as a piece of tradition that transcends anything that happened to Jesus, or involved his pre-Easter life. It belongs to the category of faith, of typology, legend and metaphor. It has to do with Christ as the Ground of Being and with us, and our human condition, more than it has to do with Jesus as a figure of history. And, yet, it does have to do with the Jesus of history.

Interestingly enough, neither Bornkamm nor Borg discusses it at all. Crossan approaches it as a piece of Markan ingenuity. What Mark did was to "retroject" the two angels that appear in the *Cross Gospel* (a work now embedded in the *Gospel of Peter*), by having them appear as Elijah and Moses, rather than as witnesses to the resurrection. Mark did this because he wanted to eliminate any thought that Jesus was an innocent sufferer, rescued by a resurrection; rather he wanted to present Jesus as a martyr whose death will be vindicated at an imminent parousia.[7] His followers will experience the same, if they truly follow him. No miracle will rescue them.

One has to appreciate this tough, no nonsense reading of the Transfiguration. What is uncanny, though, is that the disciples undergo no transformation, though they observe Christ's transfiguration. For this reason, I think it contains a dual purpose. It points back to those moments of growing revelation within the leadership of the early Church, as well as forward as a metaphor for Christ's followers. In the case of the latter, it poses a question: Are we the disciples who have yet to experience transfiguration or transformation? Certainly, Paul raises this possibility. In the case of the Church's leadership, the story hints of that elusive period during which time the Church "saw" the now crucified, pre-Easter Jesus as the risen and glorified Christ.

"Transformation" is the central focus in two of the texts: Mark and Matthew's. The word in Greek is *metemorphothé*, as pregnant a word as any Mark could have used. In Mark and Matthew, it implies that Jesus underwent a physical change, but in Rom 12:2 and 2 Cor 3:18, it stands as a metaphor of spiritual transformation. Luke reports that Jesus' *appearance* (*eidos*, image, or archetype) became different; but no *metamorphosis* occurs. 2 Pet 1:16–21 also reflects on the Transfiguration, though not by name. If one looks closely at the Synoptic texts, then at 2 Peter, a progression of the Church's wrestling with what to make of Jesus' life slowly unfolds. At least three stages emerge. In the first, the Church's "conclusion" is reported: Yes, Jesus is the Messiah, but to be understood as the Suffering Servant. Mark and Matthew present this step. Both agree that as Peter, James, and John

---

7. Crossan, *Historical Jesus*, p. 389.

came off the mountain, Jesus explained that Elijah had already come. But they are not to divulge this secret, or their "vision," until after his death. At what point after Jesus' execution it occurred to them that he must have been the Christ, we cannot know.

Luke introduces the second stage. The story is somewhat similar, but no mention is made of Jesus' *command to keep silent*; rather the disciples *keep silent on their own accord*. At what time they broke that silence, because of their new awareness of Jesus, escapes pinpointing. No explanation on Jesus' part about Elijah having already come is included in Luke's story, at least not at this point. At some point, however, it became apparent, i.e., literally *appeared* to them, that the pre-Easter Jesus could be interpreted as the Suffering Servant of prophecy. The latter especially so; in fact Luke alludes to this "event," or process, in Acts 8:32–33, in which the Ethiopian eunuch quotes to Philip verses from Isa 53:7–8: "like a sheep he was led to the slaughter." Then the eunuch goes on to explain the *euangellion* "starting with *this* scripture" (Acts 8:35).

2 Peter 1:16–18 preserves the third and final stage. The text is worth reading in its entirety: "For we did not follow cleverly devised myths (*mythois* in Greek) when we made known to you the power and coming of our Lord Jesus Christ, but we had been eye witnesses of his majesty. For he received honor and glory from God the Father when that voice was conveyed to him by the Majestic Glory, saying, 'This is my Son, my Beloved, with whom I am well pleased.' We ourselves heard this voice come from heaven, while we were with him on the holy mountain."

This text is quite transparent, to say the least. It was precisely a *mythos* that they employed to make known the power and coming of Jesus Christ, who received this power from heaven in the form of the prophetic voice of Ps 2 and Isa 44:1–2. Ironically, the writer of 2 Peter was using myth as a form to symbolize his community's understanding of the meaning of the pre-Easter Jesus' life.

As a mythical event, the Transfiguration story is latent with metaphorical value for Christ's first followers as well as his disciples today. The story has to do with one's spiritual transformation as much as with the pre-Easter Jesus' "transformation" in "glory" in the eyes of the Church. In fact, at some point Jesus' own views about himself, God, and the world had changed, or undergone a metamorphosis, just as he hoped others' views would change. Jesus' glimpse of that other world, that other possibility, whether as a Cynic, or as Borg's "spiritual man," pervades the text. So too, the disciples were granted a glimpse of that other world, that other possibility, but it took time for them to move from the "vision" to incarnating it in their lives.

To pass from one world to another and back again lies at the heart of mystical experiences. When this occurs, new insight and potential is awakened in the traveler. Writes Campbell: "myths do not often display in a single image the mystery of the ready transit. Where they do, the moment is a precious symbol, full of import, to be treasured and contemplated. Such a moment was that of the Transfiguration of the Christ."[8] For Campbell the myth displays Jesus as "the guide, the way, the vision, and the companion of the return." The glimpse into that other world was brief. Blinding light, shining garments, the Christ's face aglow, the heavenly voice, and the mystical cloud that overshadows them, all too soon pass away. The disciples had to shield their eyes; in Luke's version, they are overcome with sleep.

What is the "tenor" of this event? asks Campbell. In his view, the fact that three disciples, and not just one, witness the apparition and together see that other world *through Christ*, lies at the heart of the story, along with his conviction that the three "had extinguished their personal wills . . . by complete self-abnegation in the Master."[9] That may be an overly rosy conclusion, but Campbell reminds us that just after this event, especially in Mark's Gospel, Jesus says: "Whoever loses his life will find it." For Campbell, the meaning of the myth should be transparent. Whoever gives up his attachments to himself, along with all his idiosyncrasies, dreams, and fears, and accepts the self-abnegation necessary to receive rebirth, becomes free to live and accept whatever comes to pass. He becomes "anonymous" to himself that the true and higher self of Being may flourish in him.[10]

Jung offers a slightly different possibility. For Jung, transformation stories, or transfiguration archetypes, encourage "rebirth." He notes that a *metamorphosis* can symbolize three types of change: 1) a literal, physical change, 2) a "rebirth," or *Wiedergeburt* in German, or even *renovatio* in French (Latin), and 3) finally, a symbolic rebirth experienced during rites of transcendence. The latter include the Eleusinian Mysteries and the Catholic Mass. By participating in these rites of transformation, a catharsis occurs in the participant. In the case of 2 and 3, one's personality is renewed, but not basically changed. Only "parts of the personality are

---

8. *Hero with a Thousand Faces*, p. 229.
9. Ibid., p. 236.
10. Ibid., p. 237.

subjected to healing, strengthening, or improvement."[11] As might be expected, he favors 2) and 3). He observes that life requires constant renewal and a continuous transformation of the self. To be able to identify with a cult hero, whether in the Mass, or elsewhere, brings eternity into time, and thus *renovatio*.

Without belaboring the point, a brief consideration of Ovid's *Metamorphoses* is worth inserting. The Roman poet (Pubilus Ovidus Naso) lived between 43 BC and AD 17. His earlier works focused on love: *The Book of Love, The Art of Love*, and *The Remedies of Love*. The works were both satirical and erotic. The second, *Ars Amatoria* written around 2 BC to AD 2, was especially playful and personal, and, some say, critical of an affair Augustus was having with his daughter, Julia. Whatever the case, Augustus exiled Ovid to Tomis (now in Romania) on the Black Sea, where the poet would remain until his death. Augustus exiled him in AD 8, the very year in which the last of Ovid's fifteen books comprising the *Metamorphoses* was completed. Ovid's books were banned, too.

Ovid's older contemporary and fellow poet, Virgil, had completed his masterpiece, *Aeneid*, in 19 BC. It was composed in the heroic style similar to Homer's works and glorified the fall of Troy, the exploits of Aeneas, his return to Italy, and the founding of Rome. It was a veiled epic, celebratory of Augustus and the peace he had brought the empire. Its praise of war, glory, conquest, and fallen heroes endeared it to Augustus and the empire's citizens. Ovid took a different approach. His *Metamorphoses* has no central character, no particular plot, no chronological consistency, contains numerous digressions, and appeals to the salacious, the libidinous, and the macabre. It is often anti-military, anti-autocratic, antinomian, anti-male, and anti-heroic. Love, lust, boundless freedom, the reversal of gender roles, along with life's mistakes, conundrums and brevity receive primary attention and replace the older laudatory language dedicated to empires, warriors, and the violent arts.

The one recurring theme is metamorphosis. Life is forever changing, and human beings change, too. His philosophical sources appear to be Lucretius, Epicurus, and the pre-Socratic, Pythagoras. Toward the end of Book XV, his Pythagorean figure says: "Nothing lasts long under the same appearance. Our bodies go through ceaseless change. We pass from the span of fleeting youth to middle life and begin the downhill path of declining age. Nothing remains its own form. But Nature, the great renewer, makes up forms from other forms. Yet nothing perishes. It does but vary and renew its form. Death is but the cessation of a former state,

11. *Collected Works*, ix., pp. 114–18.

as birth is but the beginning of what once was."¹² As Bernard Knox has noted, what Ovid presents is life's "movement from metamorphosis to metempsychosis."¹³ Plato adopted this view, too. And in some respects, the Apostle Paul's "Resurrection" passage in 1 Cor 15 echoes many of these views: "What is sown is perishable, what is raised is imperishable. It is sown in dishonor; it is raised in glory. It is sown in weakness, it is raised in power. It is sown a physical body, it is raised a spiritual body" (1 Cor 15:42–44). The "transformation" motif returns, too, in just a few verses beyond: "Listen, I will tell you a mystery [*mysterion*]! We will not all die, but we shall be changed [*allagésometha*], in a moment, in the twinkling of an eye . . . For the trumpet will sound . . . and we will be changed [*allagésometha*]" (1 Cor 15:51–52).

When the author of 2 Pet 1:16 writes: "For we did not follow *cleverly devised myths* . . . but we had been eyewitnesses of his majesty," one has to wonder if he had Ovid's old book in mind. Or, if tradition is right about John Mark's being the redactor of the Gospel of Mark, and, if he were in Rome about the time of Peter's martyrdom, as well as having been a missionary with Paul on the latter's first missionary journey to Asia Minor, might he just have known about Ovid's *Metamorphoses*, and the changes that its gods passed through, even if he had never read the work? Although Ovid's disdain for Augustus never diminished, his book ends with Julius Caesar, the murdered hero of the old Republic, being apotheosized by the gods. He is raised to heaven by Aphrodite's own arm.

> Venus caught up the soul of her Caesar from his body, and . . . as she bore it she felt it glow and burn, and released it from her bosom. Higher than the moon it mounted up and, leaving in its wake a fiery train, gleamed as a star.¹⁴

Whatever the case, we are dealing with mythical material in the Transfiguration story, and it has to do as much with the reader's spiritual transformation, as with the pre-Easter Jesus and his own apotheosis, witnessed by Peter, James, and John, and the ghosts of Elijah and Moses, as Olympian attendants.

---

12. *The Metamorphoses*, New York, 2005, p. 295, altered.
13. Norton edition of Ovid's work.
14. *Metamorphoses*, p. 310, altered.

Cross

Crossan doubts that any of the arrest, trial, abuse, crucifixion, and burial narrative is history per se. He prefers to label it "prophecy historicized." He does not question that Jesus was executed, but the cross scene, as narrated by the Synoptic writers, reveals more about the post-Easter Church than the pre-Easter Jesus' death. The traditional version, in Crossan's estimation, may be traced from the existence of a *Cross Gospel*, embedded in the *Gospel of Peter*, to Mark and eventually to the other writers. Crossan maintains that the *Cross Gospel* contained an "innocence rescued model" instead of the "martyrdom vindicated model" that Mark preferred. The *Cross Gospel's* "innocence rescued model" followed a fivefold scheme: 1) an innocent person is 2) accused falsely before a court, 3) condemned, but is 4) rescued before the sentence can be carried out, and 5) enjoys restoration. The *Gospel of Peter* preserves all five motifs, restoration being in the form of the resurrection. But what makes this "prophecy historicized" and not history is the fact that buried under the narrative's surface are the following prophetic elements:

> Authorities at the trial, from Ps 2:1
>
> Abuse and torture, from Isa 50:6–7, Zech 12:10
>
> Death among thieves, from Isa 53:12
>
> Jesus' Silence, from Isa 50:7; 53:7
>
> Lots for garments, from Ps 22:18
>
> Darkness at noon, from Amos 8:9
>
> Gall and vinegar, from Ps 69:21
>
> Death cry, from Ps 22:1.[15]

Crossan also presents a list of nine elements, included in the *Cross Gospel* (now in the *Gospel of Peter*), that do not appear in Mark, since they did not enhance his "martyrdom" model, such as Pilate washing his hands, guards at the tomb, Jewish people repenting, and others.[16] Crossan reasons that prior to the *Cross Gospel*, followers of Jesus had been content to collect his sayings, but eventually a more sequential record was wanted, which led to the passion narrative of the *Cross Gospel*, then to the *Gospel of Peter*, and finally to Mark. All of this had been preceded by groups within the Christian communities discovering passages in the Old Testament that appeared to "predict" what had happened to Jesus. Having said all

---

15. Crossan, *Historical Jesus*, pp. 384–87.
16. Crossan, *Who Killed Jesus*, San Francisco, 1995, p. 138.

Nativity, Transfiguration, and the Cross

this, Crossan himself rejects the "martyrdom vindicated model," as it still retains an *apocalyptical eschatology* rather than a *sapiental eschatology* with an emphasis on *sarcophilia* in which the kingdom is incarnated in the here and now.

Crossan's analysis is difficult to best. Sufficient textual evidence seems to support his position. It appears as acceptable as any. But this makes the passion narrative, more than ever, a "fabrication" of the Church, and hence a prime example of mythmaking on the part of the four Evangelists, or five or six, if we include the *Cross Gospel* writer and the redactor of the *Gospel of Peter*. Nevertheless, the narrative is a "fabrication" only in the sense of its details. One does not invent symbols, or *eideos*, or archetypes. The archetype of the hero-god, descending from heaven to assist humanity, suffering rejection and retuning to the heaven as an apotheosized god-man, was not new. Nor was it an "invention." We are compelled to objectify ontological and cognitive dimensions of our existence in order to acknowledge and resolve the mystery of our human plight. That's what makes myth existential, directive, and numinous.

The fact that the Cross story contains mythical elements does not mitigate the reality of Jesus' death, punishment, or execution. Crucifixions had long been in practice in Jerusalem. According to Josephus, Publius Varus had 2,000 insurrectionists crucified following the chaos that erupted after Herod's death. Prior to that, Alexander Janneus had ordered 800 Jewish Hasidim crucified during his own time. He had their wives' and children's throats slit before their eyes.[17] Nor does the Cross story undermine the universal or archetypal values that the early Church read back into it. Theirs was the age of myth, of archetypes, of *eideos* objectified and personified as realities that assist one to fathom the manifestation of the mystery of life. To throw out this story is tantamount to abandoning the Christ once again as a crucified innocent, who wasn't rescued; a Cynic, who met his death because he dared to challenge his time, who lost the battle and became a kind of spiritual Spartacus. If that is the case, then Schweitzer did the right thing. He underwent a metamorphosis and changed from being a New Testament scholar into becoming a medical missionary.

What are some of the archetypal elements of the Cross?

The first is the *death of the estranged self*. "Unless a grain of wheat fall into the earth and die, it cannot bear fruit" (John 12:24). "If any want to become my followers, let them deny themselves and take up their cross and follow me. For those who want to save their life will lose it, and those who lose their life . . . will save it" (Mark 8:34–35). The cross symbolizes that

---

17. *Wars of the Jews* 2.5.2; 1.4.6; *Antiquities* 2.5.2; 13.14.2.

death: the willingness to stop trying to save oneself; thereby one becomes open to the deeper and larger self that leads to freedom and completeness. It is a self-abnegation, an extinction (*anatta*) in the Buddhist sense, a death without guarantee. "My God, my God, why hast thou abandoned me?" (Mark 15:34; Ps 22:1). If one did not feel God-abandoned, it would not be "death." There would still be hope, a glimmer of rescue. By identifying with the dying Christ, the individual dies, too. He or she dies to that self that is marked by estrangement—from itself, from others, and from the Eternal Archetype that it knows in itself.

Second, the cross provides *that sacred space where (1) the transcendent Archetype and (2) the estranged self meet face to face*. As the Tree of life, the cross represents that vertical line between the upper and the lower, heaven and earth, God and the soul, the archetype and our individualization. Its crossbeam symbolizes the ontological mystery of our twofold existence: as dust and spirit, *athama* and *ru'ah*, the unconscious and the conscious; while the nails and crown of thorns attest to the pain, uncertainty, and anguish of the crucifixion that precedes wholeness. It also symbolizes the *reality of suffering*. To live is to suffer. In that sense, suffering is universal. Or as C. S. Lewis preferred to explain it: pain, evil, and suffering are part of a larger system, which God wills. He dubbed it a "tribulational system."[18] The cross symbolizes that spiritual nexus where the soul of God embraces the ontological pain that is inseparable from mankind's pride and loss of being.

Third, the cross symbolizes the *mystery of grace*. Grace occurs wherever and whenever the Eternal embraces time, the upper bends to the lower and the lower reaches toward the upper. When heaven touches earth, and the conscious and the unconscious yield and accept one another, grace occurs. For the Apostle Paul, such is a gift. "For by grace you have been saved through faith, and this is not your own doing; it is the gift of God" (Eph 2:8).

Jung refers to the cross as a *quaternion*: that geometrical figure that embodies the mystery of the psyche in its struggle for wholeness. The Christ on the cross symbolizes that wholeness; indeed, he is that wholeness in archetypal form. The Father embracing the Son, the Son revealing the Father! You and I being the Son, revealing in our self-less death our unity with our higher self, the Father! Writes Jung; "Christ undoubtedly represents the self." He represents "the apotheosis of individuality, . . . expressing the totality of conscious and unconscious contents."[19] But this

18. See Lewis's *The Problem of Pain*.
19. *Aion*, pp. 62–63.

psychological phenomenon can only be described in "antinomian terms," i.e., in opposites: such as good and evil, time and eternity, the spiritual versus the chthonic. Thus the *quaternion* displays in pictorial imagery the complexity of the phenomenon of the psyche in its wholeness.

Campbell has his own way of explaining the cross. He concurs with Jung concerning the power of participating in rites of renewal, especially in the Roman Catholic Mass. By participating in the Mass, one participates in Christ's crucifixion.

> And that sense of the Crucifixion is twofold. One is that the divine transcendent has come into the world and has accepted the crucifixion of life; the other is that the individual has yielded his individual self to the grace of a transcendent realization. The Cross is the threshold of the passage of eternity into time and of time into eternity; and in participating in this, you are giving yourself to the Christ—and the Christ in you, namely the knower of the Father.[20]

Fourth, the cross represents *catharsis*. For "by his bruises we are healed" (Isa 53:5). After analyzing Aristotle's definition of tragedy, Princeton's Walter Kaufmann offered his own:

> Tragedy is (1) a form of literature that (2) presents a symbolic action . . . and (3) moves into the center immense human suffering, (4) in such a way that it brings to our minds our own forgotten and repressed sorrows as well as those of our kin and humanity, (5) releasing us with some sense (a) that suffering is universal—not a mere accident in our experience, (b) that courage and endurance in suffering or nobility in despair are admirable . . . and (c) that fates worse than our own can be experienced as exhilarating.[21]

By identifying with the Archetypal Man, whether as the pre-Easter Jesus or the post-Easter Christ, mankind's bruises, repressions, and forgotten sorrows are healed.

Christianity is not the only religion with a crucifixion at its center. The *Tree of Enlightenment*, under which Siddhartha Gautama sat, extinguishing his own claim to existence, was as much of a cross as Jesus's. There he overcame his own experience of estrangement, phrased as the universality of *dukkha*, or suffering, by putting to death the multiple levels of *tanha*, or craving, that constitute the human condition. Only then came release and enlightenment. And it took time after that before his followers could

---

20. *Open Life*, pp. 68–69.
21. W. Kaufmann, *Tragedy and Philosophy*, Princeton, 1968, p. 85.

incarnate the same, and I suspect time for the Buddha, too. He spent the rest of his life fulfilling the awakening that came to him on that day of days.

So also the Plains Indians of the American West had their cross. They knew it as the Sun Dance, in which they hung lashed to leather thongs from their *Tree of Suffering*: a cottonwood pole. It was their way of giving back to Father Sky a part of their Mother Earth, their own flesh. It symbolized the dance of life, that holy cycle that cradles us from "the tomb of the womb to the womb of the tomb." Once healed of their wounds, they rose from their beds of skins and matted grass, renewed, cleansed, strengthened, and "reborn," *Wiedergeburt*!

Among the Greeks were two brothers who also endured "crosses." Each was condemned by Zeus to suffer punishment: Prometheus for stealing fire and giving it to mankind; Atlas, for attempting to overthrow his father. Prometheus was chained to a *rock*, where for 30,000 years he was sentenced to suffer a vulture's daily feeding on his liver. Zeus forced Atlas to bear the *weight of the world* on his shoulders. Heracles rescued Prometheus and for a period of time supported Atlas's burden on his own shoulders, to give the weary Titan rest. Campbell refers to Prometheus's rock as a "crucifixion . . . on the rock of his own violated unconscious."[22] For Jung, Prometheus's ordeal was a "fit punishment," but he quickly notes that a "crucifixion evidently betokens a state of agonizing bondage and suspension."[23] This the Christ bore, as does the Christ of the self.

The Aztecs ripped out the beating hearts of their victims to give to their gods. The devotees of Kali did the same for her. The Ammonites, Phoenicians, Israelites, and Carthagians hurled live babies into the glowing furnaces of Moloch. Ancient Judaism substituted a ram, a scapegoat, in place of babies. A red cord would be tied about the animal's horns; the priests would spit on it. Then it would be driven into the wilderness to die for human sin. The Romans cut up whole animals to look through their entrails. Even Ovid found that disgusting. But then "crucifixion . . . betokens a state of agonizing bondage and suspension." We cannot fault the archetypes for mirroring the truth, however, our individuations of them may be skewed. The descent into hell is universal. Thus, by identifying with Christ's crucifixion and Christ's descent, we make that transition from God the "enemy" to God the "companion" within ourselves. It is the journey that every self must make. "Only you are your best helper," said the Buddha. "Unless a grain of wheat fall into the earth and die, it cannot

---

22. Campbell, *Hero*, p. 37.
23. Jung, *Collected Works*, ix, p. 236.

bear fruit." "It is no longer I who live, but Christ Jesus who lives in me" (Gal 2:20).

By identifying with the Christ as the supreme archetype of the self, we are able to acknowledge our own foibles, failures, and forfeiture. At the same time, we are able to unite with that spiritual mystery that haunts our consciousness and which our unconscious keeps compelling us to consider until we make peace with it. Tillich referred to that mystery as the Ground of Being. Eastern wisdom knows it as the Tao, the Buddha essence, or Brahman. The cross makes possible the healing conjunction of the two: our forfeiture healed by that transcendent other we cannot flee. Its memory and presence are in us, whether we interpret the transcendent as God, the universe, the Tao, or as a million years of the collective unconscious witnessing to that incredible potential we possess but cannot seem to unlock short of pain.

In Volume Two of his *Systematic Theology*, Paul Tillich focuses exclusively on mankind's estrangement from himself, his neighbor, and the ground of his being, and how the cross symbolizes the overcoming of this estrangement. For Tillich, the marks of estrangement are addressed theologically as *sin, unbelief, hubris,* and *concupiscence*. Man knows that he is not what he ought to be. States Tillich: "Man is not a stranger to his true being."[24] The fact that he feels under self-judgment and becomes hostile toward God only exacerbates his separation from God.

Sin expresses the individual act of turning away from the ground of one's being. The concept's "sharpness" lies in its capacity to remind man that such an act is his choice for which he is responsible.

Unbelief characterizes the depth of this act, in which one loses his total sense of direction and essential unity with the ground of being. Theologically, God no longer stands at the center of life. The doctrine of Total Depravity was the Reformed Tradition's way of viewing this act. It did not mean that man is incapable of reasoning or achieving good, but that he has lost the capacity to reverse his Fall.

Hubris has to do with self-elevation. It is concomitant with the loss of the center. With self-elevation, one's estrangement is intensified. Mankind's original dignity and greatness, symbolized by the *imago Dei*, are diminished. The desire to become like God, or to replace God at the center, exposes mankind to his weaknesses and finitude. Ignorance, insecurity, loneliness, and anxiety rise to the top. The more one attempts to secure one's existence, the more one loses it. This is precisely what Jesus

---

24. Tillich, Vol. II, *Systematic Theology*, Chicago, 1957, p. 45.

saw and why he urged his followers to let go of such fruitless self-elevation. The Buddha realized the same many centuries earlier in his own culture.

Once the center is lost, *concupiscence* claims one's life. For Augustine, turning away from God results in ignorance, lust, and death. It means that sex, power, and wealth, isolated from their essential unity of man's good, dominate his life and make him less than he knows he could be. Tillich defines concupiscence as "the unlimited desire to draw the whole of reality into one's self."[25]

As a consequence, one's *guilt* is compounded. Guilt, too, becomes a mark of existential estrangement. Thus the cross becomes that singular place, where human sin, unbelief, hubris, concupiscence, and guilt are "put to death," and unity with God is restored. By identifying with Christ, one overcomes the harrowing negatives of existence and enjoys reunion with the ground of one's being again. Indeed, one even becomes a new being.

This interpretation of the cross belongs entirely to the *category of faith*, to the *category of myth* in its richest depths, but it would not have been possible without the *category of history* to sharpen it, without the life of the pre-Easter Jesus who inspired the Evangelists. The archetype of the savior has always been present across the eons. For Paul, "the whole of creation has been groaning" for such a redeemer (Romans 8:22). But the way this universal archetype has been individualized in Christianity has made the Christ "the living myth of our culture," as Jung put it. I see no disvalue in stating this, or claiming this as the truth that innerves a Christian today.

---

25. Ibid., p. 52.

10

The Resurrection

IN THE New Testament, the resurrection does not stand as an isolated event, either historically or spiritually. Resuscitations (1 Kgs 17:22; 2 Kgs 4:35), ascensions (Gen 5:21–24; 2 Kgs 2:11; Acts 1:9–11), appearances (Matt 28:9; Luke 24:31, 37; John 20:14, 19, 26; 21:4; 1 Cor 15:5–8), and revelations (Gal 2:2) precede, accompany, or follow the resurrection story, reinforcing the Evangelists' beliefs that Jesus "is risen." In light of that, it is possible to posit a five-stage process through which the Church passed in its struggle to assimilate the pre-Easter Jesus in post-Easter settings. The process involved a movement from 1) perceiving Jesus, the teacher, as the living voice of wisdom, to 2) experiencing his spiritual presence during gatherings and communal meals, to 3) recognizing his continued work through acknowledged leaders, to 4) a vision of him as a vindicated martyr, and, finally, to 5) experiencing in one's own life a sense of the eternal. These stages were not sequential but probably occurred in clusters, as 1 and 5 are compatible, just as 2 and 3.

The Post-Easter Jesus as the Living Voice of Wisdom

If one begins with Q, then proceeds to the *Gospel of Thomas*, and concludes with the *Dialogue of the Savior*, these earliest of the early documents have one thing in common: Jesus is the living voice of wisdom. His teachings are still cherished, and so is he. His wisdom is eternal, illuminating, meaningful, and aretetical. His words reveal the eternal wisdom of God, thus making Jesus a conveyor of eternal wisdom himself.

One saying, in particular, in Q captures a truth, which by now we have seen is central to Jesus' whole message and mission: "Whoever tries to protect his life will lose it; but whoever loses his life . . . will preserve it."[1] This timeless insight cuts to the core of human existence. A second saying reinforces the above: "Where your treasure is, there your heart will

---

1. Mack, *The Lost Gospel*, p. 80.

also be."² From Q² comes still another: "if your eye is good, your whole body will be full of light."³ These aphorisms may sound innocuous at first, but they point to a wisdom grounded in Being and inseparable from mankind's highest potential. All of Q captures and preserves Jesus' maxims and injunctions that endear him to Q's various communities.

It is in the *Gospel of Thomas* that we first meet the phrase "the living Jesus," whose words lead to life. "These are the secret sayings which *the living Jesus* spoke . . . Whoever finds the interpretation of these sayings will *not experience death*."⁴ Throughout the remainder of Thomas, many of Jesus' sayings link life, the Father, wisdom, light, immediate insight, and a former perfect state with eternal life. For all who can grasp Jesus' teachings, death is no more. Through grasping Jesus' teachings, followers return to their primordial home of eternal life and light. They will never perish, or taste death. Especially relevant are the following chapters; 1, 3:4, 11, 18:3, 19:4, 24, 30, 37, 49–51, 58, 61–62, 69, 70, 77, 79, 82, 84, 85:2, 101:3,108, 111:2, 113.

The Seminar Fellows find none of this material traceable to the Jesus of history. It is too loaded with the language of the Church, especially with the Thomean theology of his Gnostic community. It is highly improbable that the historical Jesus ever referred to himself as a revealer, or Messiah, or as the eschatological Son of Man, or Son of God, or in anyway saw himself as God's incarnate wisdom, or as a heavenly being who had descended to earth to reveal the Father's glory, wisdom, or mystery, or that he ever spoke of the All, Pleroma or Apérion. For certain, he would not have approved of Thomas' community's elitism, disdain for the flesh, or eagerness to escape life. All that would have been foreign to him. Nonetheless, what the *Gospel of Thomas* reveals is that a vibrant, persistent, and dedicated early group of Christians perceived the post-Easter Jesus to be this kind of revealer. He was their living voice of wisdom; their return ticket home to that paradisiacal realm from whence they had fallen, come, or descended. Since the *Gospel of Thomas,* as a written document, is believed to precede any of the other Evangelists' works, it marks an early stage in the Church's attempt to relate to the Jesus of history in a post-Jesus world.

The *Dialogue of the Savior* is an expanded collection of sayings in dialogue form, rather than a mere collection of sayings. In his book, *The Other Gospels*, Ron Cameron, a member of the Seminar Fellows, notes that

---

2. Ibid., p. 95.
3. Ibid., p. 92.
4. *Other Gospels*, p. 25, italics for emphasis.

the *Dialogue* was possibly composed in the second half of the first century AD, and that it continues the sayings tradition preserved in the *Gospel of Thomas*. Like its predecessor, the *Dialogue of the Savior* pursues an order of "seeking-finding-marveling-ruling-resting."[5] The work juxtaposes both realized and futuristic eschatological views. Cameron sees it as a precursor of John's Gospel. It equally presents Jesus as a wisdom teacher and revealer of God's truth. The *Dialogue* refers to Jesus as God's "only begotten Son," whom God has "taken" to himself that Jesus might rest in Him. Here, too, we meet the language of "not tasting death," for God's own "do not die nor do they perish, for they knew their consorts and him who will take them to himself."[6] Furthermore, what the disciples seek is already within them. When Matthew asks to see the place of "life" and "light," Jesus replies: "Everyone of you who has known himself has seen it." Or again, "I say to you, truly the living God dwells in you and you dwell in him."[7] "He who is from the truth does not die." And "those . . . who understand this . . . live forever."[8]

It is interesting that this early Gnostic interpretation of Christ, apparently both Syrian and Egyptian in origin, should emerge so early and yet be utterly rejected by the time of Constantine. Conflicting emerging traditions found it too esoteric and non-representative of the pre-Easter Jesus that other communities remembered or knew. One still has the right to wonder. Might Jesus have been in part an esoteric? Jesus' Gnostic-like sayings in the *Gospel of Thomas* and the *Dialogue of the Savior* underscore the possibility. Moreover, John's "I am" sayings and the Apostle Paul's phrase, "all in all" [*panta en pasin*] (Eph 1:23; 1 Cor 15:28), and "Christ is all and in all" (Col 3:11; 4:6), suggest a mindset that hungered for a monistic solution to the mystery of the created order. Paul might never have used the word *apérion*, but the idea of an all-pervasive heavenly power, governing and guiding the universe toward its completion, certainly appealed to him. As for the Pléroma, he refers to it twice in Colossians: "For in him the whole fullness [*pléroma*] of the deity dwells bodily" (2:9; cf. 1:19).

Jesus as Spiritually Present

A different tradition seems to have flowered equally about this same time. The concept of Jesus as spiritually present at gatherings and communal

---

5. *Other Gospels*, p. 39.
6. Ibid, p. 41.
7. Ibid., pp. 43 and 45.
8. Ibid., pp. 46 and 48.

meals had taken hold. As Crossan has pointed out, many of Luke's post-resurrection *appearance*s are associated with eating and egalitarian concerns. This is true both in the Gospel of Luke and in its sequel, the Book of Acts. Luke's first post-resurrection appearance story involves the couple on the road to Emmaus, who, upon meeting the inquisitive stranger, inform him of their Master's' recent life: how "Jesus of Nazareth, a prophet mighty in deed and word," was handed over to the authorities, who condemned and crucified him. How they had hoped "that he was the one to redeem Israel!" (Luke 24:13–21). Then follows a hint of that interim movement, during which period groups of devoted followers pored over the scriptures as they sought to assimilate Jesus' words and mission and make sense of his life. "Beginning with Moses and all the prophets," his life slowly begins to unfold, and their "hearts burn within." Back at Emmaus, the couple and Jesus arrive at the couples' home. Jesus is invited to stay, and while they are "breaking bread," they suddenly recognize him. Then, immediately in the following passage, Luke presents another meal gathering, in which the disciples are present. Once again, the meeting becomes an occasion for studying scriptures, which reveal the mystery of the Master, as they search "the law of Moses, the prophets, and the psalms" (Luke 24:44). Finally, the narrative ends with an *ascension* story, as Jesus is "carried up into heaven" (Luke 24:52), much like Ovid's Julius Caesar.

The Continuation of Jesus' Work under the Guidance of Recognized Leaders

No passage is more instructive of this development than Luke's depiction of the Jerusalem community's effort to actualize Jesus' emphasis on commensality. As Luke notes in Acts 2:42, following one of Peter's sermons, Jesus' followers "devoted themselves to *the apostles' teaching* and fellowship, to breaking of bread and prayers." Acts 4:32–35 expands this program to include the donating of property as part of commensality. Later, in Acts 6:1–6, problems associated with these efforts result in renewed attempts to address gaps in the movement's egalitarian experiment. Demands on the Apostles' time necessitate the election of deacons to attend to community issues. As the story progresses, the work of the Apostles' teachings receives increased emphasis, as communal needs slip into the background. Nevertheless, the latter never disappear and continue to resurface throughout Luke's volume. Issues of ethnicity, place of origin, race, class, kosher laws, religious background, and gender command attention, but the ongoing work of the leaders receives priority. Of notable interest is Paul's rise to dominance, as Peter fades entirely from the scene and James emerges as the mother church's leader in Jerusalem. By now, Jesus is known under a growing list of titles: Christ Jesus, Lord Jesus, Jesus Christ of Nazareth, Son of God, Lord and Messiah, Leader and Savior.

The most striking development throughout this stage, however, revolves around several terms that are employed by Luke to describe the post-Easter Jesus' role and whereabouts. He "was taken up" [*aneléphthe*], "lifted up" [*epéthe*]; "he was taken up from us" [*aneléphthe aph 'emon*], as Luke puts it in Acts 1:3, 9, 22. Or again, for example, his phrase "raised from the dead" [*egeiren ek nekron*], which he uses in Acts 3:15, 4:10; 13:30 captures one's attention as well. In all three cases, it is God who does the "raising," who causes "the rising" to occur. These phrases tend to precede references to the "resurrection" [*anastasis*]. Another verb, *anistémi*, is also used for "raise up" and appears in Acts 2:24 and 3:22, 26. In its context, 3:22 is actually a quotation from the *Septuagint*'s version of Deuteronomy 18:18. The Lord is speaking to Moses: "I will *raise up [anastéso]* to them a prophet of their brethren, like thee." According to Acts 3:22–26, this promise to "raise up" a future prophet has been fulfilled in Jesus, whom "God raised" [*anastésas*] (Acts 3:26), and of whom God promised in Psalm 16:10 that "his holy one would not see corruption" (*Septuagint*). Therefore Psalm 16:10 is used in conjunction with Deuteronomy 18:18 (in Acts 2:27–31) to prove that the pre-Easter Jesus has surely been raised, is alive, and not dead, since scripture has promised that he could not see corruption. All this enables the reader to piece together the sequential threads of thought that led the post-Easter Church to proclaim the Christ's *anastasis*, or "resurrection," as an event that has already occurred.

The above provides a transparent example of prophecy being historicized rather than history fulfilling prophecy. The extent to which church leadership, or popular acclaim, promoted this transition may never be known. It seems likely, however, that the Church's leaders, and possibly scribes who were attracted to the movement, initiated the linkage between the historical Jesus and Israel's longing for messianic deliverance, which John's preaching in the wilderness had ignited.

Moreover, the concept of "raising up" does not necessarily require a bodily resurrection. As late as Ecclesiastes (cir. 300 BC), Qoheleth's chapter 12:7 states: "the dust returns to the earth as it was, and the breath returns to God who gave it." In other words, what belongs to God returns to God and what belongs to the earth returns to the earth. It is similar to Hera's view about permitting Heracles into heaven. Why not "raise up his father's part?" Furthermore, 2 Macc 7:1–42 (136 BC) had endorsed the hope of a future resurrection of the just who are martyred for God's cause. As the first of seven brothers, who were put to death by Antiochus Epiphanes, replies to the king: "You accursed wretch, you dismiss us from this present life, but the King of the universe will *raise us up* to an everlasting renewal of life, because we have died for his laws" (2 Macc 7:9; italics for emphasis). Paul would waffle on this point himself, acknowledging that "what is sown is perishable, what is raised is imperishable. . . . It is sown a physical body, it is raised a spiritual body" (1 Cor 15:43–44). If this is so, then for Paul, Christ is alive in the *spiritual sense*, as one who is "imperishable," "in glory," and "in power," but not necessarily endowed with any physical, flesh. This is Crossan's view as well.

Jesus' Resurrection as an Aspect of Vindicated Martyrdom

As Paul's theology came more and more into prominence, Jesus was viewed as God's universal archetype for resolving the human predicament. "For while we were yet sinners, at the right time Christ died for the ungodly" (Rom 5:1). His death on the cross portends salvific value for all mankind. In Romans chapters 5 and 6, Paul expounds the meaning of the cross in great detail and concludes with his own view of the resurrection. "For if we have been united with him in a death like his, we will certainly be united with him in a resurrection [*anastaseos*] like his . . . . We know that Christ, being *raised from the dead* [*egertheis ek nekron*] will never die again; death no longer has dominion over him. The death he died, he died to sin, once for all; but the life he lives, he lives to God. So you also must consider yourselves dead to sin and alive to God in Christ Jesus" (Rom 6:5–10; again, italics for emphasis). If we adopt Paul's metaphor of "sowing" as a means of interpreting "raised," then Paul's doctrine of the resurrection implies a life presently lived in hope and power, based on Christ's raised status, while one anticipates "meeting the Lord in the air" at the end-time (1 Thess 4:17). That will be the crowning vindication of Christ's death and the beginning of true glory, when one "will be with the Lord forever" (1 Thess 4:17). Such a "meeting in the air" complies perfectly with Paul's notion of a "spiritual body," rather than a "corruptible body," being raised from the dead.

All this prepared the way for the *Gospel of Peter* to present its vision of Jesus' resurrection as a vindication of his martyrdom. Mark incorporated this Gospel, while presenting his own emphasis on *an empty tomb*. Christ is not in a tomb. The post-Easter Jesus has been "raised," "lifted up." You will not find the Jesus of history in a grave. He is "risen." God has "taken him up." The heavy stone that the women feared they would be unable to roll away has already been rolled from the tomb. That is not a problem anymore. There are no physical barriers to block one's encounter with the risen Lord. What troubles Crossan, however, is that a vindicated martyrdom model shifts the focus from a *sarcophilial* identification with Jesus to a savior of the world model, which undermines the historical Jesus' message and mission. Even the Evangelist John expresses some concern over this in his *incarnational* approach, in which he stresses eternal life as a present reality, a realized eschatology, and not simply as a futuristic hope.

Christ's Resurrection as an Archetype of Experiencing the Eternal Now

As noted earlier, Ron Cameron views the *Dialogue of the Savior* as a forerunner of the Gospel of John. Its format allowed its author to create longer discourses between Jesus and his disciples. Interestingly enough, the three interlocutors of the *Dialogue* are Matthew, Miriam, and Judas. Nothing pejorative remotely arises concerning the gender or virtue of any of the three. Jesus is presented as a teacher of arcane wisdom and as a revealer of God's sacred truth. The major emphasis falls on one recognizing his or her *pre-existence with God and one's unity with the divine reality or Pleroma*. The creation of the universe, one's identification with the Pleroma (yet distinct essence as a self), along with one's discovery of the role of light and darkness, flesh and spirit, and mind and soul, constitute the subjects that occupy the interlocutors' time with the Savior, or "the Lord," as he is also called. Because of the document's fragmented condition and missing words, one feels one's self drifting in and out of a nightmare that Plato might have had, or sifting through discarded poems and epical scraps that Hesiod rejected in creating his lists of archons and eons. It is a challenge to read the *Dialogue*, but it contains remarkably enlightening statements.

It is in John's Gospel that "realized eschatology" is presented with vigor. The idea of the eternal now is ever present. In the 1950s and early '60s, it was common for seminary professors to speak of "the shadow of the cross, falling across the Gospels." Professor Donald G. Miller of Union Theological Seminary (VA), was fond of this expression, especially in association with Luke's passage: "he set his face to go to Jerusalem" (Luke 9:51). But if the Synoptics reach their climax in the passion narrative, under the *shadow* of the cross, John's Gospel celebrates throughout its 21 chapters *eternal life*. The eternal Son, whose *light* illumines a world lost in darkness, and in whom *life* is available to all who heed his call, has come to earth from his Father's realm. As John writes: "All things were made by him, and without him was not anything made that was made. In him was life; and the life was the light of men" (1:3–4). Note how *life* precedes *light*. And it is "out of his fullness" [*pléromatos*] (1:16) that all have received grace.

It is worth noting that beginning with 3:15 and continuing through 20:31, the phrase "eternal life," or "everlasting life" (*zoén aionion*), appears 36 times. To know God and the Christ, whom God has sent, is to have *zoén aionion* now (John 17:2–3). This eternal life begins with one's "rebirth," one's birth "from above," as Jesus explains to Nicodemus. Many of Jesus' seven signs have to do with "rebirth," *renovatio*, or *Wiedergeburt*. This is especially true in the case of the healed nobleman's son, the dispirited lame man by the pool, the hunger beneath the surface of the 5,000 who ate the loaves, the man born blind who now sees, and the dead Lazarus who walks out of his tomb at Christ's command. These are marvelous stories that attest to the eternal now, to the realization that all forms of alienation have been overcome. One can be reborn, walk again, see again, never hunger or thirst again.

Most scholars view John's Gospel as a repudiation of Gnosticism. If the latter is defined by its belief that 1) a lesser god created the universe, that 2) flesh and body are material and essentially evil, or prone to evil, that 3) mankind contains a spark of divinity captured within this material, that 4) God's representative, the Christ, therefore, who has come down from heaven, could not have taken on such flesh, and that 5) mankind requires a special spiritual wisdom in order to return to God, then John's Gospel definitely rejects tenets 1 and 4. Nevertheless, elements of Gnostic belief influence his overall view. These elements could be equally Platonic, since they have to do with a disdain for the body. "What is born of the flesh is flesh, and what is born of the Spirit is spirit" (3:6); if one does not believe Jesus about "earthly things," then how can one belief him about "heavenly things?" (3:12). "It is the spirit that gives life; *the flesh is useless*" (6:63, italics for emphasis). "You are from below, I am from above; you are of this world, I am not of this world" (8:23). "I have conquered the world" (16:33). "My kingdom is not from this world" (18:36). Elements of darkness, the demonic, and the chthonic also haunt John's Gospel. "Walk while you have the light, so that the darkness may not overtake you" (12:35). "You are from your father the devil" (8:44). "I do not have a demon; but I honor my Father" (8:49). "Now is the judgment of this world; now the ruler of this world will be driven out" (12:31).

The Resurrection

At the same time, this very Word of life "became flesh" (1:14); "without him was not anything made that was made" (1: 3), and unless "you eat the flesh of the Son of Man and drink his blood, you have no life in you. Those who eat my flesh and drink my blood have eternal life" (6:53–54).

By way of summary, then, "the living Jesus" was experienced in multiple ways by the first Christians: as the living voice of wisdom; as spiritually present at communal gatherings, work, and meals; as present in the preaching and activities of recognized and elected leaders; as a vision of vindicated martyrdom and symbol of future resurrection for the elect; and as the Eternal Now.

From a symbolic point of view, the resurrection signals rebirth. The bonds of alienation have been broken. Anxiety, guilt, finitude, sin, and death have lost their power. Yes, we experience anxiety; we regret choices that we cannot reverse; we know ourselves to be finite, limited, and mortal, and know that one day we must perish. But none of these existential marks of the human condition needs to have the last word. It is all right to be mortal, finite, and anxious of life's demands. That is normal. The Buddha experienced them until he was "reborn." And probably continued to do so, for they were often in his thoughts, as his collected sayings reveal. The Easter proclamation that "he whom you seek is risen" speaks to the very essence of the human condition. The lower within us can be lifted into the upper, the darkness turned into light, what has been deaf enabled to hear, what has been blind replaced with sight, depression transformed into wholeness, and deadness called back into life.

The latter requires an especially stark image, which is what the empty tomb stories and the Lazarus miracle are all about. All four Gospels report an empty tomb. In all four the "stone" has been rolled away. There is no need to seek "the living among the dead." The Jesus they love has been "raised."

From a psychological perspective, the *stone* that has kept us in our tombs is really of our own making. We are its creators, and it is we who have rolled it on ourselves. Or we have blamed others for entombing us and have quietly lain there, or sulked, or bitterly complained, as we clutch our grave clothes and bemoan our fate. Modern therapies know all too much about this form of depression and the devastating consequences of self-victimization. However, the Easter story proclaims that this *stone* has been rolled away. All that has separated one from God is gone.

In particular, the Lazarus miracle is ripe with metaphor. The stench of Lazarus's corpse is matched only by the unkempt grave clothes, which ooze with the seepage of death. "Roll the stone away!" Jesus commands. Once this is done, Jesus "cried with a loud voice, 'Lazarus, come out'"

(John 11:43). Then Jesus said: "Unbind him, and let him go" (11:44). The resurrection symbolizes the same for modern mankind. We must roll the stone away from our present entombment, come out of that grave, and take off the death cloths. We must do it for others as well as ourselves, if we are to have a whole society. Freud, Jung, Adler, Horney, Sullivan, and countless others since them have sought to assist humanity to do this. So have religious figures and spiritual guides. The process is hard and long. A death is involved before rebirth can occur. Even Jesus had to cry in "a loud voice." Reuniting aspects of repressed psyche phenomena, freeing suppressed goals and desires, integrating the anima, or the individualized unconscious with the conscious, or making peace with oneself, the universe, and God, all take time, a lifetime, and never end in the process of seeking wholeness. The resurrection story assures us that this can happen, did happen, and does happen. Without that story, mankind would still be in despair. It is what "forgiveness" means. God has set mankind free. Now there can be new life.

At a theological level, the resurrection means that we are no longer estranged from God, from the above, the Infinite, the world of the Great Spirit, the Buddha essence, or Ground of Being. There is nothing we have to do to placate God or the mystery of being. Where is God? "God is wherever man lets him in!" Where is God now? God is within us, just as the kingdom is. The Gateless Gate is open. The stone has been rolled away. That gnawing *tanha* that has caused so much *dukkha* can be eliminated and healed. We will never know which Asian pagodas contain the true ashes of the Buddha. In a similar way, the Christ is not to be found in a grave. For the post-Easter Church, he knocks at the door of every heart and longs to enter. The pre-Easter Jesus, as a human being, belongs to the category of history. This Jesus was "crucified, dead, and buried." But the post-Easter Jesus, who belongs to the category of faith, who comes down from heaven to unite mankind with the eternal, that Jesus is still alive and "risen."

From still a third perspective, or an ontological one, the resurrection symbolizes the truth of humanity's condition. In order to fathom the depth of the mystery of mankind's existence, death has to be addressed. We are mortal. Life is itself a miracle between the two great silences of before our birth and the one to come after our death. Ontologically, we are finite and must die. The resurrection assures and comforts us with the good news that this miraculous interim is worth living and that death is part of life. It is all right to die. It is OK to accept death when death comes. It is always sad when death is the result of war, or disease, or poverty, or hate. That is part of life, too. But death comes to all. To know this, as the Buddha said, fills one with enlightenment. It quickens our sense of personal purpose and of how precious time is—for ourselves and for others. It is all right to die. To give oneself back to the earth, dust to dust, and our spirit to the Spirit of life. We have come from an unfathomable ground of being and shall return to that mystery. To call it Father Sky and Mother Earth, or to personalize the mystery as a Thou, or as God, or Jesus, or Allah, or Black Elk's Tunkashila, or Brahman, or Vishnu, or Shiva matters not. But to accept this mystery, to love what life we have, and to live it with Spirit and joy, with mercy and justice toward others, is to participate in eternal life, in what never dies, whatever happens to the body or its spirit. To return to this mystery is OK. As Rabbi Bunam said to his wife, as he lay dying: "Why are you crying? My whole life was only that I might learn how to die."[9]

There is also the symbolism of the two angels in the *Gospel of Peter*, who emerge from the tomb with Jesus between them. Their light streams upward into heaven and Jesus' even higher. The two angels comfort Mary in John's Gospel, become one in Matthew's account, a young man in Mark's, and two men in Luke's. All are dressed in glowing raiment, causing awe and terror among the women. They sit casually on the stone, or beside the place where Jesus was laid. But they all bear good news. Jesus is risen. That both sides of the human dimension—the upper and the lower, the hidden and the unveiled, the heavenly and the earthly, the conscious and the unconscious—participate in the resurrection of the dead has enormous cathartic value in unleashing human potential. They represent the elimination of complexes when the latter are brought into consciousness. Also the fear and sorrow which the women feel as they arrive at the tomb, along with their shock at the sight of the apparition, rings of Aristotle's definition of tragedy, which results in catharsis through fear and pity. Through the women's fear and pity, we too are enabled to stare into the tomb of death and marvel at the presence of a glory and light that overcomes the worst.

In addition to their fear and sorrow, is the "recognition factor." The couple on the road to Emmaus did not recognize "the risen Jesus" until after their journey, their reflection on scripture, and their evening meal. So, too, Mary Magdalene, weeping in the garden, does not recognize "the living Jesus" at first. He has to call her by name: "Mary." Recognizing one's potential, awaking to its presence, realizing that the stone has been rolled away takes time. Often it takes assistance. The attending angels in the *Gospel of Peter* appear to be supporting a weakened Jesus. Angels also minister to Jesus at the end of his Temptation experience (Matt 4:11). Did

9. *Tales of the Hasidim*, Vol. 2, p. 268.

not the gods do the same for Heracles, Jason, Dionysus, and Odysseus? Do not the angels release Peter, James, and John from prison? (Acts 5:19). It is all right to need assistance. The early believing communities provided such assistance for their own. Even Buddhists retire to sanghas, to communities of fellow monks or sister nuns, as do Hindus to ashrams and spiritual leaders. Twice-born Hindus even carry the footprints of their spiritual preceptor, or guru, on a special cloth, tucked against the heart. We need community, a brother/sister's care, and frequent re-immergence in participatory rites.

Finally, the resurrection stories end with commissions. From John's "feed my sheep" and "follow me," to Luke's disciples becoming "witnesses in Jerusalem, in all Judea and Samaria, and to the ends of the earth" (Acts 1:8), to Matthew's "Great Commission" of 28:18–20, the endings are all alike. The disciples are to preach, teach, baptize, and live the Jesus mission until the end of time itself.

The resurrection is a call to life, to bear witness to the transcendent Ground of Being in gratitude and hope, to bear witness to one's own inner creative energies, and to help others fulfill their potential. It is a summons to become a Christian bodhisattva, dedicated to assisting others along their own journeys of liberation and enlightenment, which God in Christ has made possible.

Of course, the ultimate questions remains unanswered. Is there life after this life? Did the historical Jesus believe in an afterlife? One must assume so. Even if one were to eliminate John's Gospel, too many parables in the Synoptic Gospels point in that direction. But like belief in God, belief in an afterlife cannot be proven. One simply stands before the last gate of reason. Only faith can open that last gate. To believe in the transcendent God of biblical faith is to believe in the eternal. It means to entrust oneself to God and to all that is holy and good, just and merciful. Such belief fills one with a profound solace that lifts the heart above life's gnawing desolation and ennobles one with a peace and consolation that mortal sorrows may test but never take away. As Paul Tillich so aptly expressed it:

> There is *one* power that surpasses the all-consuming power of time––the eternal: He who was and is to come, the beginning and the end. He gives us forgiveness for what has passed. He gives us courage for what is to come. He gives us rest in His eternal Presence.[10]

---

10. Paul Tillich, *The Eternal Now*, New York: Charles Scribner's Sons, 1963, p. 132.

11

Jesus as Metaphor

The New Testament assigns many titles of a metaphorical nature to depict the role and personal identity of Jesus of Nazareth. Jesus of Nazareth is itself one such title. Others include: Lamb of God, the Good Shepherd, Son of God, Son of Man, Son of David, Christ Jesus, the Vine, the Door, the Light of the world, the Resurrection and the Life, the Way the Truth and the Life, and from the Old Testament, the Prince of Peace (Isa 9:6). There are others as well: Lord, Master, Teacher, Rabbi, and above all, Savior. It is doubtful if Jesus ever selected any of these or approved of them, other than the common one, "Lord," meaning, "Sir." These titles belong more to the post-Easter Jesus era than to the pre-Easter Jesus. If Crossan is correct, such titles would never have occurred to Jesus; they would have embarrassed him. Certainly, they would have compromised his radical egalitarianism and undermined his disdain for masters, lords, rulers, and princes who oppressed the poor and lowly. Let your yes be yes and your no be no was adequate enough for him. From the perspective of the *category of history*, we can understand why Jesus might not have welcomed or promoted titles. Yet, as new communities of followers emerged, they found such designations helpful. They used them to describe what the pre-Easter Jesus meant to them, even if the titles belonged to the *category of myth*, or faith, or legend, or national hopes and aspirations. Within that category lies their relevance for humanity today. They still have the power to convey a sense of wholeness and hope for contemporary mankind.

Jesus of Nazareth

Perhaps no other title is so complete in itself. Who was Jesus? He was a Galilean from Nazareth. He was a *tekton*'s son. He roughed in buildings; he worked with his hands. His friends were laborers, too. Most were from Galilee. Some were fishermen, workers like himself. One may well have been a converted tax gatherer, another a Zealot hoping to stir up trouble, to get back at Rome. His mother was Mary, his father, Joseph. He had four brothers and at least two sisters. He might have been married; probably was. If not, he seemed comfortable enough around women: Mary Magdalene, Martha, her sister Mary, and many others. What Bornkamm, Borg, Crossan, and Vermes have pieced together about him as a man seems highly likely. Yet, his title: "Jesus of Nazareth," imports something infinitely more. We hear it in his voice, see it in his actions, feel it in his words, sense it as he moves through the crowds to teach, challenge, cajole, heal, kiss a cheek, or hold a trembling hand. We feel his presence, imagine his eyes staring into our own, wish we could have been there when he trailed his fingers through the dust, while the frightened woman cried. We run to look over his shoulder, wince at his scourging, stand behind Mary at his cross, fall into silence upon his death, and mourn with Joseph of Arimathea, as he takes his body down, and lovingly lays it in his own tomb. "O lustrous comrade with silver face in the night!" as Whitman put it in his *Leaves of Grass*.

> But O heart! heart! heart!
> O the bleeding drops of red,
> Where on the deck my captain lies,
> Fallen cold and dead.

His spell still haunts us some 2,000 years after his death. "Jesus of Nazareth! Why do our hearts still quake at the thought of your name? Because you confront us with that *Other—in yourself and in us*. And it speaks to us, frightens us, heals us, and challenges us—all at the same time. You make us want to become whole, even while we resist. We cannot forget you. Jesus of Nazareth."

Sentiment aside, many scholars dismiss the name entirely, faulting Matthew's misuse of "Nazorean" (meaning "branch" from Isa 11:1) for the corruption (Matt 2:23).

Lamb of God

The title [*ho amnos tou theou*] is used twice, and only in John's Gospel. However, the metaphor "lamb" [*arnos*] appears some 28 times in the book of Revelation. All are in reference to Jesus, who has now become a conqueror. How ironic that the slain lamb of the Gospels should become a slayer by the time of the Apocalypse! What did his followers mean? What were they thinking? What horrors were they suffering?

In the Old Testament, the lamb symbolizes innocence, purity, and gentleness. It became the favorite animal of sacrifice. It was certainly less painful to sacrifice lambs than little children, although the latter re-occurred under Ahab and Manasseh and possibly under Solomon. Lambs were sacrificed, in all likelihood, from the most ancient of times (Gen 4:4), down into Jesus' era. Not only were they killed at Passover but during special lunar phases and during all the major feasts: Passover, Feast of Weeks, Day of Atonement, and Tabernacles. They were regularly included in morning and evening burnt offerings. From a figurative viewpoint, they aroused compassion and sympathy and provided a window into the soul of God. As Second Isaiah puts it: "He will feed his flock like a shepherd; he will gather the *lambs* in his arms, and carry them in his bosom" (Isa 40:11). As sacrificial offerings, they inspired Isaiah's creation of the Suffering Servant figure: "He was oppressed, and he was afflicted, yet he did not open his mouth; like a *lamb* that is led to the slaughter, and like a sheep that before its shearers is silent, so he did not open his mouth" (Isa 53:7).

Both these figures are employed by New Testament writers: in Mark 6:34 and Matt 9:36: "For they were like sheep without a shepherd." The writer of the Gospel of John carried it one step further by coining the phrase "lamb of God." John's Gospel credits John the Baptizer with making the connection: "Behold, the lamb of God, who takes away the sin of the world" (John 1: 29; 35). According to Luke, however, this connection was not drawn until after Jesus' death (Acts 8:32–33). As God's Son, the Christ became God's own offering to cover the sin of the world. It is what it *costs* God to redeem fallen humanity. It is what Bonhoeffer meant by his phrase, "costly grace," as there was nothing "cheap" about it. Christianity has also reflected on this in its *theologia crucis*, or theology of the cross, which was especially dear to Luther.

As an archetypal event that impacts mankind's salvation, Jesus' role as the Lamb of God symbolizes the quintessential gift that humanity requires to be whole again. A sacrifice has to be provided if mankind is to be lifted out of its estrangement with the Eternal, with itself, and others. "We are not the source of ourselves," as Karl Jaspers has expressed it. "Man is fundamentally more than he can know about himself." Sometimes a second party is required to arouse man out of his stupor. Or again, as Jaspers explains: "we know that we do not owe ourselves to ourselves." Without "transcendence" we cannot even "become aware of ourselves," which makes "man a being who exists in relation to God."[1] Jaspers rejects atheism as an answer to the mystery of the human condition, because man is not the Ground of his own Being. For Jaspers, it is only the extent to which we are drawn out of ourselves "by transcendence" that we come

1. K. Jaspers, *Way to Wisdom*, New Haven, 1974, pp. 63–65.

to know and experience our fullest potential. That this insight should be buried deeply within our collective unconscious, which the lamb figure awakens, makes both psychological and theological sense.

There is an additional phenomenon with respect to the sacrificial aspect of the Lamb of God that almost dwarfs other considerations and is so obvious as to be overlooked. It is Christ as the *Paschal Lamb*, sacrificed to spare Israel's true spiritual descendants on the very eve of Passover, which celebrates Israel's rescue from bondage. It is interwoven so quietly into the four Gospels as to go unnoticed. None of the four writers calls unusual attention to it. The Synoptic Evangelists simply state: "On the first day of Unleavened Bread, when the Passover lamb is sacrificed, his disciples said to him: 'Where do you want us to go and make the preparations for you to eat the Passover?'" (Mark 14:12; Matt 26:17; Luke 22:7). John sets the meal a day earlier (John 13:1). All the symbolism of sacrifice, exodus, and deliverane from bondage coalesce here. Paul never once mentions the Passover; for him the escape from bondage is Christ's cross, which frees one from the curse of the law. Yet he speaks eloquently of the freedom of this event. "For freedom Christ has set us free. Stand firm, therefore, and do not submit again to a yoke of slavery" (Gal 5:1). The slavery in that passage, however, refers to Hagar's condition, not to the children of Israel.

As for the "victor" side of the Lamb, Christianity has long hailed the post-Easter Jesus as Lord and Savior. The warrior Lamb of Revelation, reformulated as the *Christus Victor* motif of Gustaf Aulen, symbolizes Jesus' "lordship." The image of Jesus as the lamb with the cross in its arms and the crown on its head heralds Christ's victory over all evil, especially "the evils of existential self-destruction," to borrow Tillich's words.[2] Christ has obtained the victory. The crucified one has prevailed. Like the supreme archetype of the self, individuals too can become victors as they embrace the transcendent, symbolized in the Christ, that addresses their estrangement and leads them to become whole persons again, or new beings in the New Testament sense. What they could not reverse has been blotted out.

In the Book of Revelation, this victory of wholeness over chaos is presented in myriad symbolic and figurative forms, especially in 5:6—6:17. All the hosts of heaven gather about the Lamb, prostrate before it, while thousands and thousands of angels and creatures sing: "Worthy is the Lamb that was slaughtered to receive power and wealth and wisdom and might and honor and glory and blessing . . . forever and ever!" (5:12). Then the Lamb begins to open the seals of the sacred scroll that contains God's fixed purposes, and out thunder the four horses of the Apocalypse:

2. Tillich, Vol. II, *Systematic Theology*, p. 160.

a white horse, representing the triumphant Christ; a bright red horse symbolizing war; a black horse, symbolizing famine; and a pale green horse, symbolizing disease and death. The self-destructive forces of estrangement are allowed to run their course. The victory has been assured, but the rider's name of the pale green horse is "Death," and "Hades" follows fast after him. They will claim thousands in this macabre raid of death. But even if the Elect fall under the sword during these raids, their union with God, the Ground of Being, cannot be broken.

Buber was scornful of Jung's idea of the quaternary, because it elevates a dark element into the mystery and fullness of God. Buber charges that Jung recast the Jewish and Christian concept of God by making Satan (in the Old Testament) into a servant of Yahweh's, while in the New, he enlarged the Trinity "to a Quaternity in which the autonomous devil is included as 'the fourth.'"[3] Nonetheless, the four horses of the Apocalypse certainly qualify as a quaternary. They draw together the cycles of life about themselves, beginning in the North (white) and moving rapidly to the East (red) then back to the West (black) and end in the South (green). This mandala, or circle of wholeness, as the apocalyptic views it, must be conquered if true unity is to arise. As long as the self is torn asunder by its own marks of estrangement, the Lamb cannot be said to be its ruler. That the Lamb permits this time of transition to last as long as it must does not undermine the assurance of victory, or the reunification of one's psychic forces in the process of individuation. Accepting the Ground of Being as one's ultimate goal alone brings wholeness to the self in search of itself.

Not all quaternaries, however, contain solely menacing elements. Among the Oglala Sioux, white stands for old age, a time to enjoy one's final years, the winter of one's life; red symbolizes the dawn, the morning, the East, the sun, a new day, a rebirth, a time for new wisdom and opportunity; yellow (green) represents summer, warmth, growth, maturation, the time to harvest before winter returns. Black symbolizes the Thunder Beings, the West, the clouds bearing down across the mountains, bringing thunder, lightning, and rain. Wisdom, generosity, and courage are associated with the east, south, and west respectively. Black was the favorite color of the warrior, as he swept across the plain toward his enemy, or displayed courage in the face of mounting odds. In the Old Testament, Psalm 29 depicts Yahweh moving swiftly like a storm, bearing out of Lebanon, bending the mountains' magnificent cedars like reeds in its thunderous path.

The four horses and horsemen of the Apocalypse are in all likelihood patterned after the four riders, four horns, and four blacksmiths of

---

3. Buber, *Eclipse of God*, p. 90.

Zechariah. Of interest is the color of Zechariah's horses: red, sorrel, and white. It is night and Zechariah sees "a man riding on a red horse." He is standing among myrtle trees in a glen and behind him are the other horses. When he inquires about these horses and their riders, an angel informs him: "They are those whom the Lord has sent to patrol the earth" (Zech 1:10). Later, Zechariah introduces another quaternary, this time of four chariots pulled by different colored horses: red, black, white, and gray. They represent the "four winds of heaven going out" across the earth, principally north, west, and south. They are harbingers of the messianic age. Promises of restoration and the rebuilding of Jerusalem and its Temple are proclaimed. Then comes the Prince of Peace, the Good Shepherd, who disposes of three worthless shepherds, before the final purgation and last battle of good against evil.

A further word about these biblical colors, however, is in order before drawing this section to a close. According to Daniel C. Matt's *The Essential Kabbalah: The Heart of Jewish Mysticism*, red, white, and green represent profound mystical powers. In the Kabbalist frame of mind, God's left arm is symbolized by red. It is God's *gevurah*, or power, and stands for God's strict judgment. God's right arm is symbolized by white, and stands for God's *hesed*, or loving-kindness, God's grace and mercy. The world cannot function without justice and mercy. They are aspects of God's mystical beingness. But their purpose is to achieve *tif'eret*, that is, beauty and harmony, symbolized by the color green. Along with other mystical qualities, these three attributes in particular represent the unfathomable mystery of God.[4]

By way of summary, then, the lamb as a *symbol of sacrifice*, and Christ as the *Lamb of God*, together signal hope. Beyond justice and mercy, lies still a higher harmony. In spite of a world continuously raided by the ever-returning riders of the Apocalypse (decrepitude, disease, death, and the demonic), life is worth living. It is worth sacrificing for, worth renouncing all that is evil and rotten in favor of what is just and merciful. These are the values that endure, the crown that is worthy of the Prince of Peace. Sometimes the wrathful raiders are complexes within ourselves, repressed fears and missed opportunities that require purgation and release. Sometimes they are the consequences of global sorrows in conflict with repressed desires, and sometimes they represent the centuries-old scourges of poverty, ignorance, concupiscence, pride, sin, guilt, and shame. And beyond our highest human capacity to reason or dream, the arms of God are there to guide believers toward their ultimate fulfillment.

---

4. D. C. Matt, *Essential Kabbalah*, Edison, NJ, 1977, pp. 8 and 168.

"Behold the Lamb of God who takes away the sin of the world!" We are that Lamb! Along with the Christ! And the mission is crystal clear. The seals have been broken and the scroll lies uncurled before us. "Go forth!" it declares on every page. Death has been swallowed up. There is nothing to fear.

Son of God and Son of Man

We have to do here with more than the union of opposites. We have already probed the divine-son figures of Greek mythology enough to know that this pattern was widespread and influential across the Empire of Jesus' time. There is no doubt that the Evangelists used it similarly to convey their communities' interpretations of Jesus. Especially of interest is the deification of Augustus Caesar, conferred by the Senate of Rome in September of AD 14. With his victory over Mark Antony and Cleopatra of 31 BC, the period of peace that ensued led to his becoming hailed as *Augustus* and ushered in a favorable era for the Mediterranean world. He was popular and considered divine. An inscription to him in 7 BC reads: "The birthday of the god was the beginning of good news." In other words, Augustus was already encoded within *euangellion*. Moreover, his mother contributed to the mystique by swearing—seriously or otherwise—that Apollo was his father. Octavian, embarrassed or not, liked the idea. Virgil's *Aeneid* was written at Augustus' request, adding only more luster to his popularity as an Emperor "god." We can see, therefore, how easily the Evangelists could have moved from Jesus of Nazareth to Jesus Christ, Son of God, whose mother, like Caesar's, "pondered these things in her heart" (Luke 2:51).

For the most part, the Seminar Fellows consider the title "Son of God" to be a fabrication of the storyteller, whether we find it in Mark, Matthew, Luke, or John. The title *huios theos,* or its genitive *huiou theou,* appears numerous times in the Gospels. It is employed primarily to (1) recognize Jesus' special relation to his Father (i.e. God), and (2) to account for his unique authority, including his gifts of insight and healing. This explains why people are "astounded" by his teachings and why the exorcised demons are able to recognize him. "They were astounded at his teaching" (Mark 1:22). Or as the unclean spirit shouts: "I know who you are, the Holy One of God" (Mark 1:24). Matthew and Luke's versions expand on these examples with additional content of their own.

The title itself, as I have indicated earlier, had its origin with the people of Israel. All three Synoptic writers incorporate two significant texts from the Old Testament which they conflate. The texts are Ps 2:7 and Isa 42:1.

You are my son; today I have begotten you (Ps 2:7).

Here is my servant, whom I uphold, my chosen in whom my soul delights;
I have put my spirit upon him; he will bring forth justice to the nations (Isa 42:1).

By the time the New Testament communities began writing gospels, these texts had found their way into the interpretative process concerning the pre-Easter Jesus of history. He was viewed as God's chosen, as God's son in the Davidic sense. The latter idea, in turn, owed its derivation to 2 Sam 7:14: "I will be a father to him, and he shall be a son to me."

As "Son of God," Jesus enjoyed the full authority of, and relationship to, God as ascribed in these texts. He was the Davidic King apparent! He was God's son in every respect of Nathan's prophecy: the truly anointed One and Servant whom Isaiah prophesized as the "delight" of God's soul. These texts, more than any Roman adulation for Augustus, probably inspired the Gospel writers' sense of Jesus' uniqueness, though the former cannot be ruled out.

As the Seminar Fellows maintain, it is doubtful if Jesus ever used this title to describe himself. It simply doesn't fit his model as a Cynic, or mendicant wisdom healer. I think the evidence is on their side. Save for "Rabbi" and "Lord," the other titles are weighted with meanings and theological innuendo that could have flourished only after Jesus' execution. Nonetheless, the hope that Jesus might have been the "Son of God" in the Old Testament sense, surely crossed his disciples' minds before his death and quickened his audiences' wildest dreams.

That does not eviscerate their value for the post-Easter Church, or its many believing communities. Luke provides an example of this in his genealogy of Jesus, in which he traces Jesus' lineage all the way back to "son of Seth, son of Adam, son of God" (Luke 3:38). In tracing Jesus' family's forbears in this way, he universalizes the process for all mankind. We are all "descendants of God," if this is the case. The same may be said of Ps 8:5, where the Psalmist asks first about "mankind," or *mahish*, and then about the "son of man," *ben-atham*, or "son of Adam." The plain meaning of the text can be nothing less that every one is God's son or daughter.

Once again, from a mythic, or metaphoric, perspective, Christ incarnates the supreme archetype of the self. What we have projected outward onto him is actually a vision of our self, as Ludwig Feuerbach expressed it. "Consciousness of God is self-consciousness, knowledge of God is self-knowledge.... God is the manifested inward nature, the expressed self of a man."[5] Jung took the same position from a psychological view, which also explains why Buber rejected Jung's analysis of God and religion. There is too much truth in Feuerbach and Jung's analyses, however, to reject them out right. By participating in the "risen Christ," we are able to claim back all that has been projected onto the Christ. The issue is, is God, or the risen Christ, purely a phenomenon of the self, or is God a reality apart from our psyche? Since no one can either prove or disprove God's reality, it falls beyond our cognitive level to know. But what cannot be denied is the reality that we are compelled to fathom the mystery of our human existence, and in doing so, God emerges as the Transcendent Ground of Being, without whom nothing would exist. We are not self-caused, as Jaspers reminds us, along with Tillich. Or with Buber, for that matter, who insists that by relating to the Eternal as a Thou, and not as an It, our lives take on a depth of possibility undreamt of otherwise. To define God as the manifestation of the mystery of our human condition is not purely subjective. We feel drawn to that Other that we know defines us, whether that Other is God, the Tao, the Buddha-essence, Brahman, Vishnu, Shiva, Allah, the Great Spirit, Tunkashila, or the universe itself. This makes all mankind "sons and daughters of God," in the broad, universal sense. We are the "royal heirs," the hope of the world, the anointed ones whose kingdoms are urged to promote justice and mercy, and whose lives are encouraged to become like the Buddha's "shining mountains," or Jesus' "light of the world." This is our hope and destiny, nobility and dignity, and upon us are the world's chastisements laid.

Having said this, however, the Gospel of John goes one step further. It was a necessary step, if not a logical step, and became forever after that part of the post-Easter Jesus' identity. John refers to Jesus as "a father's *only son*, full of grace and truth" (John 1:14); and again "No one has ever seen God. It is God the *only Son*, who is close to the Father's heart, who has made him known" (John 1:18; italics for emphasis). For the post-Easter communities, Jesus' sonship is unique. That is why he and he alone is the universal archetype. Mankind needs no other. Even Luke came to share this view: "For there is no other name, given among men, by which we must be saved" (Acts 4:12). This claim has become an embarrassment for many; still it belongs to the expanding post-Easter Church's understanding of Christ and why anything about him was worth retaining.

The title "Son of Man" carries an equally ambitious and ambiguous quality about it. The Seminar Fellows translate it as "son of Adam."

---

5. See *Essence of Christianity*, cit., in J. Hick, *Classical and Contemporary Readings in the Philosophy of Religion*, Englewood Cliffs, 1990, p. 149.

The phrase "Son of Man" appears 85 times in the Bible. In the Synoptic Gospels, the writers use the expression in at least three different ways: 1) as the Son of Man with authority on earth, 2) as the Son of Man who must suffer and die, and 3) as the Eschatological Son of Man to come in an imminent future. The expression is hardly unique to the Gospels, as it appears in a variety of settings in the Old Testament. Compounding the problem for many readers is the fact that, whereas the RSV translated *ben atham* as "son of man," the NRSV translates the phrase as "human beings," or "mortals." Under the older RSV version, at least three distinct usages of the expression are noticeable. In Ps 8:3 we read: "what is man that thou art mindful of him, and the son of man that thou dost care for him?" Here "son of man" appears to mean nothing other than mankind in general, or mortal, or human being. A second usage appears in Job 25:4–6, in which humanity is likened unto a worm. "How then can man be righteous before God? . . . Behold, even the moon is not bright and the stars are not clean in his sight; how much less man, who is a maggot, and the son of man (*ben atham*), who is a worm." In this instance, it is humankind's weakness and claim to status that is the issue. A third usage, and the more important one for New Testament research, appears in Dan 7:13–14, where we read: "I saw in the night visions, and behold, with the clouds of heaven there came one like a son of man (*bar ehnash*), and he came to the Ancient of Days and was presented before him. And to him was given dominion and glory and kingdom, that all peoples, nations, and languages should serve him; his dominion shall not pass away, and his kingdom one that shall not be destroyed." In this instance, the "son of man" appears to be a futuristic figure, or an apocalyptic savior to come. In the book of Ezekiel, however, the phrase "son of man" (*ben atham*) is used multiple times, and, in general, refers to the prophet himself. Following the incredible series of convoluted visions that seize the prophet (Ezek 1:1–28), from that point on, Ezekiel is addressed as the "Son of man" (*ben atham*). In other words, Ezekiel is the mortal, the human being, to whom the visions are being revealed.

How did such an innocent title become the center for so much controversy? About five or six decades before Jesus' birth, a document appeared in which the long-hoped-for Messiah was described in glowing eschatological terms. The document is known as *Psalm of Solomon 17*. Its language suggests that its intended audience was the Judah of the post-Pompeian invasion (63 BC), along with its corrupt Jewish officials whom Rome put in power. The Psalm foresees that day in a "time known" only to God, when God will "raise up" the "son of David" and send him to purge Jerusalem of its gentiles and unlawful henchmen. He will "judge peoples and nations in the wisdom of his righteousness." He will be "compassionate," "free of sin," "powerful in the holy spirit," "wise in counsel," "righteously shepherding the Lord's flock." His strength will lie in "his word," not "on horse and rider and bow, nor will he collect gold and sliver for war."

It is not an impossible leap from the post-Easter communities of the New Testament to the inclusion of this prophecy in their interpretations of the pre-Easter Jesus. His life conformed to the Psalm's vision of its "son's" peaceful mission. In the same way in which the post-Easter communities pored over Old Testament's passages in Isaiah, Daniel, Malachi, and the Psalms, here was still another text to be deciphered. Mark's Gospel, which Matthew and Luke absorb, portrays Jesus as employing the expression "Son of Man" multiple times. Few scholars believe that Jesus ever used it as a reference to himself, but it is possible that Jesus used it to speak of the Psalm's "coming one." John certainly seems to have been charmed by the hope. Perhaps, Jesus fashioned something of his own ministry in light of the anticipation of the "coming one" before branching off on his own, either before or after John's arrest. But this would assume that both he and John the Baptizer were aware of *Psalm of Solomon 17*. The mood in the country was certainly ripe. The community of Qumran in its fervor to create a new Israel attests to this development. In all likelihood, Jesus did use the expression but not in reference to himself. Nevertheless, many of Jesus' usages of the phrase are in reference to mankind, as the Seminar Scholars seek to demonstrate. The best example of this appears in Q and the *Gospel of Thomas*. "Jesus said: 'Foxes have their dens and birds have their nests, but human beings have no place to lie down and rest'" (*Thom* 86:1–2); "And Jesus says to him, 'Foxes have dens, and birds of the sky have nests, but the son of Adam has nowhere to rest his head'" (Matt 8:20); and "Jesus said to him, 'Foxes have dens, and birds of the sky have nests; but the son of Adam has nowhere to rest his head'" (Luke 9:58). In all three instances, the *Five Gospels'* translators render "son of man" as either "human beings" or "son of Adam."

Much more could be said of this expression, but "son of man" is a fitting metaphor of Jesus' followers themselves. We are the sons and daughters of mankind. In our effort to fathom the mystery of the human condition, it is we who are addressed by that Ineffable mystery within the self. "What are poets for in a destitute time?" asked Holderlin. "They sing the wine god's song from night to holy night." It is we who hear that song in our souls, our psyches, and who must respond. Not to respond is to close the door on our own potential. We are the ones who have the power to forgive, who are the lords of the Sabbath, who will suffer and eventually die, but until then, we can judge with righteousness and mercy and seek to expunge what is evil in ourselves and in the world.

Son of David

Son of David has to be the one title most steeped in the national consciousness of Jesus' day. Its claim to legitimacy is likewise questioned, as the very title itself designates Jesus as the legitimate royal scion who should be sitting on Judah's throne. The title nowhere appears in Q or in the *Gospel of Thomas,* nor does it ever fall from Jesus' lips. Paul refers to it only once: "his son, who was descended from David according to the flesh" (Rom 1:3). The writer of 2 Timothy says: "Remember Jesus Christ, . . . a descendant of David" (1:8). This emphasis on Jesus' descendance is as close as Paul comes to calling Jesus "Son of David." Mark and Luke also emphasize Jesus' descendancy from the house of David (Mark 11:10; Luke 1:27, 32; 2:4; Acts 2:29–31; 4:25) and place the phrase "Son of David" only on the lips of the blind Bartimaeus (Mark 10:47–48; Luke 18:38–39; cf. Matt 20:30–31). Hearing that it is "Jesus of Nazareth" who is passing by, Bartimaeus cries in Mark's account: "Jesus, Son of David, have mercy on me." As the Son of David, Jesus is on his way to Jerusalem to be crucified. How blind all are not to recognize who he is! In an earlier healing event, involving a "demoniac who was blind and mute," Matthew has the crowds ask: "Can this be the Son of David?" (Matt 12:23). The editors of *The Five Gospels* tend to play down the title and consider it to be part of the dialogue that the Gospel writers invent. In their genealogies, both Luke and Matthew trace Jesus' lineage back to David. For both of them, Jesus' legitimacy as the Son of God is inseparable from his royal descent. One could argue that they represent a late expansion of the Church's assessment of the historical Jesus. But Paul's usage of the idea implies that it belonged to a much earlier level of tradition. Demoniacs, the blind and the mute, may well have cried aloud when Jesus passed by: "O Son of David, have mercy on us!"

The Good Shepherd

Sheep and shepherd are used to present several intriguing motifs in the Gospels. All four Gospels, plus the *Gospel of Thomas,* utilize the image of the shepherd and his watchful eye. Both they and Jesus probably had Old Testament precedents in mind, namely, Ps 23; Ezek 34:23–34; Mic 5:2–5;

and Zech 13:7–9. The passages from Ezekiel and Zechariah are instructive, inasmuch as they delineate God's charges against the false shepherds of Israel. Zechariah catalogs the shepherd's crimes: 1) they have not fed God's sheep, 2) nor strengthened the weak, 3) nor healed the sick, 4) nor bound the wounds of the crippled, 5) nor searched for strays, 6) nor brought back the scattered (Zech 34:3–6). Zechariah's charges are political, insofar as the rulers of Jerusalem in 586 BC had done nothing to cope with the disaster of the city's fall, following Nebuchadrezzar's conquest. Because of this failure, Zechariah prophesizes that God himself will shepherd his people and redress their wrongs. "I myself will be the shepherd of my sheep, and I will make them lie down, says the Lord God. I will seek the lost, and I will bring back the strayed, and I will bind up the crippled, and I will strengthen the weak, and the fat and the strong I will watch over; I will feed them in justice" (Zech 34:16). It is difficult to imagine that the writer of the Gospel of John did not have this passage in mind when he depicts Jesus as the Good Shepherd. Nor can one imagine the absence of this passage in Jesus' reflection, when he told the parable of the lost sheep (in Q and the *Gospel of Thomas*). Matthew cites the Micah passage in his birth narrative, in which Micah prophesizes that the Shepherd Messiah will be born in Bethlehem, the least town of the twelve clans: "and he shall stand and feed his flock in the strength of the Lord" (Mic 5:4). Luke's reference to the "shepherds out in the field, keeping watch over the flock by night," may also allude to this text (Luke 2:8).

John's use of these texts, if he did incorporate them, shifts the focus in a more theologically pointed direction. As John sees it, Jesus is the *gate* to the sheepfold; only those who come into the community "through" him can be assured of their safety and life to the fullest (John 10:9). Other competing voices belong to "wolves," who come only to "snatch and scatter" (vs. 10). There is a slight twinge of Gnosticism to John's text, as only those who know the good shepherd can be rescued: "I am the good shepherd; I know my own and my own know me" (10:14). Compounding this is the shepherd's decision to give his life for his sheep, which he does freely. He alone has the power to lay it down and the power to take it back. This new dimension of Christ's right and power to lay down and take back his life witnesses all the more to Jesus as God incarnate, or his oneness with God. It goes beyond the idea that "God raised up this Jesus," since Jesus has the power within himself to do so. In any case, when Jesus appears to his disciples beside the sea, his command to Peter is "feed my lambs . . . tend my sheep . . . and follow me" (John 20:15–19).

This latter commandment suggests a spiritualizing of Jesus' message that takes it quite beyond the egalitarianism of Acts 2:41–44. The Johannine community's form of Christianity is both more mystical and esoteric. It offers a solace for the soul that transcends commensality, though not at the expense of the latter (1 John 3:17). It is this form of Christianity that seems to have encouraged, or been usurped by, Gnostics and which may well have found a friendlier reception in Egypt than in Ignatius, Polycarp, and Justin's northern realm.

Whatever we make of John's "Good Shepherd," his commission to Peter endures: "Feed my lambs. Tend my sheep. Follow me!" In fathoming the mystery of our human condition, we do so as fellow/sister human beings. We are not alone. We are part of the post-Easter Jesus' Great Commission. In every regard, he is still the Good Shepherd, who leads his followers beside the still waters and restores their souls for his name's sake. He is their strength and comfort in the valley of the shadow of death and stands present with them before all enemies. Indeed, their cup runs over. His sacramental table of bread and wine is ever there to nourish them.

The True Vine

It is tempting to interpret John 15 as John's response to the Eleusinian mysteries and the worship of Dionysus. That element may well be there. One should not exclude it. In addition, the idea of eating Christ's flesh and drinking his blood is too Hellenistic to ignore. However, there are Old Testament precedents that deserve investigation first. They are found in Isa 5:2, Jer 2:21, and Ezek 19:10–14. By far the most interesting passage is the one in Isaiah. Scholars refer to it as the "Allegory of the Vineyard," or the "Song of the Vineyard." It has to do with Israel and Judah failing to live up to the Mosaic Covenant, i.e., with their failure to deliver justice and righteousness. "For the vineyard of the Lord of hosts is the house of Israel, and the men of Judah are his pleasant planting; and he looked for justice, but behold, bloodshed; for righteousness, but behold, a cry!" (Isa 5:7). The accusations are similar in Jeremiah and Ezekiel. But of particular note is the Hebrew word used for vines in both Isa 5:2 and Jer 2:21. It is *soreq* and is translated as "choice vines." Commentators like to explain that *soreq* refers to a luscious red grape or vines growing just to the west of Jerusalem. If John means to imply that Jesus is this blood-red grape producing vine of the royal line of David, the true vine, then his transference of the allegory to Jesus makes perfect sense. But John doesn't seem overly concerned about Jesus' royal lineage. He is more interested in Christ's identity with the Father and with Christ's followers' abiding in the Christ. Nor do issues of justice and righteousness per se accompany his metaphor of Jesus as the vine, although John's *love ethic* does. If John is borrowing from Isaiah's allegory, he is replacing the older Mosaic Covenant with the Johannine community's emphasis on love (*agapé*). The Johannine community has become the true Israel and Jesus' love ethic the movement's defining norm.

In the *Gospel of Thomas*, the connection between the Allegory of the Vineyard and Jesus' use of the term is much clearer. For in Thomas, the issues of justice, land usage, fair wages, and oppression take center stage. Jesus is not the vine, but Crossan's theme of commensality ripples beneath the surface of the story. In *Thom* 65, an owner of a vineyard sends a slave to collect its crop from the workers. They beat him and almost kill him. The owner rationalizes that maybe the workers didn't recognize his servant, so he sends his son. But because the "farmers knew that he was the heir to the vineyard, they grabbed him and killed him" (*Thom* 65:1–7). There is no overlay of the allegory here, state the editors of *The Five Gospels*.[6] However, Jesus' story certainly alludes to the social tensions current at the time. This factor is absent in the Synoptic versions, where the son's death and expulsion from the vineyard focus on Christian claims to be the true Israel (Mark 12:1–8; Matt 21:33–39; and Luke 20:9–15).

As a metaphor, Christ as the vine and his disciples as the branches is closer to the Eleusinian mysteries than to the Synoptic versions. At first the Eleusinian mysteries were devoted to Demeter, but in time Dionysus was joined to the festivals. An air of secrecy guarded the earlier years, but with the addition of Dionysus, bread and wine and open joviality characterized the mysteries. The mysteries endured over 1,800 years, until Theodosius closed them in the late AD 380s. They constituted the ancient world's most famous and sacred religious celebration. The rites lasted for nine days. In addition to Demeter's initiates "knowing her voice," so to speak, on the sixth day revelers danced from Athens along a sacred way, passed a sacred fig tree, and entered the field of Eleusis by way of a gate called "the mystical entrance." It is difficult to imagine that John was not aware of these mysteries, at least by way of hearsay. His use of words like "door," "way," "life," "vine," "branches," "wine," and "bread" were hardly used in a spiritual vacuum. He may not have known anything of the mysteries' inner secrets, but their general contents would have been common knowledge, just as notions of the Mardi Gras festivities and the Running of the Bulls in Pamplona are commonplace today, whether one has ever participated in them or not.

6. P. 510 of op. cit.

The point of all this is simply the reminder that John's metaphors carry us well into the category of myth, or faith, if you prefer. There is nothing astonishing or startling about this. Without myth, symbol, metaphor, allegory, and parable, spiritual truth is impossible to impart. Since its language cannot be cognitive or representative, in Randall's sense, it can only *express the truths of its experience* in symbolic form. Understanding this enables a Christian, Buddhist, Hindu, Jew, or Moslem to encapsulate within themselves the sacred insights of mankind's past that still energize humanity emotionally and spiritually. Without this "knowledge," one cannot truly respond to the transcendence one experiences in fathoming the mystery of his or her human beingness. That Christ is the "true vine" and "we his branches" enriches our own journey of faith as we abide in the mystery of what gives life its true vitality. Moreover, that "pruning" must occur from time to time speaks of a truth that none can deny. There isn't a religion today that doesn't espouse such discipline. The possibility of all this being lost is too grave to be left in the hands of historians alone.

The Stone that the Builders Rejected

The three Synoptic Gospels, *The Gospel of Thomas*, Acts, Paul's letter to the Romans, and 1 Peter all refer to the "stone that the builders rejected." In turn this stone is traceable to the "cornerstone" or "stumbling stone" that Isa 8:14; 28:16, and Ps 118:22 mention. In the first Isaiah instance, it is "the Lord of hosts" who is "a stone one strikes against" and the "rock one stumbles over" (Isa 8:14). In the second passage, God is "laying in Zion a foundation stone, a tested stone, a precious cornerstone, a sure foundation: 'One who trusts will not panic'" (Isa 28:16). Both prophecies are judgments against Judah's *absence of faith* in the face of foreign aggression. The "stone" has to do with trusting God and God's covenant of justice and righteousness. In neither passage, however, is the word "rejected" mentioned. It is only implied. Its first mention is in Ps 118:22: "The stone that the builders rejected has become the chief cornerstone." As Old Testament scholars note, Psalm 118 preserves segments of an entrance ceremony required to approach the temple. The protagonist in this psalm declares his fitness to enter based on his "confidence" and "trust" in "the Lord." It is the Lord who "has become [his] salvation." His own strength is secondary.

When we move forward in time, if *The Gospel of Thomas* precedes the Synoptic Gospels, then its chapter 66 is the first written witness to Psalm 118's words being placed on Jesus' lips: "Show me the stone that the builders rejected: that is the keystone."[7] Even here, however, the editors dismiss the notion that Jesus made any such reference to Psalm 118. These words are credited to the early Church's Jesus movements and not to Jesus.

The next time this "stone" appears is in Paul's letter to the Romans. The context is Paul's anguish over his "own people," or Israel's, unbelief. Again, his emphasis, like Isaiah's, falls on "faith." "They have stumbled over the stumbling stone, as it is written, 'See, I am laying in Zion a stone that will make people stumble, a rock that will make them fall [*petran scandalou*]'" (Rom 9:33). This is the *scandal* that breaks Paul's heart, that his own people should have rejected Jesus as the Messiah. From Paul to Mark seems to have been the next step. As with Thomas 66, the words are placed on Jesus' lips: "The stone that the builders rejected has become the cornerstone" (Mark 12:10). Matthew and Luke repeat Mark's text and Luke cites it again in Acts 4:11.

If Jesus were half the sage, or half the wily Cynic, the Seminar Fellows depict him to be, then the possibility that Jesus quoted this ancient text is highly likely. He knew his program of commensality was radical, that it was meeting resistance wherever he went. Yes, *he* was being "rejected." Yes, his *program* was being "rejected." Yet, he knew its claim to truth was as solid as the "cornerstone" that Judah had rejected in Ahaz's time. He had no misgivings about this. It was the *new wine* that he was trying to pour into the old wine skins, the *new cloth* that he was struggling to sew on Israel's old rags. Jesus surely carried this burden cognizant of what was happening. It was part of his passion, and at some point it may well have dawned on him that he might be rejected, along with his dream, by his own people and by his own nation.

Were the earliest followers placing words on Jesus' lips that he never uttered? Or were they grieving with him, as Paul did, over Israel's own rejection of its native son and scion of the Davidic throne, Jesus of Nazareth? To assign these words solely to the post-Easter Church is to miss once again the mystery that made the pre-Easter Jesus the Jesus they could never forget.

Teacher or Rabbi

Crossan and others doubt that Jesus ever called himself, or allowed himself to be called, "Teacher," *Didaskalé* (voc. sing.) in Greek. The term appears no less than 13 times in Mark, 12 in Matthew, 16 in Luke, and 8 in John. Most of its occurrences in Matthew and Luke are recast narratives based on Mark's story. A "teacher" is one who instructs, teaches, admonishes, and

---

7. *The Five Gospels*, p. 511.

directs. Certainly, Jesus' most memorable aphorisms and parables, maxims and imperatives all fit this definition. To bar the possibility that Jesus' disciples (*mathētai*—who are mentioned no less than 240 times in the Gospels and the Book of Acts) called, or thought of, Jesus as a *didaskalos* borders on the absurd. Even the appellation *Rabbi* appears thrice in Mark, 4 times in Matthew, and 8 times in John's Gospel. Even more engaging is the fact that the appellation of endearment, "*rabbouni*," is used once by Mark (Mark 10:51) and twice by John (1:38; 20:16). The editors of *The Five Gospels* consider such designations, as "teacher" and "rabbi," to date to the post-Easter Church, but this supposition cannot be proven; it simply follows from their view of Jesus as an egalitarian Cynic.

Beyond what this may suggest about Jesus' identity as a "man," symbolically or metaphorically, its significance is obvious. For the New Testament community, Jesus was the "Teacher extraordinaire." Like the rabbis, or masters of the Tradition of the Elders, Jesus' "teachings" possessed aretetical and cognitive import. His voice was more than a Cynic's cry against injustice or social estrangement and decay. Yes, it was that. But theologically his *logoi* offered the clearest pathway to the knowledge of God and knowledge of mankind. His voice rang with the immanent Presence of the Transcendent God, who alone quells mankind's estrangement from himself, his neighbor, and the Eternal.

12

Jesus as Shaman, Magician, and Healer

Most New Testament scholars in quest of the historical Jesus have concentrated on his oracles and sayings. After all, the oracular period preceded any narrative period and therefore, in all likelihood, contains history's earliest glimpse of Jesus. Nonetheless, Luke's second volume, the Acts of the Apostles, indicates that memories of Jesus' acts and deeds circulated at an early timeframe, too. Unlike Q's collection of Jesus' aphorisms and maxims that concentrate on Jesus' words, Luke has Peter state that "God anointed Jesus of Nazareth with the *Holy Spirit and with power*, [who] *went about doing good* and *healing* all who were *oppressed by the devil*, for God was with him. We are witnesses to *all that he did* both in Judea and Jerusalem" (Acts 10:38; italics for emphasis). Note that the focus here falls on Jesus' actions and deeds, rather than on his words, and that most of the emphasis stresses the presence and the power of the Holy Spirit who enables Jesus to heal and cast out demons. In this heavenly struggle or contest with evil, God's power prevails.

It is somewhat sobering to think that Jesus might have fulfilled the role of a shaman or magician. Many aspects of shamanism are present in Jesus' healing activities, along with magic. Luke denounces the magic of Simon of Samaria, the famous Simon Magus of Acts 8:9–24, as well as the arts of the magician Elymas of Paphos (Acts 13:7). Yet he describes Jesus' healings as dramatic exorcisms, accompanied by commands and confrontations with demons (Luke 9:49; 11:14; 13:32), and depicts Paul doing the same in Acts 13:9–13. In fact, he describes Paul as engaging in shaman-like activity in Acts 19:11: "God did extraordinary miracles through Paul, so that when the handkerchiefs or aprons that had touched his skin were brought to the sick, their diseases left them, and evil spirits came out of them." This is known as "contagious magic," according to James Frazer in *The Golden Bough*, and is probably as ancient as Cro-Magnon Man.

If we define a shaman as a holy person, who through commands and gestures is able to coerce or expel demonic forces from possessed individuals, then the pre-Easter Jesus qualifies as a preeminent shaman. If we can suspend our prejudices long enough against any such thoughts, Jesus as a shaman, or even as a magician, need not disparage or disenchant us. It was his world. He was born into it. Psychotherapy and anti-depressant drugs were centuries away. How else was one to heal the "possessed"? To "charm out" evil? As late as the 1940s, my grandmother, a child of the Blue Ridge Knobs of Southwest Virginia, "charmed" a cluster of warts off my hand. She did it with a string of knots, rubbed gently across each wart, one knot per wart. She could read fortunes from coffee grounds and predict visitors' arrivals from the brightness of embers on a glowing hearth. It was part of the mountain lore of Appalachia. In Luke's case, he attributes Jesus' power to cast out [*ekballo*] demons to the presence of the Holy Spirit in Jesus' life. Jesus' healings represent the power of God overcoming the power of evil. These events are as much a part of the pre-Easter Jesus' legacy as his aphorisms and sayings. They mean that Jesus' sayings were already accompanied by a memory of Jesus as a healer, as an exorcist, and not only as a Cynic, or popular social revolutionary.

As an exorcist, Jesus pitted his will against the will of the possessed. Casting out demons required commanding the dark unclean forces to show themselves and come out. This was no simple task, no project for the fearful or faint of spirit. Confrontation, resistance, name calling, charges, emotional and physical violence, spirit versus spirit, power versus power, will versus will, all come into play. As the possessed man of Mark 1:24–25 charges: "'What have you to do with us, Jesus of Nazareth? Have you come to destroy us? I know who you are, the Holy One of God.' But Jesus rebuked him, saying, 'Be silent, and come out of him!' And the unclean spirit, convulsing him and crying with a loud voice, came out of him." The Gospels repeat this scene time and again, along with Jesus' commands, gestures, or spells: "Be silent! Come out!"

The reality of the phenomenon of exorcism is acknowledged not only in the Gospels but also in Josephus' *The Jewish Antiquities*. In section 2.8.5 of the *Antiquities,* Josephus relates how he witnessed in the presence of Vespasian a man named Eleazar expel a demon from a possessed victim and thus set him free. Eleazar procured the man's release by holding a ring rubbed in a special root [*baara*] under the possessed man's nose, then he slowly drew the demon out through the victim's nostrils. The man collapsed on the spot. Eleazar commanded the demon never to enter the man again. Josephus goes on to comment that: "this method of cure [exorcism] is of great force unto this day." Of equal interest is Josephus's belief that Eleazar was using conjurations with which God endowed Solomon as part of his overall wisdom. 1 Kgs 4:33, however, says only: "He would speak of trees, from the cedar . . . to the hyssop, . . . of animals, and birds, and reptiles, and fish." The Book of Tobit mentions the "gall of a fish" as possessing curative powers (Tob 6:5; 11:11), but the Gospels make no mention of Jesus utilizing such healing libations or fish oils. In the former account, however, Tobias says to his blind father, as he administers the oil, "Take courage." And Tobit replies: "I see you, my son, the light of my eyes!" (11:11, 14). Might Jesus have remembered Tobias's words and re-rendered them as "Your faith has made you whole"?

In any event, in the case of illnesses or diseases, Jesus lays his hands on the sick, or summons the ill person's faith to a higher level, or even touches the leprous and the unclean (Mark 1:41–43). Mark tells us that in the reference cited, Jesus was "moved with pity." It wasn't just Jesus' pithy and acerbic sayings that moved his hearers, but it was his compassion, his sense of a sufferer's need of God's presence and love, that drew them by the number, too. Moreover, Jesus' finger drawings in the sand (John 8:6, 8) and saliva mixed in dust (John 9:6) represent appropriate medicinal formularies of the day. How ancient these gestures are can only be surmised from Solomon's knowledge of the healing gifts of the hyssop to Tobit's use of magical potions. In our own day, the sand paintings of the Navahos and the mandalas of the Tibetan Buddhists are famous for their spiritual and medicinal powers. That Jesus utilized similar arts should come as no surprise. Luke's concern was to defend them against charges of sorcery and devil worship. Scripture condemned both, and the Teachings of the Elders did, too, as attested in the *Mishnah*'s tractate, Sanhedrin 7.7.11.

Matthew tells us that: "Jesus went about all the cities and villages, teaching in their synagogues, and proclaiming the good news of the kingdom, and curing [*therapeuon*] every disease and every sickness. When he saw the crowds, he had compassion for them, because they were harassed and helpless, like sheep without a shepherd" (Matt 9:35–36). In a still earlier passage, in which Matthew outlines the same activities, he adds: "they brought to him all the sick, those who were afflicted with various diseases and pains, demoniacs, epileptics, and paralytics, and he cured [*etherapeusen*] them" (Matt 4:24). However late Matthew's Gospel might be dated, he clearly holds in juxtaposition Jesus' three principal activities: teaching, proclaiming, and healing. He treats these as simultaneous and not as invented events by later storytellers. I think there is too much truth in this to deny it. The sayings and parables of Q might well belong to the synagogue visits, along with Jesus' statements about the Kingdom. Q and the *Gospel of Thomas* readily attest to his sayings. They simply don't tell us the when and the where. Matthew and Luke locate them in fields and on hilltops, or while Jesus is in transit, but many may well have been voiced in synagogues. That Jesus practiced his exorcisms on such occasions, or nearby, seems feasible, too. The crowds were astonished and amazed; the authorities were displeased. Both these results fit in quite reasonably with Crossan's own assessment of Jesus. He delighted the poor, gave hope to the harassed, while angering the powerful and elite.

Matthew's usage of the verb *therapeuo* is of interest, insofar as Asclepius's medical priests were known as *therapeutae*. Asclepius, or Askleipios, was the Greek god of medicine. It was an art he had learned from his father Apollo—Greek god of light and healing. That Jesus combines both these gifts of illumination and healing would not have struck the post-Easter Church as contradictory or unthinkable. Socrates thought highly of the god and throughout Greece, temples were raised in his honor. The Greek traveler Pausanias reports that Alexander the Great dedicated his breastplate and spear to the god. By Jesus' time, Asclepius had achieved universal acclaim. In his book *Hellenistic Religions*, Luther Martin explains that part of the healing attributed to Ascelpius was transmitted in dreams and their interpretations and that much of the god's power lay in his devotees finding release from "the malaise of Hellenistic existence." In contrast to the medical practices traceable to Hippocrates, "the medicine of Asclepius was divine and sought to heal this existential malaise and its physical symptoms."[1] Walter Burkert explains further that acts of ritual and overnight visits to the Ascelpian shrines demanded time and expense on the part of any suppliant seeking release.[2] Jesus performs all this free, yet he encouraged the healed, especially lepers, to seek out a priest and make appropriate offerings to God (Mark 1:43). In this regard, Jesus' pattern follows quite remarkably the universal practice throughout Asia Minor and elsewhere. He was acting in conformity with the consensus of his time, or at least the Gospel writers perceived him as following that venue. This takes some of the edge off of what the editors of *The Five Gospels* maintain. Time and again in their comments on Jesus' healings and exorcisms they dismiss them as "inventions of the storyteller." One must suspend their opinion and rethink each case. In the final analysis, all this suggests that there was more to the historical Jesus than just fascination with his biting aphorisms and maxims. He was a Palestinian Asclepius, through whom the healing arts and catharsis of God could be seen and felt, heard and touched, offered and received. This aspect of his ministry was not a fabrication but appears based on fact. Moreover, it is in perfect harmony with what one should expect of a mendicant teacher, gadfly, and sage. The courage required of both—rabbi and healer—fits Jesus to a T. They render

1. L. Martin, *Hellenistic Religions*, New York, 1987, p. 51.
2. Burkert, *Greek Religion*, p. 268.

even more believable his fashioning of the infamous whip to drive out the Temple's moneychangers and his strength to survive the punishing ordeal he suffered before and throughout his crucifixion.

Also central to Jesus' healings are his *farewell prognoses* following several of his cures. Granted they are found only in the Synoptic Gospels, and thus constitute single attestation, they are nonetheless in tune with the historical Jesus' approach and "effrontery," so to speak. They constitute Jesus' closing remarks, or pronouncements, repeated no less than seven times, three with respect to the woman who suffered from hemorrhages (Mark 5:34; Matt 9:22; Luke 8:48), two concerning the blind Bartimaeus (Mark 10:52; Luke 18:42), and two unique to Luke (Luke 7:50; 17:19). The closing pronouncement is: "Your faith has made you well." Mark 5:34 and Luke 8:48 add: "Go in peace." The idea that faith should make one well belongs within the parameters of the historical Jesus. Isn't that what his vision was all about? Its symbolic truth is as relevant for our time as his. The riddle of the human condition can only be resolved by an act of faith. In many respects, these farewell prognoses portend today's CBT: "cognitive behavioral therapy." By replacing his "patients's" thoughts of worthlessness and depression with thoughts of self-worth, a capacity to believe, and a resumed sense of self-responsibility (Your faith has made you well; go in peace), Jesus released them from their demons and healed their hearts. As John T. Carroll has pointed out, what the Gospels' healing narratives proclaim is "the fundamental conviction that God wills the wholeness of human beings," indeed, the "transformation of human life" itself.[3]

Lastly, by way of addendum, it is important to note that there are 56 references of various tense endings of the two verbs *iaomai* (to heal, or cure) and *therapeuo* (to heal, cure, render service, or serve) in the Synoptic Gospels. Many of these healings are administered to the demon possessed or those possessed of an unclean [*akathartos*] spirit or demon. It seems highly unlikely that Mark would have "invented" the dozen or so that appear in his Gospel, which Matthew and Luke reproduce, as well as those which they add of their own. The unclean can be ceremonially unclean as well as morally unclean, and the texts do not always discriminate between the two. In either case, confronting the "unclean" would not have been an unusual phenomenon for the historical Jesus to have tackled. The clean and the unclean, the fit and the unfit, have haunted Judaism since its inception. Thus to assign the inclusion of these "healings" to the post-Easter Church seems more of a "fabrication" than to accept them at face value.

---

3. See John T. Carroll: "Sickness and Healing in the New Testament Gospels," *Interpretation* Vol. 49. April 1955: pp. 130–42.

13

The Pre-Easter Jesus as Wonderful Counselor and Prince of Peace

Is THERE any material in the oracular period that attests to Jesus as an unusual counselor [*pele' yo'es*, i.e., "extraordinary counselor" in Hebrew], the symbolic mighty God, everlasting father, and prince of peace [*shar-shalom*] of Isa 9:6? If so, such material would balance the over-emphasis on Jesus as a Cynic and lend credence to the Synoptic Gospels' view of Jesus as Israel's long-awaited Messiah and Davidic Prince of Peace.

The Old Testament abounds with promises of 1) divine *comfort* and *counsel* and with 2) two critical references to the Messiah as a *prince of peace [shar-shalom]*. Concerning the first, the Psalmist of 119:50, 52, and 76 extols the "comfort [from] distress" that God's promises and God's ordinances afford. As the Psalmist declares: "Let your steadfast love become my comfort, according to your promise to your servant" (119:76). Or as Isaiah 40:1 proclaims: "Comfort, O comfort my people, says your God." Or again: "Sing for joy, O heavens, and exult, O earth; . . . For the Lord has comforted his people and will have compassion on his suffering ones" (Isa 49:13). Or again in chapter 51:2: "For the Lord will comfort Zion; he will comfort all her waste places." And still again: "I have seen their ways, but I will heal them; I will lead them and repay them with comfort" (Isa 57:18). Above all is Isaiah's vision of the Suffering Servant's task: "The spirit of the Lord God is upon me, because the Lord has anointed me; he has sent me to bring good news to the oppressed, to bind up the brokenhearted, to proclaim liberty to the captives, and release to the prisoners; to proclaim the year of the Lord's favor, and the day of vengeance of our God; to comfort all who mourn; to provide for those who mourn in Zion" (Isa 61:1–3). Jeremiah repeats a similar promise (31:13) as well as Zech 1:17.

Although references to the Messiah as "prince of peace" occur only twice (Isa 9:6; Ezek 37:25), they nonetheless underscore the Messiah's role as national healer and prince of justice. In Hebrew, *shar* means not only prince, but also chief, chieftain, captain, and ruler. His role is to lead as well as to protect, to guide as well as to defend. In Isaiah 9, his goal is to champion Yahweh's justice and righteousness, which all nations await. It is this image of the Redeemer that Isaiah promulgates in his inimical symbol of the Messiah as a mothering figure: "As a mother comforts her child, so I will comfort you" (Isa 66:13).

This last prophecy finds its way into Q, which both Matthew and Luke preserve. "How often have I desired to gather your children together as a hen gathers her brood under her wings" (Matt 23:37); or again in Luke: "How often have I desired to gather your children together as a hen gathers her brood under her wings" (13:34). Notice that in translation the saying is identical in both Gospels! The Seminar Fellows suspect its usage, as the two evangelists incorporate the saying in a passage of judgment against Jerusalem, which, at the time of their writing, had already fallen. Thus the Seminar scholars conclude that the saying cannot be relied on for historical information. That the saying appears in Q, however, and is virtually similar in Greek in both passages, attests to the fact that before the Gospels were written the Jesus movement already retained images of Jesus as a comforting voice of counsel and hope. Such an image of Jesus is preserved throughout Q as well as in *The Gospel of Thomas*. Consequently, it strengthens the post-Easter Church's perception of the pre-Easter Jesus as a revealer of God, of the everlasting Father's sacred wisdom and love, of his commitment to justice and peace, and of his image as an extraordinary counselor.

On *anxiety*, Jesus' saying, "do not worry about your life" is found in Matt 6:25–34, Luke 12:22–31, and *Thom* 36:1–3. Its emphasis on unqualified trust in God is one of Jesus' foundational principles.

On *impoverishment*, his saying: "Blessed are the poor" is found in Matt 5:3, Luke 6:20, and *Thom* 54:1. Its opposite, "woe to the rich" (Luke 6:24), is equally a reminder of divine priorities. To neglect the poor is tantamount to rejecting God.

Of *grief*, his saying: "Blessed are those who mourn" appears in Matt 5:4 and Luke 6:21 (not found in Thomas). "Mourning" here is more than a sign of depression or victimization; rather it is symbolic of God's divine balm, which alone heals.

On *hunger*, "Blessed are those who hunger" is preserved in Matt 5:6, Luke 6:21, and *Thom* 69:2. Again, its opposite, "Woe to you who are full now" (Luke 6:25), underlies mankind's common bond and Jesus' commitment to God's concern for all disadvantaged persons.

On the *homeless*, "the son of Adam has no place to lay his head," likewise receives double attestation in Q (Matt 8:20, Luke 9:58) and *Thom* 86:2. Far beyond any dispute of the "son of Adam's" meaning, looms the specter of Micah's charge against the elite of Judah's wealthy classes during Ahaz's and Hezekiah's era: "They covet fields, and seize them; houses, and take them away; they oppress householder and house, people and their inheritance" (Mic 2:2). Jesus took Micah's counsel to heart. The landless poor were a stark reminder of prophetic calls for justice. The prophet's verse might well have inspired Luke's community of Acts 2:44–46 as well.

On the *restless and inquisitive*, "Ask, and it will be given you, seek and you will find, knock and it will be opened to you," in Matt 7:7–8, Luke 11:9–10, and in *Thom* 2:1, 92:1, and 94:1. For Jesus, God is open to all who seek him. All are welcome before God. To acquiesce in hopelessness is not an option for Jesus. One has the right to challenge injustice and cruelty, to seek self-improvement and to confront the status quo.

On *burdens*, "Come unto me, all you who are weary and carry heavy burdens, and I will give you rest. Take my yoke upon you, and learn from me; for I am gentle and humble in heart, and you will find rest for your souls. For my yoke is easy, and my burden is light" (Matt 11:28–39; *Thom* 90:2). One would expect this saying to have shown up in John's Gospel rather than in Matthew's or Thomas's, but that the latter two preserve it speaks volumes of the pre-Easter Jesus' attempt to nurture and provide guidance, along with respite and encouragement.

These sayings witness as much to Jesus' empathy as they do to Jesus' public criticism of the political, social, and economic conditions of the day. For that reason, the Gospels' portrayal of the pre-Easter Jesus as one who had "compassion" for the crowds and whose words brought hope and solace to his hearers (Mark 6:34, 8:2; Matt 9:36, 14:14, 15:32, 20:34; and Luke 7:13, 15:20) is justified and not necessarily an editorial supplement to enliven the evangelists' stories. At the same time, the topics italicized above attest to the horrendous social and economic state of affairs that persisted in first-century AD. Palestine. The hunger, poverty, and hopelessness of his people were never far from his mind. To what extent he was as haunted by Isaiah's text as Isaiah himself, we can only surmise. In addition to Micah, Jesus might well have had Psalm 34 in mind, too. "The young lions suffer want and hunger, but those who seek the Lord lack no good thing. . . . When the righteous cry for help, the Lord hears, and rescues them from all their troubles. The Lord is near the broken hearted and saves the crushed in spirit" (Ps 34: 10, 17–18).

In the preceding chapter, it was pointed out how many of Jesus' healings were prompted by his concern for the plight of his people's sufferings. That Luke's sources remembered Jesus as one who "went about doing good" (Acts 10:38) corroborates this facet of Jesus' itinerant program. In fact, it is impossible to analyze Jesus' life apart from his welcomed words of hope and wisdom. That people flocked to him wherever he went, speaks for itself.

When one compares Jesus' burden for the poor with Hesiod's views on poverty, one can understand why Jesus' followers received him with such enthusiasm. Hesiod's views, though datable to the seventh century BC, reflected much of the Greco-Roman world's attitude toward the poor in Jesus' day. In his *Elegies*, Hesiod writes: "Bad men are often rich, and good men poor." Yet, "Ah Poverty, you slut! Why do you stay? Why love me when I hate you? Please betray me for another man." Again, "Thus poverty gives birth to impotence." Still again: "The sentiments of all men are the same. They all love rich men, and despise the poor." And once more:

> O wretched Poverty, why do you sit
> Upon my shoulders, bringing me disgrace
> In mind and body? I, who know the good
> And beautiful, of all men, I have learned
> Many vile things from you, against my will.[1]

Hesiod's observations are poignant and reveal a troubled conscience, but his maxims fail to address the underlying injustices that contribute to the plight of the poor. Hesiod wanted only to escape them.

The Gospel of Thomas clearly supports one of Mark's pivotal narrative sections, in which Jesus asks the disciples, "Who do men say that I am?" (Mark 8:27). According to *Thom* 13:1–4, Jesus asks, "Tell me what I am like." Peter answers: "You are like a just angel." Matthew adds: "You are like a wise philosopher," and Thomas: "Teacher, my mouth is utterly unable to say what you are like."[2] In all three of these responses, the absorbing character of Jesus as someone different and special takes center stage. Echoes of Isaiah's "wonderful counselor" [*pele' yo'es*] reverberate in Peter's reply of "just angel," as well as in Matthew's "wise philosopher," and Thomas's "utterly unable to say." What did they see in the pre-Easter Jesus to evoke such responses? Was it a charisma that sparked political hopes? Or was it something more? Something that nudged the very essence of their being and made them want to touch his robe?

It is impossible to read Matt 25:31–46 without being grasped by a sense of the same. The Seminar Fellows reject the passage's sayings of Jesus, because in their estimation the cluster is not a "parable" but a "portrayal

---

1. Hesiod, *Hesiod and Theognis*, New York, 1963, pp. 107, 109–10, 118–19.
2. *The Five Gospels*, p. 480.

of the last judgment."³ The point they overlook, however, is its cumulative impact on the post-Easter communities' memories of Jesus. Whether a parable or not, many of Jesus' sayings, like this one, address a final judgment. The Fellows' methodology and presuppositions have limited their sphere of authentic sayings to the point that anything Jesus might have said about the End-Time is simply ignored by them. Few passages, however, ring as true of the pre-Easter Jesus of even Crossan's reconstruction as this text. "I was hungry and you gave me food, I was thirsty and you gave me something to drink, I was a stranger and you welcomed me, I was naked and you gave me clothing, I was sick and you took care of me, I was in prison and you visited me" (Matt 25:35–36). Why would any community "invent" or "fabricate" such a passage, unless there were sufficient rudimentary oracular material to support it? As in the case of Matthew's "Sermon on the Mount," what Matthew appears to have done is to piece together the sayings in a notable story, worthy of Jesus' highest vision of *commensality*. Five centuries later, Islam's *Hadith* would place three of these sayings on Mohammed's own lips: "I was sick, and you did not visit me; . . . I asked food of you, but you gave Me no food; . . . I asked drink of you, but thou gavest Me nothing to drink."⁴⁴

Perhaps nowhere is Jesus' legacy as *pele' yo'es* and *shar-shalom* more highlighted than in Paul's letters and in the subsequent Pauline epistles. Since mankind is no longer under condemnation, Paul can celebrate the unfathomable consolation that Christ has brought believers, as there is nothing "in all creation" that can "separate [them] from the love of God in Christ Jesus" (Rom 8:39). As a consequence, believers may now walk in Christ's Spirit of "love, joy, peace, patience, kindness, generosity, faithfulness, gentleness, and self-control" (Gal 5:22–23). By bearing "one another's burdens," they "fulfill the law of Christ" (6:2). They may "forget what lies behind" and "not worry about anything," as "the peace of God, which surpasses all understanding, will guard [their] hearts and minds in Christ Jesus" (Phil 3:13, 4:6–7). Paul has already experienced such peace: "for I have learned to be content with whatever I have. I know what it is to have little, and I know what it is to have plenty" (4:11–12). Note how he differs from Hesiod, who learned only "vile things" from want! In contrast, Christ's followers may now clothe themselves with "compassion, kindness, humility, meekness, and patience." They may "forgive each other" and "let the peace of Christ rule in [their] hearts" (Col 3:12–15). All this Paul has

---

3. Ibid., p. 258.
4. See van Voorst, p. 327.

garnered from his own "revelations" and wrestling with the traditions that had been handed down to him.

In retrospect, "wonderful counselor" or "extraordinary counselor" is a surprising metaphor when seen in its historical perspective. Isaiah had watched the kingdom of Judah deteriorate under Ahaz. To the north, the house of Israel was in total disarray. The Syro-Israelite League was intent on humbling Judah. Ahaz possessed none of the Davidic charisma required to thwart the League's threats. Yet Isaiah's heart burned with zeal for Yahweh. His vision of Yahweh's glory on the occasion of Jotham's coronation had seared itself indelibly on his soul. "Holy, Holy, Holy is the Lord of Hosts. Who will go for us?" the seraphim had chanted (Isa 6:3,8). How could Isaiah not volunteer? Was not God capable of redeeming Judah, the house of David, of sending a king to correct the decades of decay and corruption? To send a "wonderful counselor" would be just like Yahweh, in spite of all the malaise that Judah had suffered. Isaiah never doubted Yahweh's *hesed* loyalty to Judah.

If Jesus were half the figure the Evangelists portray him to be, he had to be haunted by Isaiah's vision, too. It obsessed him, transformed and molded him as much as anything Jesus experienced. He wasn't simply a Cynic offering memorable maxims and shocking aphorisms. He was a dreamer, himself, filled with the ancient sound of prophetic hopes and promises resounding in his soul. He took those promises to heart, gave them voice, and lifted the spirit of his people. And it inspired them with a vision of God that rekindled their will in the season of their national despair.

Who among mankind does not need rekindling, renewal, and redemption? I venture that this was the Jesus the crowds pressed about in order to touch the hem of his garment. Such men are rare in any culture, and to know them is to know "the power of God unto salvation" (Rom 1:16). Is it not appropriate that the woman of Luke 7:37–50, who knelt before Jesus, wept and covered his feet with her tears, kissed and dried them with her hair, and anointed them with oil should remain nameless? She is a metaphor for all who understand the depth of their human condition and longing for a savior.

To be truthful, Jesus as the Prince of Peace is problematic and symbolic. If we mean peace as the absence of conflict, struggle, or standing for principles, No! But if we mean peace as wholeness, justice, fairness, and as the comprehension of that "peace which passes all understanding," Yes! Jesus is quite blunt: "I have not come to bring peace, but a sword" (Matt 10:34). "Do you think that I have come to bring peace to the earth? No,

... but rather division" (Luke 12:51). "They do not know that I have come to cast conflicts upon the earth: fire, sword, war" (*Thom* 16:2).

The word "fire" [*pyros*] is of particular interest in this list and appears frequently in the New Testament. Q preserves John the Baptizer's blistering phrase, "unquenchable fire," which awaits the unrepentant at Judgment (Matt 3:11–12; Luke 3:9, 17), along with the phrase that "he who comes after me" will baptize with the "Holy Spirit and fire" (Matt 3:12; Luke 3:16). Thereafter, Matthew employs the phrases "thrown into the fire," "hell of fire" [*géenan tou pyros*], and "eternal fire" no less than seven more times. All these phrases are attributed to Jesus. They refer to the fate of "evildoers" at the End Time, or Last Judgment. Mark includes the intriguing "salted with fire" that Jesus' disciples must also endure. As a symbol of justice and discipline, Jesus' *fire motif* reminds all of the magnitude of the kingdom's significance and of God's watchful care of life's dispossessed. His phrase, "salted with fire," especially captures attention when one recalls the symbolism of fire in the Old Testament: from the burning bush, to Elijah's contest with the priests of Baal, to the glowing ember placed on Isaiah's tongue. Fire represents the sacred cleansing presence of God, the commissioning prerequisite that prepares His ambassadors for service to God. The gift of the tongues of fire at Pentecost perpetuates the same theme.

The editors of *The Five Gospels* reject the above sayings as authentic utterances of the historical Jesus, as he would not have referred to himself as having a mission from God. Plus, the *fire motif* has to do with *apocalyptic eschatology* and not *sapiential eschatology*. Still, the presence of these sayings in both Q and Thomas underscores the Church's memory of the pre-Easter Jesus as a type of Israel's ancient *shar-shalom*, her mighty God, her incarnated Father. His role as counselor and prince echoes all the way back to Samuel's era and Israel's plea for a king [a *melek* in Hebrew]. Did they really need a *melek*, Samuel asks, a king like the kings of the Ancient Near East? Such a king would financially and morally bankrupt Israel. Would not a prince, a *nagid*, whose love of God and unquestionable obedience to God, be far more preferable than a *melek*? (I Sam 8–12.)

In pursuance of Samuel's very advice, Matthew's famous collection of Q, known as "The Sermon on the Mount," contains scores of aphorisms that witness to Jesus' commitment to, basically, non-resistance. Certainly, Jesus had counted the cost and knew that an armed insurrection was out of the question. Plus, it was foreign to his spirit, his nature as a holy man, healer, and sage. His maxims urge patience, caution, restraint.

Blessed are the meek (5:5); Blessed are the merciful (5:7); Blessed are the peacemakers, for they will be called children of God (5:9); Do not be angry (5:22); Do not be unfaithful to your spouse (5:27); Do not swear falsely (5:33); Do not resist an evildoer (5:39); Love your enemies, pray for those who persecute you (5:44); Be perfect as your Father is perfect (5:48); Store your treasures in heaven (6:20); Do not worry about tomorrow (6:34); Do not judge others (7:1); Do unto others as you would have them treat you (7:12); Enter through the narrow gate (7:13); Build your life on solid ground (7:24).

Luke adds to this list: Do good to those who hate you; Bless those who curse you; Pray for those who abuse you. Turn your cheek; Lend without expecting anything in return; Forgive and you will be forgiven; Give and it will be given to you (Luke 6:27–30, 35, 37–38).

If we turn to the ancient world for similar advice, Seneca's essay, "*De Clementia*," or "On Mercy," is the closest approximation to Jesus' largesse of spirit. Written for and sent to Nero, the essay encourages the fickle emperor to exercise mercy and restraint in cases requiring appropriate redress of personal and national wrongs. Seneca cites the generosity of Augustus when dealing with his own foes. Seneca rejects any thought of pity, but he extols mercy, for it is the preeminent sign of strength and wisdom.

If we look to the gods, we search in vain, for they were not that keen on peace and often quarreled among themselves. Athena's olive branch, at best, symbolizes her patronage of agriculture, not peace. After all, she is depicted wearing a helmet and carrying a spear. She is Athens' warrior-goddess, defender of the city-state and guardian of her father, Zeus's, thunderbolts. Oddly enough, however, the Athenians did cherish peace. Lempriere reports in his *Classical Dictionary* that the city's inhabitants acknowledged the goddess Pax. The city raised a statute in her honor and placed the god Plutus—an offspring of their beloved Demeter—in her lap. Plutus and Pax symbolized the prosperity and opulence that cities enjoy during times of peace. The Romans represented her with a horn of plenty and an olive branch in her hand. Vespasian erected a temple in her honor, which became a depository for the writings of learned men. When it burned to the ground during Commodus' reign, immense deposits of literature and wealth were lost.[5]

Perhaps it is not surprising that Plato discusses peace in his dialogue *Laws*. He prefers it to war. In the dialogue, the laws of both Crete and Lacedaemon are attributed to gods—Crete's to Zeus and Lacedaemon's to Apollo, god of enlightenment and light. Plato's protagonist, "an Athenian

---

5. Lempriere, *Classical Dictionary*, London & Boston, 1972, pp. 452–53.

stranger," learns that the Lacedaemons define civic stability as an outgrowth of conquest in war. Plato's "stranger," however, is forced to ask:

> Ought not everyone always make laws for the sake of best? . . . But war is not the best. Peace with one another and good will are best. The happiness of the individual and the state depend on peace. If there must be war, it can only be for the sake of peace.[6]

Aristotle, in his *Politics*, adopts a similar view.

Is it possible that Jesus' statement about rendering to Caesar the things that are Caesar's and to God that which belongs to God draws from this ancient pool of common wisdom: that matters of war and peace belong to the province of the state, but peace is always best? Paul's adaptation of the same appears to have guided him in his counsel to the Romans. "For rulers are not a terror to good conduct but to bad" (Rom 13:3). The state is "God's servant for . . . good" (vs. 4). He might also have been drawing from Wisdom 6:1–3 and its injunction for rulers: "For your dominion was given you from the Lord, and your sovereignty from the Most High." Jesus' reply to Pontius Pilate certainly echoes the text. "You would have no power over me unless it had been given you from above" (John 19:11). If Jesus did not actually say as much, John's community embraced the principle, along with admiring Jesus' courageous humility before authority and calm in the face of raw power.

Long after the Synoptic writers had completed their works, the Johannine community could not help but recast much of the above in one of John's most memorable adages of Jesus: "Peace I leave with you; my peace I give to you. I do not give to you as the world gives. Do not let your hearts be troubled, and do not let them be afraid" (John 14:27).

In a similar vein belongs another Johannine text attributed to Jesus. It too is part of the Jesus-Pilate dialogue. "My kingdom [*basileia*] is not of this world. If my kingdom were of this world, my followers would be fighting to keep me from being handed over to the Jews. But as it is, my kingdom is not from here [*enteuthen*]" (John 18:36). Like a Platonic idea or universal form, Jesus' kingdom transcends the mundane orders of human greed and power, fear and oppression, order and taxes. Yet, Jesus' ideal is both other and earthly. It holds before us that shining vision of what might be, could be, and can be, if we but muster the will to incarnate his Transcend Ideal in our own world. In this regard, Crossan is entirely right to emphasize a kingdom of *sarcophilia*. It isn't "of this world!" It's not the way the world thinks. Yet, what could be better?

---

6. *Laws*, Jowett trans., Vol. II, p. 411, text slightly altered.

Whatever we make of Jesus as the Prince of Peace, his symbolism as what "is best" is ancient. If Plato had met him, Plato's Socrates would have responded with a feisty and intense dialectic of give-and-take. John's Pilate and Jesus provide but a faint glimmer of how profound such a dialogue might have been.

When late in life Leo Tolstoy discovered the Jesus of the Gospels, his former fame as a writer meant less and less to him. He gave away massive amounts of his wealth, dressed in the blouse of his estates' serfs, took up his hoe and toiled with them. Too old to fight anymore, he endorsed the tenets of the emerging pacifist movement. He found himself compelled to question his government, its courts, its ministries of justice and law, its penchant for war, its system of conscription, its cruelty, barbarity, and indifference to suffering. His view of the Russian Orthodox Church was equally jaundiced. He wanted nothing more to do with its power, hierarchies, priests, vestments, sacraments, or orders. His one obsession was the Jesus of the Gospels—the Jesus of peace, meekness, poverty, kindness, and love. His re-encounter with Jesus resulted in numerous books and short stories, the most dramatic of these being *The Kingdom of God is Within You*. It was his call to pacifism, his call to end Europe's preoccupation with war and military conquest. It was his call for justice and peace. But did anyone listen? Scarcely four years after his death, The Great War enveloped them all.

14

The Chief Priests, Scribes, Elders, Pharisees, and Essenes

A BRIEF word concerning Jesus' enemies certainly deserves attention. In particular, in the Synoptic Gospels the "chief priests, scribes, and elders" are associated time and again with the coming Passion and the Passion Narrative itself. Since Crossan considers the latter narrative to be an invention of the Church, it behooves one to reexamine the chief priests' role, as assigned by the Gospels.

Chief Priests, Scribes, and Elders

As early as *The Gospel of Peter*, an *instrumental* role had been assigned to the chief priests. Writes the author: "But of the Jews none washed their hands, neither Herod nor any of his judges" (*Gospel of Peter* 1:1, in Cameron). In this document, the judges or chief priests have served as an apparent judicial body: trying, rejecting, and convicting Jesus as worthy of death. Mark, Matthew, and Luke will adopt this motif and incorporate it in Jesus' Passion sayings and throughout their respective Passion Narratives. The "Jews" or "chief priests, scribes, and elders" (presumably of the Sanhedrin) are the official judicial instrument implicated in Jesus' rejection and death. However neatly this refrain may echo Isaiah 53 and Ps 118:22, the fact remains that Jesus' crucifixion implies a trial of some sort, a judgment, and a sentence by some group or legal entity. That the precursor to Mark's own Gospel should report this may not historically prove the event, but it certainly lends credence to a trial that led to a conviction that resulted in Jesus' death.

An instrumental role, however, is not the only purpose for which "chief priests, scribes, and elders" are remembered. An *apologetic* and *theological* role is also incorporated into the Gospel stories. The writer of *The Gospel of Peter* expressly mentions that following Christ's crucifixion, the "Jews and elders and the priests" began to lament their deed: "Woe on our sins, the judgment and the end of Jerusalem is drawn nigh" (*Gospel of Peter* 7:25). Recognizing how "righteous" the Christ was, they implore Pilate to provide guards "lest his disciples come and steal him away" (8:28–30). Matthew picks up on this theme and repeats the story of the guards and the "theft" of Jesus' body in his own resurrection story (Matt 18:13).

More importantly, the Christian community appears to use this story to justify its separation from official Judaism, since "the stone which the builders rejected has become the chief cornerstone." Symbolically, the Christian community will look back on this official rejection as a warning to itself. To reject the Christ, the historical Jesus as the Messiah, is to bring a judgment of sorrow upon oneself, equal to that suffered by official Judaism. Just as Jerusalem's own judgment had drawn nigh, its walls breached and temple destroyed, Christians living in the post-Jerusalem era of the late 70s and 80s—seeing God's "righteous" hand in Jerusalem's fall—could deduce the same possibility for themselves. Whether this makes the *Gospel of Peter* later than AD 70 or contemporaneous with Mark's Gospel, its apologetic purpose holds. The gulf between Judaism and the Christian community's embracement of Jesus as the Christ was well underway. John's Gospel also attests to this movement in his story of the blind man who now sees. Like the *Gospel of Peter*, John refers to the Jewish leaders as "Jews." The blind man's parents are afraid to answer the authorities, "for the Jews had already agreed that anyone who confessed Jesus to be the Messiah would be put out of the synagogue" (John 9:22).

Pharisees

The Pharisees are assigned still another role. It is both *aretetical* and *legislative*. One is to avoid the "leaven of the Pharisees" (Matt 16:6). Unless one's righteousness "exceeds that of the scribes and the Pharisees," one is not fit for the in-breaking kingdom (Matt 5:20). Jesus' "Sermon on the Mount" and teachings in Q and elsewhere present a radically different approach to common problems, human needs, and one's awareness of the will of God than the Pharisees' teachings contain. The commandments to love, forgive, and embrace everyone (Crossan's "commensality" motif), set the Christian community apart from Judaism's then-present direction. The Pharisees' interpretations and applications of ancient Israel's laws no longer represent the aretetical values and legislative parameters for the new community of Christ's followers.

Although the Gospels' representations of the Pharisees are considered questionable by today's scholars, the New Testament's communities of faith understood what Pharisaism symbolized. In the mind of the developing Christian churches, it denoted a rejection of grace, humility, love, and commensality. It represented a flawed legalism that led to bondage, resulting in pride, hypocrisy, exclusion, and the aggrandizement of the self. The Gospel writers held this view though they possibly knew that its greatest rabbinic teacher, Hillel, advocated a message similar to Jesus's. Perhaps the Gospel writers were not so much interested in denigrating Judaism's teachers per se—though that they do so is undeniable—but in admonishing Jesus' followers to adhere to a new order of values, or a higher set of principles, which only words like "grace," "love," and "faith" could capture.

Today's disciples are meant to benefit from the Gospels' reminders of a symbol of pride and arrogance that erodes Jesus' potential impact on one's life and its fulfillment. Rather than dismiss the Gospels' harsh treatment of the Pharisees (however inaccurate it might be), the *aretetical* and *legislative* value of a converse way of life deserves to be emphasized. Faith, hope, and love are to be the new hallmarks of spirituality. Nothing exceeds them in either Luke, John's, or Paul's view. Why? Because love best captures the mystery of Jesus' own life. Like love, he could be patient and kind. He was neither envious nor boastful nor arrogant, although he could be confrontational and exasperated by human pride. Still, he never rejoiced at wrong but only in the truth. He bore all things, hoped all things, and endured the cross for his Father's sake and the coming kingdom's. He may have been blunt at times, intent, and focused, but he was never mean-spirited. "Make love your aim," Paul would write (1 Cor 14:1), for there is nothing higher than love, other than Jesus himself.

References to the Pharisees also serve a positive *theological* purpose. After all, they believe in the resurrection, angels and other spiritual beings, a coming judgment, life after death, and the doctrine of providence. Josephus' *Antiquities of the Jews* underscores all these principles as beliefs of the Pharisees (see *Ant.* 13.5.9, 13.10.6, 17.2.4, and 18.1.3). Josephus explains that they had "the multitude on their side," yet were a "cunning sect" and possessed prophetic powers. He emphasizes their value of "tradition," i.e. the handing down of the precepts of their fathers, along with their emphasis on "reason." Josephus had been a Pharisee but considered himself a modestly liberated intellectual desirous to impress his Roman readers with the better aspects of his nation's laws and history.

The Gospels acknowledge worthy facets of the Pharisaic movement, such as Nicodemus' attraction to Jesus' person and teachings and the former's role in assisting Joseph of Arimathea in preparing Jesus' body for burial. Luke's Gospel also retains a story of Jesus' attractive qualities to a Pharisee named Simon. The latter invited Jesus into his home only to become overawed by his guest's forgiving spirit and words of hope to a fallen woman who wept at his feet. It is one of Luke's more powerful stories and underlies the essence of Jesus' humanness and appeal (Luke 7:36–50). Luke also identifies the Gamaliel of Acts' Sanhedrin as a Pharisee whose trust in God's providential wisdom "softens" the sentence (the disciples were flogged rather than executed) passed against Peter and the accompanying apostles (Acts 5:34).

Essenes

From a historical perspective, it is Josephus' rather lengthy paragraphs on the Essenes that are most noteworthy. With careful and obvious admiration for the sect, he adumbrates their principles and practices: that they ascribe all things to God; teach the immortality of the soul; esteem the rewards of righteousness; share all things in common; no longer desire or keep servants; serve and minister one another; and appoint able stewards to receive and oversee their revenues (*Ant.* 18.1.6). Luke's account of the early Church's commune in Jerusalem reiterates many of these themes (Acts 24:43–47; 4:32–37; and 6:1–6). More amazing is Luke's reference to the community's number of 5,000, insofar as Josephus numbered the Essenes to be about 4,000. One almost wonders if Luke's writings don't betray knowledge of Josephus' *Antiquities*. If so, that would date his Gospel and Acts of the Apostles after the first century.

Whatever the case, the Gospel stories portray Jesus as one whose presence and message, actions and dreams, ignited hopes that created a community who hailed the historical Jesus as the long awaited Messiah and whose life transformed their own. It is this reality that underlies all the Gospels, whether those of the canonical collection or the numerous writings that have come down to us in the non-canonical works. In the light of this evidence, it seems immensely shortsighted for modern New Testament scholars to want the Christian community to substitute "the post-Easer Jesus" as the preferred assignation for the "Christ Jesus of faith."

15

Jesus and the Sabbath

The Synoptic Gospel Writers clearly understood the significance of the Sabbath. Luke mentions the Sabbath more than the other two, notwithstanding his numerous references to the Sabbath in the Acts of the Apostles. All three of the writers employ the Sabbath as a timeframe in which to set critical pronouncement stories, which magnify Jesus' person. Nonetheless, the stories provide a glimpse into Jesus' activities on the Sabbath and his views of its intended purpose. The employment of the Sabbath also occurs with reference to the synagogue, where members of the Jewish Palestinian community could gather for praise, worship, and study. In general, one can make at least five observations about the Synoptic Gospels' references to the Sabbath and Jesus' corresponding views: 1) the writers understood the Sabbath's historical place in Jewish life; 2) they understood its importance, in conjunction with the synagogue, as providing a time and place for Jesus' teachings, 3) for his miracles, 4) and for presenting his key theological principles, 5) along with providing a ray of enlightenment concerning Jesus' sense of sacred time.

Tradition

All four Gospel writers understand the role and place of the Sabbath in Jewish life, if not in Jesus' as well. Mark reminds us that Mary Magdalene and the women who accompanied her to the tomb, waited until "the Sabbath was over" (Mark 16:1). Matthew alludes to the same (Matt 28:1), while Luke notes that Jesus' death occurred just before "the sabbath was beginning," and goes on to state that the women who planned to prepare his body in the tomb, rested "on the Sabbath . . . according to the commandment" (Luke 23:56). John explains with equal sensitivity that, following Jesus' crucifixion, "because it was the Jewish day of Preparation," Nicodemus and Joseph of Arimathea laid Jesus in the Joseph's tomb, out of respect for the lateness of the hour and the tomb's close proximity to Golgotha. Earlier, during his version of Jesus' End-Time speech, Matthew has Jesus lament that, hopefully, when the "desolating sacrilege event" occurs, it may not be "on a Sabbath" (Matt 24:20), because of distance limitations that Torah prescribed. In none of these occurrences, do the writers express any negative attitudes toward the Sabbath.

A Time for Teaching

Matthew, Mark, and Luke all report that Jesus sought out synagogues, even on the Sabbath, that he might attend them in order to teach (Matt 9:35, 12:9, 13:54; Mark 1:21; 6:2; Luke 4:16, 4:31, 13:10). Mark 6:2 is especially noteworthy, as it reads: "On the Sabbath he began to teach in the synagogue, and many who heard him were astounded. They said, 'Where did this man get all this? What is this wisdom that has been given to him? What deeds of power are being done by his hands!'" Matt 13:54f and Luke 4:16f retain this pericope, repeating it almost word for word. Luke's version, however, varies more than Matthew's, inasmuch as Luke reworks the time and setting to shape Jesus' identity as the Suffering Servant of Isaiah 61:1, 2:58. After reading the text (in the synagogue at Nazareth), Jesus sits down to expound his Torah. He announces the fulfillment of the text, and "all spoke well of him and were amazed at the gracious words that came from his mouth" (Luke 4:22). But as Jesus begins to apply his message to the synagogue's members, they become enraged, for his Torah probes the depths of their unpreparedness to accept God's kingdom and to do God's will. What appears to be central in his message is Jesus' conviction that now is the time for the scripture's words to become reality. The Sabbath is not merely a time for "hearing" the word, or hearing it "read." It is a time for launching the will of God, for "letting God in," as the Hasid would later commend. It is not simply a moment for escaping life's harsh edges, or for hearing "gracious words." Even the Sabbath is a time "to bring good news to the poor, to proclaim release to the captives, the recovering of sight to the blind; to let the oppressed go free; a time for proclaiming the year of the Lord's favor" (Luke 4:18–19). It is this insight that guides Jesus' actions and vision of the value of the Sabbath, along with its purpose.

Time for Healing

It is not surprising, therefore, that Jesus uses the Sabbath and the synagogue as settings for healings, for engaging in exorcisms, and the casting out of demons. All three Synoptic Gospels, along with John, note Jesus' proclivity to heal and cure the sick and the lame on the Sabbath, for the

Sabbath represents a time, as holy as any time, filled with the goodness, nearness, and power of the Spirit of God. Time and again, Jesus heals on the Sabbath to the shock and consternation of those who have accepted it as their duty to protect and consecrate the Sabbath wholly unto God. Does he not recognize that what he does is "unlawful?" Matt 12:10: Mark 2:23–24; Luke 6:9; John 5:18, 7:23–24 all raise the question. But Jesus will not be deterred. In the process, he cites three principles, all based on scripture, which illuminate his unique visualization and activity.

Jesus' Principles for Guidance on the Sabbath

Jesus employs at least three criteria. One has to do with immediacy, or humanitarian need. When hunger or danger is clearly manifest, actions to relieve discomfort and suffering fulfill the intention of the Torah; they do not undermine it. Even the priests of Nob fed David's men when they were hungry, providing them with nothing less than the holy showbread itself! See Mark 2:21–27; Matt 12:1-14; Luke 6:1–11. As Jesus adumbrates for his stunned and sullen critics, "The Sabbath was made for humankind, and not humankind for the Sabbath, so the Son of Man is lord even on the Sabbath." Human need takes precedence over rigid formality. If a sheep "falls into a pit on the Sabbath; will you not lay hold of it and lift it out?" (Matt 12:11). "Does not each of you on the Sabbath untie his ox or his donkey from the manger, and lead it away to give it water?" (Luke 12:15).

A second principle has to do with Jesus' concept of "good" (*agathon*). *Agathos* refers to that which is generous, virtuous, profitable, and beneficent. Not only does "need" take precedence over inactivity and "gracious words," but "good" actions, or deeds, engaged in for the purpose of enhancing the welfare of those who suffer, reflect far better the intention of the Sabbath than correct observance of a hallowed day. Sabbath activity is not meant to be blind-sided by even a well-intentioned piety; rather "good" is preferable to inaction. "Lawful" or "unlawful" no longer define God's purposes on the Sabbath. Rather, helping, healing, curing, assisting, or rendering something "good," more appropriately fathoms the spirit of God's will for the Sabbath. To the question: "Is it lawful to cure or not?" Jesus replies: "Is it lawful to do good or harm . . . to save life or to kill?" (Mark 3:4). Luke's Jesus, in a similar text, is even more blunt. The leader of the synagogue argues that "there are six days on which work ought to be done; come on those days and be cured, and not on the sabbath" (Luke

13:14). But Jesus rebukes him: "Is not the Sabbath the perfect day on which to be set free from bondage?"

His third criterion, by way of deduction, follows from his reference to "harm," or "neglect." To neglect the lost sheep, the tied burro or oxen in its stall, or force a suffering man or woman to come back tomorrow, denies the very power and will of God to release those who suffer *now*. Jesus' sense of God's desire and availability to bring wholeness *now* overrides the older, more ancient custom of refraining from any unnecessary "work" on the Sabbath. That is why the Son of Man is lord of the Sabbath. For God's Sabbath, God's hallowed day of "rest," implies renewal and wholeness, not neglect, delay, postponement, or indifference to more suffering. Tomorrow will be replete with problems enough (Matt 6:34). God's will is ready for action today.

Jesus' Sense of Sacred Time

All this suggests that Jesus' sense of sacred time clashed with his contemporary world's traditional view. His rising early in the morning to go into the hills to pray, his belief that God hears best in the silent and secret places of the heart, his own frequent penchant for praying alone reveal a personally private and quiet side of Jesus' overall psychological makeup. He was complex, with many facets to his personality. The veil between himself and God, his soul and his Abba Father, permitted the immanence of God to revive Jesus' strength every day, as well as prompt him to seek God's will every day. Is it not possible, therefore, that Jesus' sense of his Father's daily presence obviated his need to consecrate one day in seven to the task of advancing his Father's will? In that respect, every day was a Sabbath for Jesus.

To move beyond the Jesus of history debate means incorporating Jesus' own insights as ours. It breathes new life into the mystery of God's intended Sabbath. It can lift us, too, out of the pits into which our piety falls and release us from the stagnant stalls of meaningless preoccupation. To do "good" on the Sabbath, to find and offer wholeness to others, as well as claim it for our selves, was Jesus' unique challenge for his time to grasp, as well as ours.

16

The Historical Jesus and the Apostle Paul

Paul and Jesus

IN ONE of his major works, *Paul: An Apostle of the Heart Set Free,* F. F. Bruce identifies no less than eight Pauline passages, which reflect Paul's knowledge of Jesus' words. Six of these appear to be based on Q; the other two are found in Mark. Bruce prefaces these texts by reminding his readers that as early as 1 Corinthians (AD 51–53), Paul was already in possession of the kerygma, which the Apostle attributed to the "tradition" that he had "received," presumably from Peter and James (1 Cor 15:3). That tradition is mirrored in Jesus' central *passion* statements, associated with the Son of Man oracles, found in all three of the Synoptic Gospels. 1) That Christ died for sins, 2) that he was buried, 3) that he was raised on the third day, and 4) that he appeared to many afterwards. Bruce also notes that Paul's doctrine of justification by faith is the theological underside of Jesus' parable of the Prodigal Son and other parables that emphasize grace (Good Samaritan, Dives and Lazarus), as well as a doctrine that may be inferred from Jesus' miracles (the healing of the man lowered from the ceiling, e.g.).

The eight "sayings," which Paul quotes, are found in 1 Cor 7:10; 9:14; 10:27; Rom 12:14; 13:7; 13:10; Gal 6:1 and 1 Thess 5:2–5. In the order in which they are listed, they have to do with divorce (Mark 10:11), laborers (Matt 10:10 and Luke 10:7), food set before one (Luke 10:8), blessing those who persecute believers (Luke 6:28), rendering Caesar his due (Mark 12:17), love as the fulfillment of the law (Matt 22:37–40), restoring one in a spirit of meekness (Matt 18:15), and the day of the Lord coming as a thief in the night (Luke 12:39). Half of these reflect authority issues and the other half seem to wrestle with appropriate ethical conduct for the era's new founded churches. The shadow of Jesus' emphasis on commensality is present.

Paul also cites a tradition, which he "received from the Lord" (1 Cor 11:23). It contains the first written instructions concerning the Lord's

Supper. It is one of his most famous passages, because it mentions Jesus' "betrayal," the loaf that symbolizes the broken body of Christ, the cup that represents his blood necessary for the establishment of the new covenant, and the proclamation of his death until his eschatological return. This tradition reveals quite clearly that by Paul's time, in the mid-first century, Jesus' followers were already interpreting the pre-Easter Jesus in the light of Isaiah 53, Jeremiah 31:31, Exod 24:8, and possibly *Psalm of Solomon 17*. None of this appears to be original with Paul, but something he has "received" and in turn wishes to "hand on." Since he never knew the pre-Easter Jesus, he only knows the post-Easter Christ. This knowledge may well have inspired his "revelations," which enabled him to interpret the meaning of Jesus' life at a deeper level than any of his Christian contemporaries had heretofore done.

There are at least eleven insights that Paul brings to his "knowledge of Jesus" that illuminate the post-Easter Christ for him. 1) Christ is the universal man, or principal archetype, who represents mankind before God (Rom 5:1–21; 1 Cor 15:42–56). 2) In his death, the righteousness of God has been revealed (Rom 1:16–17). What no man could do to satisfy the law, Jesus fulfilled (Rom 3:21–26; 7:14–25)). The law now represents the will of God, but its purpose is to prick the conscience and lead one to Christ. 3) This redemptive event is a gift that cannot be earned (Eph 2:4–10). It can only be received by faith. 4) As God's Son (Rom 1:3) and archetype of all mankind, Christ willingly descended from heaven to take on human form (Phil 2:5–8). He was indeed human: "descended from David according to the flesh" (Rom 1:3), "born of a woman, born under the law" (Gal 4:4). 5) He was crucified for mankind's sake (Rom 5:6–11). 6) He died a martyr's death (Phil 2:8–9). 7) Nonetheless, God raised him and has given him the name above every name (Phil 2:9–11). 8) Through faith in him, his believers enjoy a mystical union that will continue into eternity (Gal 2:19–21). 9) The present world is soon to end. But when Christ returns, the faithful will meet him in the air, or if they should die, their unique personhood will be raised imperishable (1 Thess 4:13–18). 10) At that time, one will know the Eternal God face to face (1 Cor 13:12). 11) Even creation will experience its long-anguished *teleos* toward wholeness (Rom 8:18–25), a foreshadow of the *shekinah* rising to *tif'eret* again.

How many of these views Paul inherited, versus those he conceived entirely on his own, we may never know. But it is obvious at a glance that his understanding of Jesus influenced the Evangelists. The extent to which he wove Greco-philosophical and mythic elements into his "revelations" is likewise difficult to establish. The pattern of the descending God who takes on human form is certainly embedded in his theology. The consuming of bread and wine, or flesh and blood, at the Lord's Supper rings of the Dionysian cult, yet also of the Passover. But if the latter is the case, it is strange that Paul never mentions it. Also making its debut is the Platonic universal man, in whom participation and identification with enhances life and sets one free from the bondage of the "flesh." Nevertheless, Isaiah 53, Psalm 2, Hab 2:4 and Gen 12:4 are equally important. In addition, Paul's use of the word *mystérion* to describe the work and purpose of Christ introduces an intriguing element of its own. He uses the word no less than 14 times, excluding its two appearances in 1 Tim 3:9, 16. Christ is the *mystérion* whom God has kept secret for ages, "as a plan for the fullness [*plēroma*] of time, to gather up all things in him, things in heaven and things on earth" (Eph 1:9–10).

A glance at his letter to the Galatians reveals the independent way in which Paul used scripture. In two of its most important chapters (3–4), Paul alludes to the Old Testament no less than 14 times. He quotes from the *Septuagint* no less than 5 times. He employs *typology*, *allegory*, and *symbolism* in all but one of his quotes and/or allusions. Though the scriptures might well be his material principle, justification by grace through faith is his normative principle. It demonstrates the freedom with which Paul approached his own biblical sources. From this we might infer that many followers during this timeframe felt free to do the same.

In none of this was Paul betraying the tradition he had received. Rather, he subjected it to the highest norms of his faith's sources, namely, that God is one and had promised his long-suffering people a Savior and Messiah. To this, he brought his keen mind, trained both in Greek philosophy, I suspect, and in the Hebrew Scriptures, or at least, the *Septuagint*. After all, he was from Tarsus, a "no mean city," where Cicero himself had resided in 51–52 BC, which Julius Caesar visited in 47 BC, where Mark Antony established his headquarters before his break with Rome, and to which Augustus sent his favorite tutor, Athenodorus, the Stoic, about the time of Paul's birth. Paul was a learned son of Tarsus, as well as a Hebrew through and through. I belief he drew from the best of both sources, biblical and Greek, in fathoming the meaning of Jesus of Nazareth, God's Son, the Messiah, and Redeemer of the world.

One last addendum is worthy of note. It is Paul's use of the word *sophia* (wisdom). He employs it 27 times: 6 in reference to God, 3 in reference to Christ, and 18 with respect to mankind. Not even the Gospel of John once mentions *sophia*. Let us consider the *divine* references first.

Paul mentions God's wisdom in Rom 11:33; 1 Cor 1:21; 2:6, 7; and Eph 1:8; 3:10. In the Romans text, it is God's "depth of wisdom" that Paul cites. He quotes from the *Septuagint*'s version of Isa 40:13 and Job 35:7 to support his point. God's wisdom is simply unsearchable, especially with respect to God's plan for Israel (the context of 11:33). The 1 Corinthian passages refer to God's "secret and hidden" wisdom, "decreed before the ages" (1:21 and 2:6–7). Paul does not cite any Old Testament texts to clarify his theme, but he could be alluding to Proverbs 8 or Plato's eternal ideas, which are unchangeable, and participation in which enrich the physical life. In his letter to the Ephesians, it is by means of God's wisdom that "the mystery of his will" is manifested and equally by means of the Church that God's eternal purpose "might now be made known to the rulers and authorities in the heavenly places" (Eph 3:10). This mythic realm "in the heavenly places" is left undefined, although it appears to pertain to the angelic beings mentioned in 1 Cor 4:9. That same passage refers to the Apostles' sufferings as a "spectacle to the world, angels and to mortals," possibly constituting an allusion to death in the arenas of the Empire. In any case, all six of these references to God's wisdom have to do with God's eternal plan to send the Christ as the savior of the world.

The three passages that pertain to Jesus identify him as "Christ the power of God and the wisdom of God" (1 Cor 1:24), "who became for us wisdom from God" (1 Cor 1:30) and "in whom are hidden all the treasures of wisdom and knowledge" (Col 2:3). This is as close as Paul ever comes to endorsing any kind of *sophia theology* with respect to Jesus. If he knew outright of any Gnostic communities, his views of Christ as the conveyor of God's wisdom is subsumed under God's "eternal purpose" to send Christ as mankind's Mediator. Paul was not interested in a hidden wisdom that leads to salvation apart from Christ. As he warns the Colossains: "See to it that no one takes you captive through philosophy and empty deceit, according to human tradition, according to the elemental spirits of the universe, and *not according to Christ*" (Col 2:8; italics for emphasis). This may have been Paul's way of separating himself from Plato's universal archetypes that, however useful, were not associated with the historical life of the pre-Easter Jesus.

In the case of Paul's 18 references to human wisdom, most are designed to reveal human wisdom's shortcomings. In comparison with God's wisdom, "God made foolish the wisdom of the world" (1 Cor 1:21; 3:19). He actually destroys "the wisdom of the wise" (Isa 29:14—*Septuagint* version, quoted in 1 Cor 1:19). "Greeks desire wisdom, but we proclaim Christ crucified" (1:22). "God's wisdom is wiser than human wisdom"

(1:25). Paul reminds the Corinthian congregation that when he came to them, he employed neither "lofty" nor "plausible words of wisdom," nor language based on "human wisdom" or "earthly wisdom" (1 Cor 2:1, 4, 5, 13; 2 Cor 1:12). Nonetheless, Paul returns to a more Platonic note in Col 2:23, where he admonishes the Colossians to dismiss regulations that have to do with the "things that perish." Such regulations "have indeed the appearance of wisdom" but "are of no value." Finally, there are four wisdom references that acknowledge that the *sophia* associated with God's plan in Christ is a gift of God, or a gift of the Spirit, to be used to communicate the Gospel as well as edify the Church. These may be found in 1 Cor 12:8; Eph 1:19; and Col 1:28; 3:16).

Beyond doubt, Paul shaped the legacy of Jesus more than any other figure of the first century AD. He may not have created Q, known any of the rich details about the historical Jesus' life, ever heard his voice (Paul does not verify Luke's appearance reports on the road to Damascus), or witnessed his miracles, but he saw in the historical man Jesus what his own nation and the world had been seeking since its foundation. He applied that to the post-Easter Christ and, in doing so, became a conduit himself of mankind's knowledge of God and knowledge of self.

Paul has never been Faith's enemy. It is superstition, blind credulity, misplaced literalism, ignorance, spiritual pride, human recalcitrance, power, spite, lust for revenge, and inflexible dogma that plunge the Church into inertia and irrelevance. But where Paul's summons to "love, joy, peace, patience, kindness, generosity, faithfulness, gentleness, and self-control" prevails, there the Spirit of the living Christ never dies (Gal 5:22–23).

Bornkamm's Critique

Gunther Bornkamm's assessment of Paul's knowledge of Jesus should not be ignored. For Bornkamm, the subject of Paul's proclamation is hardly the coming Kingdom. Rather, it is Christ himself, the salvation made possible through Christ's cross, his resurrection, and exaltation as Lord. Paul's starting point is not the life of Jesus, but Christ's death and resurrection. Nowhere does Paul expound the teachings of the historical Jesus. He knows nothing of the "rabbi from Nazareth," or of his miracles or camaraderie with tax collectors and sinners, let alone his "Sermon on the Mount," or his parables, or controversies with the scribes and Pharisees. Not once does he mention the Lord's Prayer. Contrary to Bruce's view, when Paul does cite Jesus' words, Bornkamm argues that they scarcely represent what Jesus said. They are merely tidbits of tradition that Paul gleaned here and there. Paul never knew or met the historical Jesus, and even if he had, it would not have mattered, since Paul chose to disregard Jesus "in the flesh" in favor of the new being his death and resurrection made possible. After all, the "old has passed away" (2 Cor 5:16–18).[1]

Bornkamm dismisses any thought of Paul's having turned Jesus into a mythical, divine being, like the gods and deities of pagan religion. It was Christ's resurrection that empowered and awakened the apostle. Moreover, Bornkamm doubts that the young Paul was ever trained in Greek philosophy, certainly, not to the extent of Philo of Alexandria. However, Bornkamm does venture that Paul absorbed "a number of elements of Greek culture," especially concepts associated with Stoicism and the art of rhetoric.[2] Nonetheless, Bornkamm concludes: "To lead man as confronted by God to self-understanding, and thus to reflection on his salvation and life in the world, this is the steadfast aim of the apostle's preaching and teaching."[3]

The Roman Empire's Reaction

Paul was careful not to offend Rome or Rome's imperial prerogatives. According to Luke, Paul prized his Roman citizenship (Acts 16:37–38; 22:25–29) and relied on it for his defense in times of trouble. Above all, he recognized Rome's magistrates' roles and consuls' authoritative positions. His assessment of the state's magisterial rights is well known:

> For rulers are not a terror to good conduct, but to bad . . . [For] the authority does not bear the sword in vain . . . [Therefore] pay to all what is due them—taxes to whom taxes are due, revenue to whom revenue is due, respect to whom respect is due, honor to whom honor is due (Rom 13:3–7).

All this, however, was before Nero burned Rome and blamed it on the Christians. Nonetheless, seeds of discontent had been sown as early as Claudius' reign. Somewhere around AD 49, Claudius expelled the Jewish community from Rome, because they had "caused continuous disturbances at the instigation of Chrestus."[4] Whatever this means, it implies that Rome was beginning to associate "Christ" and "Christians" with disorderly conduct. Tacitus' *Annals* allege that even more alarming issues emerged with respect to the burning of Rome. In his mind, however wrong Nero was in

---

1. Bornkamm, *Paul*, New York, Harper & Row, 1971, pp. 109–18.
2. Ibid., p. 9.
3. Ibid., p. 119.
4. See Seutonius, *The Twelve Caesars*, New York: Penguin Books, 1979, p. 200.

his brutal treatment of the Christians, he was right to punish these "notoriously depraved Christians," so named for their "originator, Christ, . . . who had been executed in Tiberius' reign by . . . Pontius Pilate." Nonetheless, their "deadly superstition had broken out afresh," and Nero was wise to have them condemned "for their anti-social tendencies." Although Tacitus "pitied" their plight, he concluded that their "ruthless punishment" was "deserved."[5]

It is only with Pliny the Younger's letters to Trajan (AD 98–117) that Jesus' followers' "crimes" become of serious concern to the Empire. Pliny was sent by the emperor to the province of Bithynia and Pontus to report back on domestic affairs. A number of Christians had ceased to present honors both to the cult of the Emperor and to the Roman gods. Pliny found Christ's followers' behavior unacceptable. Nevertheless, Pliny reports that their "guilt" amounted to nothing more than that they

> had met regularly before dawn on a fixed day to chant verses . . . in honour of Christ as if to a god, and also to bind themselves by oath . . . to abstain from theft, robbery and adultery, to commit no breach of trust and not to deny a deposit when called upon to restore it.[6]

In any event, Pliny felt justified in torturing two "slave-women deaconesses" to garner more information. All he discovered, however, was "a degenerate sort of cult carried to extravagant lengths." As for those who refused to reverence the emperor's statute or make offerings to the gods, he ordered them executed, on the grounds that such "stubbornness and unshakeable obstinacy ought not to go unpunished."[7] He was disgusted, if not disillusioned, to discover that there were Roman citizens "similarly fanatical."[8]

In the next generation—AD 185—the pagan writer and Greek philosopher Celsus would carry this attack a step further. In a wide and rambling, yet tightly argued defense of paganism—entitled *On the True Doctrine*, Celsus accused Christianity for its radical monotheism and religious exclusivity that would destroy the Empire's culture, if left unchecked. He found nothing original or logically consistent about the Christian faith. Consequently, he dismissed it for its followers' incredu-

---

5. See *Tacitus: The Annals of Imperial Rome*, New York: Penguin Books, 1956, p. 354.

6. See *Pliny: Letters and Panegyricus*, vol. II, LCL, Bk. 10:96, Cambridge: Harvard Univ. Press, 1969, p. 289.

7. Ibid., p. 287.

8. Ibid., p. 289.

lity and "salvation-hungry people" whose notions of wisdom were utterly unworthy of the greatest teacher of the past: Plato. In his estimation, the doctrines of incarnation and resurrection were especially shallow. Based on a Platonic disdain for the flesh, he argues: "No god or son of God has come down to earth."[9] Nor could they. As for the resurrection: "what sort of body is it that could return to its original nature or become the same as it was before it rotted away?"[10] Paul would have probably agreed and might even have shared this philosophy.

What is one to say? First, there is an air of modernity about Celsus' complaints, to say the least. Perhaps this is why Christ as symbol, metaphor, and myth must never be shunted aside as irrelevant to the post-Easter Christ's reality. A historical Jesus, shorn of his believers' faith in his "risen presence," is no savior, after all. It is that Jesus, in his risen presence, that the Evangelists preserve and that the Church would apotheosize in its creeds and counsels: "Who for us men, and for our salvation, came down from heaven; and was incarnate by the Holy Ghost of the Virgin Mary, and was made man."[11]

Second, Christianity was more than a mystical movement, ideal for the individual in his or her solitariness. To that extent, scholars like Crossan are right in identifying the pre-Easter Jesus and the post-Easter Church with social, class, and political issues whose purpose was to challenge and transform society. Perhaps the perception of "Jesus as a Cynic" fails to capture the full essence of his mission or due justice to his followers' enthusiasm to replace *Romanitas* with Christian zeal. That might not have been their original intention, but Christendom was the net result. How to balance faith and culture, or faith and reason, with the inner and the outer, and with the individual and society, still haunts the present age. No reconstruction of the Jesus of History can evade the problem.

---

9. See *Celsus: On the True Doctrine*, trans. by R. J. Hoffmann, New York: Oxford Univ. Press, 1987, p. 85.
10. Ibid., p. 86.
11. See The Nicene Creed.

17

The Pre-Easter Jesus and the Creeds of the Church

ON THE surface, a vast gulf separates Jesus of Nazareth from the Second Person of the Trinity. In all honesty, it is highly unlikely that the historical Jesus ever thought of himself as the incarnation of God. He lived and died as a human being, just as we must do. But that he thought of himself as a child of God, or *huios* of God, in the universal human sense, is surely unmistakably the case. We all think of ourselves as God's sons and daughters. What believing Christian hasn't prayed to his or her Heavenly Father, regardless of circumstance or need? I dare say, all have. But the issue goes beyond that. The Nicene Creed and Chalcedonian Formula brought to an apex four hundred years of pondering the Jesus of history's legacy. Was God truly in Christ, reconciling the world unto himself? And if so, how could divinity and humanity indwell a human life, without compromising the unique nature of each? Those creeds were fashioned to answer precisely those questions. The questions were raised in all genuine sincerity, and the resolutions that were proffered were designed to witness more to the grandeur of Christ's attractiveness and his haunting authentic presence than to explain what philosophically falls beyond the realm of human knowledge. All one has to do is to read St. Augustine's *Confessions* to realize how alive God was to him and how present the "living Jesus" was in his life.

> But where was my free will during all those years and from what deep and secret retreat was it called forth in a single moment whereby I gave my neck to thy "easy yoke" and my shoulders to thy "light burden," O Christ Jesus, "my strength and my Redeemer"?[1]

If Augustine is any example of the thousands who preceded him, then we can grasp the existential hold the "living Jesus" had on them. Any notion

---

1. Augustine, *Confessions, 9.1.*, in *Augustine: Confessions and Enchiridion*, Philadelphia, 1955, p. 178.

of a Jewish Cynic, whose call to egalitarian commensality as one's burning passion, had long since faded by the third and fourth centuries AD. Yes, the monastic life was appealing, with its renunciation of the flesh and the cares of the world, but a life filled with the Spirit of Christ had become the norm, and living one's life in the *civitas hominem* or *civitas terrena* with eyes riveted on the *civitas Dei* was the summum bonum of the hour.

Into this cultural climate Constantine had battled his way to the emperorship of Rome. Desirous of a unifying principle, he chose Christianity over Mithraism. That the assembled Fathers of Nicaea of AD 325 produced the document they did, was as much a product of his determination as of their astuteness. They were not attempting to create a metaphysical metamorphosis of the Jesus of the Gospels they adored. Rather, they were attempting to be faithful to the "living Jesus" whose way and truth and life embodied the very *ousia, the very essence,* of the Godhead, as they understood God. We cannot fault them for that, nor deride their efforts to fathom the mystery of the One in whom the mystery of their own humanity seemed, at last, resolved.

> God of God, light of light, very God of very God, begotten, not made, being of one substance [*homoousion*] with the Father, by whom all things were made; who for us men and for our salvation, came down from heaven, and was incarnate by the Holy Ghost.[2]

By identifying Christ with God and themselves with Christ, they were asserting the optimal reunion possible with the Ground of Being. Cognitively and existentially, the Christ of the Creed represented the highest manifestation of life's greatest mystery they could expound in philosophical terms. He had *come down from heaven* for them. Not even Zeus had done that for the Greeks. Zeus might have *raised* Dionysus and Heracles, but neither had *come down from heaven* for mankind. Prometheus might have stolen fire, and paid the consequence, but he was more of a suffering god than a savior. Besides, Jesus of Nazareth had *actually lived*. As Ignatius had spelled it out so clearly,

> Jesus Christ, of David's lineage, of Mary; who was really born, ate, and drank; was really persecuted under Pontius Pilate; was really crucified and died, in the sight of heaven and earth and the underworld. He was really raised from the dead, for his Father raised

---

2. See AD 391 *Nicaeno-Constantinopolitan Creed*, in Schaff, Vol. II, *Creeds of Christendom*, New York, 1919.

him, just as his Father will raise us, who believe on him, through Christ Jesus, apart from whom we have no genuine life.[3]

Here is the myth of myths by which Western Christianity has lived for the past 1,700 years. This document beautifully testifies to the post-Easter Jesus of the later Fathers, as they struggled to make sense of the pre-Easter Jesus as the Christ of faith.

One thing more remained to be solved. How could the post-Easter Jesus be fully divine and fully human at the same time? If he were truly *divine*, descending from heaven to save them, how could that benefit the estranged race of *humanity*? If mankind were not represented in Him, how could He represent them? Theories abounded that made compelling sense, but none seemed free of error. Paul of Samosata, Lucian of Antioch, and Theodore of Mopsuestia all offered theological solutions. Paul's still seems the most reasonable: that the mind of the Christ's was amenable to the mind of the Logos and willingly did what God's Spirit willed. That isn't all that far from Crossan's Jewish Cynic, whose love of God and of God's righteousness inspires Jesus' mission of radical egalitarianism. By AD 451, however, the lines were drawn, and once more the Empire's bishops assembled. The creed they propounded could hardly resolve the metaphysics of the Godhead, but it could at least offer guidelines for the faithful. Whatever may be said about the post-Easter Christ, he embodied two natures in one Person, "consubstantial [*homoousion*] with the Father according to the Godhead, and consubstantial [*homoousion*] with us according to the Manhood."[4] Christ really was human, like us, he in us and we in him; yet his "divinity" could not be denied. Thus he became the supreme archetype of the self, reunited and one with the mystery of Being, just as all his followers could be, too. The Prince of Peace had opened the door for the heart's return at last. Knowing and spiritually experiencing this enables even a modern humanity to resolve the question of one's human condition. *We are created for God and are forever restless and torn until we rest in Him.* Or, more generically, we cannot understand ourselves apart from Transcendence, because our very ontological structure as human beings requires us to put our existence to the question. By embracing the Christ, we are enabled to touch base with the Ground of Being, to whom or to which, if we say, "Yes," we find both spiritual peace for the soul and guidance for living.

---

3. *Letter to the Trallians*, in *Early Church Fathers*, p. 100.
4. See *Symbol of Chalcedon*, in Vol. II, *Creeds of Christendom*, p. 62.

One must also bear in mind that the creeds of the Church, especially the Nicaeno-Constantinopolitan Creed of AD 381 (which is the popular version of the Nicene Creed recited in most churches), was and is a product of the Church. Mirroring the Trinity, its three theological paragraphs were not devoted solely to the Christ of faith. After all, the opening paragraph focuses on the role of God the Father, and the third on the work of the Holy Spirit. As students of church history know, many creeds and rules of faith preceded the Nicene Creed. Most of these reflect the intense struggle in which Christian communities were engaged in their battle against Gnosticism, Arianism, Manichaeism, Donatism and other heresies. Briefly, Gnosticism rejected the possibility that God's Son could have taken on flesh [*sarx*]; Arianism denied that Christ possessed full or co-equality with God; Manichaeism projected a dualism, in which a second and external power existed outside of God's control; and Donatism favored a Church established on the purity of its priests rather than on the purity and holiness of Christ.

The opening paragraph offers a staunchly monistic position with respect to the creation of the universe. Only one source brought it about: "one God, the Father Almighty; maker of heaven and earth, and of all things visible and invisible."[5] Everything in creation owes its existence to God. There are no hidden or competing powers outside of God. No darkness can ever overcome or thwart the Divine will. There exists no higher peace that one need seek. "Ask and it will be given you; search, and you will find; knock and the door will be opened for you" (Matt 7:7).

The third paragraph celebrates the living presence of God, who in the past, present, and future has and continues to engage humankind, first, through Israel's prophets of old, and today in Christ's living community of believers: the Church. This same Spirit of God was present at creation and indwells the living Christ. His Spirit equally indwells the Church, seeking to keep it "one, holy, catholic, and apostolic." Only one baptism is required, ever. It cherishes the "resurrection of the dead" [*anastasin nekron*], note: not the resuscitation of the *sarx*. It is one's resurrection that it hallows: one's personal, individual, and holistic vitality, along with one's neighbor's reclaimed existence. And it believes in "the life of the world to come."[6] Prophets of doom misunderstand this intent. It is God who will have the last word. It is the goodness of God that will prevail. Not chaos, violence, nihilism, or despair.

---

5. Ibid., p. 58.
6. Ibid.

All this is symbolic and metaphorical: an invitation to trust in God beyond the gates of doubt. It has to do with hope, promise, and wholeness, and with that peace which the world can never take away.

18

The Historical Jesus and the Reformed Tradition

No one person or theologian can speak definitively for the Reformed Tradition. Depending on whether one's origins are Scottish, Swiss, French, Dutch, German, or American, adherents emphasize different nuances. Yet, there are common tenets that unite this Tradition's varied communities of faith. John Leith, in his *Introduction to the Reformed Tradition*, attempted to catalog the more important beliefs. As a living tradition that has sought to "hand down" the essence of the Church's faith and life, it has centered around: 1) The Bible as the primary source of theology and life. The Scriptures of the Old and New Testament, together, form the "original witness to and interpretation of God's revelation."[1] It is the unique and irreplaceable authority. It witnesses both forward and backward to Christ. 2) No human being is above mistakes, thus the Tradition must undergo repeated submission to its biblical sources and the work of the Holy Spirit to reform human error. No human tradition may usurp this role. 3) The Tradition has been diverse, just as the "traditioning" in Scripture has been diverse. 4) The primacy of grace is central. Human beings are not the principal agents of their salvation. 5) The history of the Church's attempt to fathom the mystery of Christ cannot be ignored. Thus, the Apostles' Creed, the Nicene Creed, and the Formula of Chadcedon provide essential links with historic Christianity and its transformation over time. With its affirmation of the "one, holy, catholic, and apostolic church," the Tradition seeks to uphold what "has always, by all, and in every place" been believed.

At a glimpse, one can see that these affirmations are already in conflict with any course of critical study that would demote the historical Jesus as a figure who embodied the saving will of God. For the Reformed Tradition, the pre-Easter Jesus, who belongs to the category of history, is the same Jesus that the post-Easter Church rightly interpreted to be the Son of God,

---

1. Leith, *The Reformed Tradition*, Atlanta, 1977, p. 18.

the risen Messiah, the Lamb of God, who takes away the sin of the world. One cannot have the one without the other, the Jesus of history without the Christ of metaphor, mystery, and myth. The man of history would scarcely have been remembered, save for the Church's interpretation of his life and death as the Supreme Archetype, as the God-Man, sent from heaven, to overcome humanity's estrangement. True, intriguing fragments and esoteric documents, such that the Nag Hammadi collection contains, would have surfaced. But what would their significance have been without the Gospels and Paul's letters to provide their "normative" context?

None of this is to say that attempts to discover and construct historically adequate depictions of the Jesus of history should be set aside by New Testament scholars—Reformed, Catholic, or otherwise. But the loss of the post-Easter Jesus as mankind's savior, healer, redeemer, and guide, would constitute a cynical betrayal of the very sources and traditions that make studying Jesus even possible. We need to know who Jesus was, what he said, how he lived, what he believed, how the Church came into existence, grew, and was transformed in its understanding of God, of mankind, and the world. But, as Nietzsche put it long ago in his Madman Speech, "only a god can destroy God." To demote the *Christ* of faith by quoting the historical Jesus' "own words" is a dubious science at best, if not a questionable art and ploy of the cruelest *hubris*. Yet, something of the converse is equally true. To believe in a *Jesus* who was born of a virgin, without a male's participation, who was literally able to multiple loaves of bread, raise the dead with the call of his voice, heal the sick from a distance, walk on water, calm seas from the back of a boat, read minds, physically rise from the dead, eat afterwards, and float off into heaven, also begs credulity. Even more importantly, to create a theological system founded on a figure of history who never claimed to be what the system claims of him is likewise unconvincing. But if that claim is based on a symbolic interpretation of historical antecedents and linguistic resources available at the time, then the claim bears legitimacy. Nonetheless, the limitations of symbolism and philosophical and religious nuance still adhere. Son of God, Son of Man, and Son of David are Old Testament symbols, in reference to messianic hopes. Lord Jesus, Lamb of God, Logos become flesh, Christ Jesus, Savior, Servant of God, the Good Shepherd, the true Vine, and others are a collection of mixed metaphors, drawn from both pagan and Jewish sources. They were used by the post-Easter Church to interpret the life and meaning of Jesus of Nazareth, in whom they saw so many Old Testament prophecies fulfilled. But what encouraged this development and inspired the movement's growth, was the fact that the pre-Easter Jesus made God apparent, real, and alive to them. In doing so, their most profound spiritual yearnings received embracement, fulfillment, and healing. When these symbols are honored, then both the pre-Easter Jesus and the Christ of faith, the *man of history* and the *man of myth*, become one and minister to one's journey through life. If anything, what gave Christianity its edge over the myriad spiritual and mystical religions of the Hellenistic and Roman age, was the fact that Jesus had actually lived. At long last, all the archetypes of the soul could be seen to dwell in a true human life, which opened the way to the Eternal Now. He still possesses that gift and power today.

John Calvin, the founder of the Reformed Tradition in Geneva, may have subsumed his theology of Jesus under the rubric of Mediator, based on 1 Tim 2:5. Nevertheless, he held to the "two natures in one person" of the ecumenical councils as indispensable for faith. It was his way of affirming the reality of the pre-Easter Jesus, long before interest in the historical Jesus became popular. In Book II, chapters 12 and 13 of his *Institutes of the Christian Religion*, Calvin devotes surprising space to the humanity of Jesus. Aware of mankind's estrangement from God, and borrowing from Anselm's *Cur Deus Homo*, he reasoned that only a divine figure could initiate and fulfill the human need for restoration. Yet, he concluded that if that occurred, it had to take place in reality and not in myth only. The mystery of God would have to appear in a human life for humanity to be represented. It could not take place except in time, in reality, in history.

> The case was certainly desperate, if the Godhead itself did not descend to us, it being impossible for us to ascend. Thus the Son of God behooved to become our Emmanuel, i.e., God with us; and in such a way, that by mutual union his divinity and our nature might be combined.[2]

As an exegete, Calvin pointed out for his readers that the phrase "Son of Man" was actually *ben atham* in Hebrew, meaning "son of Adam," and thereby mankind in general: "it [is] obvious that in the Hebrew idiom, the Son of man means a true man: and Christ, doubtless, retained the idiom of his own tongue."[3] Calvin likewise adopted the Apostle Paul's interpretation of Jesus as the universal man, or the representative archetype, whose death on the cross represents every human being's life and death.

---

2. *Institutes of the Christian Religion*, 2.12.1, Grand Rapids, 1957.
3. Ibid., 2.13.2.

> Who could do this unless the Son of God should also become the Son of man, and so receive what is ours as to transfer to us what is his, making that which is his by nature to become ours by grace?[4]

Or again:

> Therefore our Lord came forth very man, adopted the person of Adam, and assumed his name, that he might in his stead obey the Father; that he might present our flesh as the price of satisfaction to the just judgment of God, and in the same flesh pay the penalty which we had incurred.[5]

In this regard, Calvin almost sounds Jungian in his perception of the saving work of Christ.

Furthermore, Calvin did not hesitate to utilize metaphors of his own to capture the redemptive role of Christ. Though he preferred the term "Mediator," he conceived of Christ's overall mission as incorporating three roles: *Prophet, King,* and *Priest* (*Institutes*, 2.15.1–6). In explicating these "offices," Calvin singled out many of the texts that the early Church identified as prophecies fulfilled: Isa 61:2; Joel 2:28; Dan 2:44; Ps 89:35, 37; Ps 2:2–4; Ps 110:4.

That a later generation of reformers tended to systematize theology along propositional lines and smother the historical Jesus under doctrines of providence and predestination cannot be denied. That a militant and fundamentalist Christianity that, for the most part, has spurned the creeds and transformed the Church's Christ into a sentimental gateway to eternity, has not helped, either. A liberal Christianity that touted the so-called Fatherhood of God and brotherhood of man, but that died in the trenches of World War I, disenchanted both Karl Barth and Emil Brunner, whose theological tomes followed the outline of the Apostles' Creed, rather than a visionary reconstruction of the life of Jesus. Schweitzer's *Quest* seemed to have rolled the stone over the tomb of such efforts, anyway. It was only with Bultmann and others, that a renewed interest in the Jesus of history took hold again. Reformed theologies have not responded well to the challenge. Even my mentor, Professor Leith, followed Barth and Brunner's lead in his own book *Basic Christian Doctrine*. Yet his lectures always centered about God's purposes in Christ, in the Christ of faith, whose grace alone transforms lives. It is time that the Reformed community awakened to the challenge that the historians of the Jesus of history movement present.

---

4. Ibid., 2.12.2.
5. Ibid., 2.12.3.

Karl Barth's handling of Jesus constitutes an interesting example. In his major work, *Church Dogmatics*, Vol. 1, Part 2, Jesus is subordinated entirely under the Nicene Creed and the Formula of Chalcedon. Barth's section "Very God and Very Man" opens with a commentary on John 1:14. It is the Triune God in the mode of the Son who "was made flesh in the entire fullness of deity."[6] If one has to ask who Jesus Christ is, "we are speaking of the Lord of heaven and earth."[7] This event is a "miracle, an act of God's mercy." What takes place in the "created world [is] unforeseen." It could never be "constructed or postulated." It flows completely from the mercy and mystery of God.[8] As for his birth, his mother's role signals primarily that he "belongs to the unity of the human race." But of equal importance is the reminder that he "who was here born in time is the very same who in eternity is born of the Father."[9] Barth continues in this vein, focusing on the universality of Jesus, rather than on his uniqueness as a person of Galilee. That Jesus became "'flesh' does not imply a man, but human essence and existence, human kind and nature, humanity, *humanitas*, that which makes a man man as opposed to God, angel, or animal."[10] In still another place, he intimates that the whole of Jesus' historical life is summed up in the Apostles Creed's paragraph: "suffered under Pontius Pilate, was crucified, dead, and buried; he descended into hell."[11] In particular, he notes: "By speaking of the passion, cross and resurrection, the Creed recalls the whole substance of the Gospel narratives."[12]

In many ways, Barth's approach to Jesus follows from his rejection of natural theology. The latter can tell us nothing of God, nor ever has. Only God can disclose himself. No analogy of being, no *analogia entis*, can tell us anything about God. For "not even in the slightest degree can we men sense the existence and mode of being of a self-disclosure of God. The self-disclosure of God can itself be known only in this divine self-disclosure."[13] This leads Barth to criticize Augustine's Neo-Platonism with amazing *hauteur*. He singles out one of Augustine's "most beautiful but also most dangerous passages in the *Confessions* IX, 10." Augustine

---

6. K. Barth, *Church Dogmatics*, Vol. I, Part 2, Edinburgh, 1963, p. 133.
7. Ibid.
8. Ibid., p.136.
9. Ibid., p.138.
10. Ibid., p. 149.
11. *Faith of the Church*, New York, 1958, pp. 69–87.
12. Ibid., p. 87.
13. In *Church Dogmatics*, Vol. II. Part I, p. 82.

is describing his mystical journey of *ascendere* and *transcendere*, in which he and his mother Monica, while at Ostia, climb spiritually from star to star in philosophical wonder of God. Barth denounces all of this. The only place for encountering God is "in His revelation and where He gives Himself to be heard and seen by men."[14] But Barth's theological arrogance would rob the Old Testament of numerous Wisdom texts and Psalms that were inspired precisely by Augustine's method, which belongs to all mankind. After all, the Wisdom writers never appealed to divine authority to authenticate their views. Perhaps, that is what endears their Psalms of praise, thanksgiving, and lament to readers today. They flow straight from the human heart to God's. It is little wonder that current New Testament scholars wince at theological pronouncements and doctrines that ignore the facts of Jesus' life.

Emil Brunner did not wish to repeat this mistake. Yet, like Barth, his central concern throughout his work, *The Mediator*, hinges on John 1:14: *kai ho logos sarx egeneto*, "and the word became flesh." For Brunner this is a historical fact; it "means that the Eternal has entered into the sphere of external fact."[15] Everything depends on this. For the Christian faith, it actually happened. Otherwise, Christianity has nothing to offer that other religions haven't also put forward. For this reason, the Christian faith "must never withdraw from the sphere of conflict, from the realm of history."[16] But having advanced this, Brunner, drawing on Rom 1:3 and 2 Cor 5:16, makes a critical distinction between Christ "after the flesh" and Christ "in the flesh." The latter has to do with John's passage (1:14) and preserves the *Christ of faith*; the former has to do with the *Jesus of history*, whose brief sketch in the Gospels may present a chronicler's view of Jesus, but one that can never replace faith. Paul claims that the Christ "after the flesh" [*kata sarka*] is of the line of David (Rom 1:3), but since his coming, as Paul explains, we no longer "regard anyone from a human point of view [*kata sarka*], even though we once knew Christ from a human point of view [*kata sarka*], we know him no longer in that way" (2 Cor 5:16). Paul's point is that it is only through faith that one grasps that "God was in Christ reconciling the world to himself" (2 Cor 5:19). That is the issue. Simply knowing about the Christ *kata sarka* is insufficient. Therefore, in Brunner's view, Christianity must avoid confusing the Christ who came "in the flesh" with the Christ "after the flesh," or the *Christos kata sarka*.

---

14. Ibid., pp. 10–11.
15. E. Brunner, *The Mediator*, Philadelphia, 1957, p. 153.
16. Ibid., p. 154.

Knowledge about the latter cannot substitute for faith, or for Christ's role as Mediator. Thus, the Lives of Jesus, however interesting they may be, can offer nothing with respect to the demands of faith. Nonetheless, it is essential that Christ came in the flesh, that the Word became flesh, or else Christianity lapses into just another religion, or form of idealism, or human ethical system, no better than any other culture's.

In contrast to Barth, Brunner endorsed a higher view of natural theology, incorporating aspects of the "Orders of Nature," as Brunner calls them, in his book *The Divine Imperative*. He also relied on Buber's I-Thou theological perspective and the belief that *encounter* is the sphere wherein God is revealed. This takes place in the arena of history, where God encounters us as the mystery alone that redeems human life. It is this mystery that became flesh in Jesus of Nazareth, whose life witnesses to that Other that only faith and metaphor, symbol and myth can perceive. Furthermore, Brunner embraced Kierkegaard's distinction between Socrates and Christ, which the Danish existentialist made in his book, *Philosophical Fragments*. Whereas Socrates awakens an individual's knowledge of the truth that a person already possesses; Christ, on the other hand, must bring the truth to us, since the truth is not in us. Even then, an encounter with the historical Jesus requires a leap of faith. Knowledge of the historical figure still leaves one in ignorance until the leap of faith is taken. That being the case, Kierkegaard argued that the first disciples enjoyed no advantage over contemporary disciples. Then and now, a leap of faith is indispensable. In truth, that assessment fits in quite well with the Post-Easter Church's own experience.

In my own situation, I have had to turn to Tillich and his interpretation of the symbols that surround Jesus to find "the best answer." But even this has been limited. The reality of the Christ constitutes the thinnest of Tillich's three volumes of *Systematics*. Still, his emphasis on Christ as the savior of the human predicament is more in keeping with the Christ of faith, or the post-Easter Jesus of the Church, than anything else I know.

Tillich's Volume II was published in 1957. He entitled it, *Existence and the Christ*. Toward the end of the volume, Tillich offered his assessment of the Jesus of history quests. He considered them a failure. Why? Because the Gospels' "reports about Jesus of Nazareth are those of Jesus as the Christ, given by persons who had received him as the Christ." Since any attempt to "separate" out the historical side from the believer's side is problematic, he concluded that all so-called "Lives of Jesus" lead, at best, to "more or less probable results," none of which can serve as a basis for either accepting or rejecting the Christian faith.[17] This has been my

17. Tillich, *Systematic Theology*, Vol. II, pp. 102–3.

own contention, independent of Tillich's. Tillich goes on to charge that such Lives only obscure the "Jesus behind the symbols," until the Christ recedes "farther and farther away."[18] Moreover, theologies based on such Lives serve to no advantage either, as they end up producing "teachings of Jesus" or the "message of Jesus," neither of which advances the Christian faith. If there is any value to an "empirical historical" approach, it lies in enabling theologians to grapple more successfully with "the Christological symbols of the Bible." These in turn speak to the human predicament and offer it the experience of becoming a New Being. Once this occurs, historical criticism loses its power to "question the immediate awareness of those who find themselves transformed into the state of faith."[19]

These are momentous days for the Christian faith. In spite of Tillich's comments, the rediscovery of the Jesus of history—if we might call it that—has to be a welcomed event of our time. Scholars like Borg and Crossan deserve our highest admiration. To know who Jesus was, what he said, how he lived his life, and what we can glean from him, has never been needed more. That he still possesses the power to attract us, to cleanse us in his mystical way, to mirror the depth of Being in his life and in the Church's interpretation of him, offers hope and peace for all who hear what the Spirit is saying. There have been so few lives that open us to the mystery of our own being and that speak to the unspeakable within us. Until God should come to earth again, I see no reason for abandoning Jesus of Nazareth, or discarding the Church's symbolic language that speaks so powerfully to the mystery of the human condition and makes us wonder about God.

---

18. Ibid.
19. Ibid., pp. 112–14.

19

Intrigue, Conspiracies, and Plots

RECENT POPULAR works, such as *Holy Blood, Holy Grail*, and Dan Brown's *The Da Vinci Code* are but two examples of a long list of intriguing studies of this sort. Albert Schweitzer, in his *Quest of the Historical Jesus*, summarizes two similar works published in 1782 and 1800, respectively. Both works were founded on the hypothesis that Jesus belonged to a Secret Essene Society that used Jesus, with his cooperation, to promote its goals. Karl Bahrdt, the first of these advocates, in his book, *Popular Letters About the Bible* (1782), named Joseph of Arimathea and Nicodemus the co-founders of the Society. Both were wealthy and influential members of the Jewish state. According to Bahrdt, both were Essenes and wanted to detach their nation's future from its hopes in a military Messiah to an endorsement of higher spiritual principles. Very early in Jesus' childhood, these two took notice of the boy from Nazareth and trained him in the philosophy of Plato. As a young man, Jesus received medical secrets and healing remedies from a mysterious Persian healer. Later, Luke made Jesus' acquaintance and taught him everything he himself knew about medicine. Jesus' cousin, John the Baptist, was also inducted into the Society and became part of the movement to change Judah's political and moral direction. The task ahead for both young men was daunting. The Society was organized into different tiers of membership, with only the top tier aware of the group's secret agenda. John and Jesus were forced to pursue their missions in a manner that the common man expected, but not for long. John was killed in the process. The Society decided to plot Jesus' death and resurrection, in order to move the nation beyond its crude Messianic expectations. Nicodemus worked to see that the Sanhedrin condemned Jesus; Joseph of Arimathea made certain that, after Jesus' "execution," his bloodied body would be taken down and his life restored. By the third day, Jesus was able to walk again. After the miracle of the "resurrection," members of the Society provided a hiding place for Jesus, where he could secretly direct the movement's future. Jesus occasionally reappeared to reassure his disciples and appeared to Paul on his journey to Damascus. Jesus later died, but by that time, the Society had fulfilled its spiritual goals.

Eighteen years after Bahrdt's work, Karl Venturini carried the tradition a step further. In his book, *The Non-supernatural History of the Great Prophet of Nazareth* (1800–1802), Venturini, adopting most of Bahrdt's hypothesis and approach, added that the Society's task turned out to be far more difficult than its members had imagined. The Society decided that the only way Jesus could accomplish its goals was for him to ride into Jerusalem and announce his Messiahship. Hopefully, he could then persuade the people to substitute his new order of the Kingdom for the more violent one they expected. His efforts failed; he was arrested, tried, and executed. The Society was caught off guard. Still, Joseph of Arimathea managed to persuade Pilate to release Jesus' body. Along with Nicodemus, they hurried to Golgotha, carried Jesus' body to Joseph's own grave, and revived him. To escape notice, Jesus disguised himself as a gardener, thus causing Mary Magdalene's failure to recognize him at first. As in Bahrdt's volume, Venturini portrays Jesus as living on for sometime afterwards before his death.

Surprisingly, Schweitzer did not condemn either author for his outlandish views. Rather, he praises them for being the "first to see" that Jesus' death was "distinctly" an act of Jesus' own.[1] He wasn't a victim; he chose the cross. He knew what he was doing. In fact, this is precisely what the Evangelists (all four) claim, and what the Jesus Seminar's thesis fails to address. In their scenarios, Jesus is executed for being a thorn in Judah's political side. It is his *sarcophilial* views that count, not his death on behalf of an estranged humankind.

In 1977, Bahrdt and Venturini's fictitious approaches were updated by Hugh Schonfield in his best-selling, *The Passover Plot*. Schonfield's study, however, drew directly from New Testament nuances and less imaginatively from fabricated episodes. While accepting the Secret Essene Society as a reality and the "resurrection" as a resuscitation event, Schonfield introduced Lazarus as the "Beloved Disciple" and the clandestine liaison who prepared the upper room for Jesus' last supper before the arrest, trail, and crucifixion could be staged. He too concluded that Jesus was revived and lived until a natural death. Not long after Schonfield's book, Barbara Thiering in 1992 published *Jesus and the Riddle of the Dead Sea Scrolls*. Her book presented many of the same findings, along with emphasizing that Jesus was of David's royal line, and that the settings described in John's Gospel about the Sea of Galilee actually depict Dead Sea ports and harbors

---

1. Schweitzer, *Quest of the Historical Jesus*, p. 47.

better. Not only was Jesus married to Mary Magdalene, but also the two had a daughter, whom the Apostle Paul wed. Schonfield's book made quite a stir at the time, but hardly of the magnitude of Dan Brown's *Da Vinci Code* or of the fascinating tome, *Holy Blood, Holy Grail.*

Central to the latter is the role that codes and ciphers play in reconstructing the hypothesis that Jesus was married, related to Lazarus, and either had a child by Mary Magdalene or left her pregnant. The book also retains the legend of Jesus' resuscitation and continued existence until his death in AD 45. Much is made of Schonfield's, Venturini's and Bahrdt's emphasis on the Secret Essene Society, to which Joseph of Arimathea, Nicodemus, Lazarus and Jesus belonged. All this, however, is predicated on the conviction that the Gospel of John is a Code-Gospel, presenting the truth about Jesus in symbolic and disguised form. Thus the wedding at Cana is Jesus' and Mary's wedding, and Lazarus' raising from the dead is a baptismal rite sacred to the Society. So also, Jesus' crucifixion occurred on private property, near or in Joseph's Garden, and was equally staged. Pilate was either in on the plot, or had at least been bribed. Plus, while Pilate was shocked that Jesus had died so quickly and thought that Joseph was requesting Jesus' corpse [*ptoma*], Joseph was actually asking for Jesus' body [*soma*] in the hopes of reviving it before Jesus could die (see Mark 15:43, 45).[2] Furthermore, the men, messengers, or "angels," who appear in the empty tomb stories of all the Gospels, are described as wearing white garments or robed in radiant vestments—the preferred attire of the higher tier of the Secret Society's members. Finally, much is made of the linen cloth that Joseph brought to cover Jesus' body upon its "burial." All this is conjecture, based principally on the supposition that John's Gospel is a coded document. But there is no way to prove this, nor does its writer pass himself off as an esoteric, nor pretend to be composing an apocalyptic or secretive manuscript. Granted his "Book of Signs" may be cited to support such, the Gospel itself emphasizes realized eschatology, not membership in a clandestine cult whose Savior survived death. Still, the mystery of the person who provided the foal for Jesus to ride and who prepared the upper room remains unsolved. Anything is possible, but hasty conclusions advanced without sufficient research to support them are of little value.

It is interesting to note that most, if not all, of the intrigue, conspiracy, and plots associated with Jesus are centered around his triumphal entry, his week in Jerusalem, last supper, arrest, trial, execution, and resurrection. In other words, these crucial events hinge on traditions preserved in the *passion narratives*. This is the very material Crossan rejects, or ques-

---

2. See *The Greek New Testament*, Philadelphia, 1966, p. 95.

tions. Yet, simply because it doesn't fit neatly into his schema of Jesus as a peasant Cynic, does not excuse New Testament scholarship from having to grapple with it. Crossan does not mention Baigent's "research" in either of his volumes, nor lend it credence, nor does he cite Thiering's work. Is it not possible that the unresolved questions surrounding Pilate's role, along with those of Joseph of Arimathea and Nicodemus, the proximity of Bethany, and the liaison who provided the foal and prepared the upper room for Jesus' observance of Passover were insoluble conundrums for the Evangelists, too? The Synoptic writers, following Mark's account, report the same story, but each in a slightly different way. Does this not suggest that even as late as Matthew and Luke's accounts, no consensus existed in the Church on exactly what happened during Jesus' last hours, or how it happened? Who did what, when, and where was still open to interpretation. John's narrative comes the closest to lending itself to conspiracy theories, yet John's principal interest was to stress the reality of eternal life now, not to engage in speculation as to the post-Easter Jesus' physical whereabouts or Jesus' continued role on earth. All that now is in the hands of his believers and in the power of the Holy Spirit. Jesus has already ascended to his Father to prepare a place for his disciples, when it is their time to come. All the Gospels assert that Jesus died. All report that he was buried. But that his pneumatic presence was with them is beyond question. The hypothesis that Jesus survived the cross can never be more than that—a hypothesis. Moreover, trying to prove it requires one to mine the non-canonical documents for supporting "evidence." It is these very sources, i.e., *The Gospel of Philip, The Gospel of Mary, The Acts of Pilate*, and others that, apart from the canonical Gospels, are so bizarre and embellished, or as in the case of *The Acts of Pilate*, forged, as to render them marginal at best. Does any scholar truly believe that by focusing on the non-canonical esoteric documents of the Nag Hammadi collection, that such a reconstructed Jesus would make any sense, apart from the Jesus of the Synoptic Gospels and Paul's letters? If the Synoptic Gospels had never been written, memories of the Nag Hammadi Jesus would have perished in the sands, and its scrolls when rediscovered become a puzzling witness to the declining years of the Hellenistic Age.

On the other hand, would it constitute an insurmountable obstacle for traditional faith to accept Jesus' marriage to Mary Magdalene, alias Mary of Bethany? How would that acknowledgement change anything the Evangelists advance? Or how would it detract from anything Paul postulates about Christ Jesus as Lord and Savior, descended *kata sarka* from the house of David and born of a woman? And would it really undermine the theological language invested in the Nicene Creed and Formula of Chalcedon? I can't see that it would alter a thing, other than our unwillingness to rethink our perceptions of the historical Jesus and the post-Easter Christ. One cannot argue from the Church's silence, one way or the other. Is it not wiser to remain open, hopeful, prayerful, and expectant rather than closed minded, inflexible, adamant, and dogmatic? After all, Jesus himself said: "Ask and it will be given you; seek and you will find, knock and it will be opened to you." The Church has nothing to fear of Jesus of Nazareth. Wherever he passes by in our hearts and minds, our sacraments and scriptures, our missions to the homeless and to the least of the brethren, *as well as in our research*, he will always be present, alive, risen, and available to heal: "O Jesus of Nazareth! Son of David! Have mercy on me!" Nowhere in *The Gospel of Thomas* do those words appear, but they do in the memory of the post-Easter Church, whose members' "hearts burned within them" when they read Isaiah and remembered the mendicant carpenter of Nazareth.

20

Conclusion: The Five Trees of Paradise

BEFORE LISTING this study's conclusions, there remains a metaphor that appears in *The Gospel of Thomas* that is too haunting to neglect. In chapter 19 we read:

> Jesus said: "Blessed is he who came into being before he came into being. If you become My disciples and listen to My words, these stones will minister to you. For there are five trees for you in Paradise which remain undisturbed summer and winter and whose leaves do not fall. Whoever becomes acquainted with them will not experience death."[1]

The symbolism of these trees evokes a warning, perhaps, a two-fold warning at that, lest one tumble into fallacies. The first is what we might call a *formal fallacy* and the second a *material fallacy*. By *formal fallacy* it would be a mistake to assume that there is an actual *norm*—however abstract or universal—or a normative principle that underlies these trees. What possible principle could it be? The writer provides none. The genre of symbolism is the closest "norm" or "form" that comes to it. Once again we are in the realm of myth and symbolism. Not even the number five can be trusted. It could have been any number the writer wanted. "Paradise" is the only normative clue he provides. And by "Paradise" does he mean the End-Time or Eden? The text doesn't say. One suspects he means "Heaven," or "Abraham's bosom," in the sense in which Jesus is reported to have said: "Today you will be with me in Paradise" (Luke 23:43; cf. 16:22). By *material fallacy*, it would be a mistake to assume that the metaphor is actually referring to trees, or for that matter, to anything material. That might not be the case at all.

At best, the five trees constitute a mixed metaphor. A Paradise with trees combines a material with a mystical dimension, similar to Paul's "imperishable bodies." Symbolically, the key to unraveling the metaphor lies in the opening statement: "Blessed is he who came into being before he

---

1. Cited from *The Other Gospels*, p. 27.

came into being." This seems to echo the Thomean belief in the Primordial Man, from whom present mankind is estranged. Once this estrangement is overcome, and one is reunited with his true self, one enjoys the Eternal again. One is reunited with the Godhead and with one's authentic self. Transcendence rules rather than discord. Paradise is regained.

If one were to take the five trees as pertaining to something of the highest elemental human importance, many intriguing possibilities "sprout up." One of the most productive of these has been suggested by Jean-Yves Leloup in his translation of and commentary on *The Gospel of Thomas*, published in 1986. He proposes that the five trees refer to the tree of thought, the tree of feeling, the tree of reflection, the tree of the intellect, and the tree of reasoning.[2] These bring to mind the five aggregates of the conditioned self that Buddhism teaches, as well as Jung's four functions of consciousness. The hypothesis is, that when we are in touch with these five aggregates or essential functions of the self, we experience harmony. Interestingly enough, the number "five" represents a "natural man" for Jung, whereas "four" symbolizes the "ideal man."[3] Perhaps that is why the Cross constitutes such a fitting symbol for Jung, in which the five wounds of Christ have been taken up into the healing quaternary of the Holy Rood.

One may also interpret the trees from a theological perspective by identifying the probable trees that flourished in Eden's mythical Garden. Since theologically the tree of the knowledge of good and evil and the tree of life would have lost their leaves after the Fall, the most likely candidates to replace them are the myrtle, the fig, the olive, the cedar, and the cypress tree. These, along with the palm tree, are the most frequently cited floras in the Old Testament. They are employed as metaphors and are plants indigenous to Palestine. From a theological standpoint, the lofty cedar symbolizes pride as well as beauty; its timbers formed the frame, ceiling, and floors of Solomon's Temple. From its earliest mention in Genesis, the fig tree became associated with guilt and the need to hide sin and vulnerability; the fragrant myrtle switch became a balm for cleansing; the olive was prized for its oil to lighten one's path, and the cypress was chosen for the construction of the ark that bore the ancestors of the patriarchs above the waters of chaos and discord. That Jesus cursed a fig tree when he needed its fruit most speaks volumes of his humanity and tortured heart on his way to Golgotha. That these trees await us in Paradise, in the

---

2. Jean-Yves Leloup, *The Gospel of Thomas*, 1986, p. 94.
3. Jung, *Archetypes and the Collective Unconscious*, in *Collected Works*, ix, 1, p. 373.

Conclusion: The Five Trees of Paradise

Eleusinian fields of our own hearts, addresses the deepest recesses of our human condition and our potential to become whole.

But who is to say that the five trees may not be the Pentateuch, the soul of Haggadah and Halakah? Or the five divisions of the books of the Psalms? Neither of which shall ever lose their leaf, in winter or summer? Or the five disciples closest to Jesus: Peter, James, John, the Beloved Disciple, and Mary Magdalene? Or Thomas Didymus?

I do not pretend to know. What we do know is that the trees stood as symbols of peace and harmony for a band of Jesus' disciples who produced *The Gospel of Thomas*. I find it disappointing that, while the Jesus Seminar Fellows embrace many of *The Gospel of Thomas*' stunning aphorisms that support their *sapiental* preference, they neglect those that address anything otherworldly, or that have to do with the Transcendent. Even though the latter may be tainted by Gnostic or Platonic influence, nonetheless, they witness to the mystery of our human condition and desire to be at one with our selves and God. That this tradition endured as long as it did, or until its members were forced underground, speaks of their hunger to have their intellects challenged and fed, as well as their ontological substructure encompassed by the Eternal. We do not have to endorse the *content* of their interpretations, but their *intent* mirrors our own.

There is a marvelous allegory preserved in 1 Enoch that explores the symbolism of the tree that grows on the slopes of the mystical mountain of Paradise. Jesus' saying in *The Gospel of Thomas*, chapter 19, might well have been inspirited by it. It is a

> tree like no other. Its fragrance was beyond all fragrance, and its leaves and blooms and wood never withered. Its fruit was beautiful, resembling the dates of the palm . . . As for this fragrant tree, no mortal is permitted to touch it till the great judgment when God's justice redresses all and brings everything to its ultimate consummation. The tree shall then be given to the good and holy. Its food shall be food for the elect. It shall be transplanted to the holy temple of the Lord, the eternal King (I Enoch).[4]

This is the hope of mankind, to be included in the "good and holy," however unholy one's past. It addresses that need for grace and salvation that the post-Easter Christ represents and which the Jesus Seminar finds in conflict with its perception of the pre-Easter, historical Jesus. In conjunction with I Enoch, there is also a fascinating passage in the first chapter of the *Zohar* that speaks of the five gates of Paradise. They are the portals

---

4. See *The Other Bible*, p. 489.

that open the passage for *shekinah* to return to God. The five portals are *gevurah, hesed, tif'eret, hod,* and *netsah.*[5]

Whatever the faults of *The Gospel of Thomas*, perhaps, for Christianity, the five trees of Paradise that possess the spiritual power to nurture contemporary man, might be reconfigured as Matthew, Mark, Luke, John, and Thomas. It is the fruit of these trees that has the power to open human eyes and hearts, to feed the never-ceasing hunger within. Like the "law of the Lord," it delights the soul of all who feed thereon. In turn, those who are nourished by God's Word become flesh become "like trees planted beside streams of water, which yield their fruit in its season, and their leaves do not wither" (Ps 1:2–3). Perhaps only such gatherers discover anew the original meaning of the tree of the knowledge of good and evil and the tree of life, guarded by the angel with a flaming sword.

Conclusions. I entertained no idea where this study would lead when I first began it. As a seminary student, I was haunted by Schweitzer's "One Unknown," who confronts us in the mystery of the Jesus of history. Even though my field of study was the Reformation and Calvin in particular, I have never ceased to be enchanted by the quests of the Jesus of history. As a professor of philosophy and world religions, I have always thought that the Evangelists' depictions of Jesus were influenced by the religious views of their own era, namely, Greco-Roman as well as Jewish. But I have always wondered which exercised the paramount edge. Earlier, in this study, I emphasized the world of Greek mythology and its influence over the emerging Christian worldview. I think now that what seems apparent is that that worldview did *regulate* but not *legislate* the Church's content. The mythical culture of the late Hellenistic and early Roman period appealed to the Gospel writers as a framework for presenting their good news. However, the content of their *euangellion* drew upon the scriptures of the Old Testament and possibly 1 Enoch and *The Psalm of Solomon 17*. They utilized metaphor, myth, legend, and parable to report their story, to enflesh the Christ. They saw him in the light of an Apollo or Dionysus become flesh, but not in the sensuous form of the Homeric or Greek godhead. Instead, he was the Son of David, the Son of God. He was the Messiah of Isaiah 53. The hope of the world! The way, the truth, and the life! The self-emptying Word that came down from heaven to restore human life. In so doing, they were compelled to use symbols, and, as in Paul's case, to draw upon the Platonic archetype of the perfect primal man. By our recognizing and employing such symbols in our own encounter with

---

5. See Daniel Matt's, Vol. I, of the *Zohar* under "References" in the back of this book.

God, we too discover our needs met, whether ontological, psychological, or spiritual.

The mystery of our human condition will forever require us to put our existence to the question. It is unavoidable—just as God is unavoidable, or Buber's Eternal Thou is unavoidable. And that is what makes religion and its symbols, its sacred figures and shamans, redemptive and instructive for lives. The Jesus of history cannot be separated from this larger milieu, both cultural and spiritual, that preserved him for Western mankind and the world. To lose Him, in His wholeness, as Savior and Lord, as Healer and Comforter, because a certain methodology can only reconstruct a peasant Cynic, is to lose the greatest legacy the Western world has ever known. We need Him as the objectification of our own encounter with that depth within us that longs for fulfillment and for oneness with the mystery that grounds our being and everything else. That mystery will never go away. It has been there since the first evolving man wondered about the stars and himself. Nothing about that is invented or fabricated. It is part of our very being. It is what makes us human, just as Jesus was human, who really lived and really died and still lives as the Supreme Archetype, Savior, and Revealer of the mystery of life.

There are other conclusions to be drawn. None escapes paradox, nor resolves the mystery.

1. Reformed communities need to look afresh at the emerging historical Jesus of Jesus research and reassess their Christologies where appropriate. The supposition that the Second Person of the Trinity must take priority over the Jesus of history may have been a logical necessity of the Council of Nicaea, but it does little to illumine the humanity of the Jesus of history. If anything, it obfuscates his individuality as a human being, which paradoxically denies his never-to-be repeated unique life. That is its irony and his saving grace.

2. Simultaneously, New Testament scholars who track the pre-Easter Jesus, clothed in the garments of the Post-Easter Christ, might hopefully consider acknowledging their indebtedness to the Evangelists, rather than spurning their narratives as "inventions of the storyteller," cloaked in "the tyranny of dogma." Neither Borg nor Crossan are this crass, but the editors of *The Five Gospels* approach impertinence at times, or appear to lean toward hasty conclusions. In addition, one might question Crossan's use of the term "commensality." The term becomes his normative principle

for interpreting the sayings and actions of Jesus, while his "material principle" is Q and the *Gospel of Thomas* in many instances. If one reads the Gospels carefully, one realizes that the idea of "commensality" belongs more to the Book of Acts and the post-Easter Church than to the period of Jesus' life. Has Crossan read back into his sources an interpretive principle that belongs to the Church, more than it pertains to the historical Jesus? It is a close one to call, but the question needs to be raised.

3. There is no one definitive interpretation of the historical Jesus that has been authorized to silence the others.

4. Psychological approaches, such as Jung's; mythological, such as Campbell's; and symbolic, such as Tillich's, enrich our understanding of the field of religion and its capacity to address our lives. Any and all such constructive approaches like theirs assist us in the redemptive processes to restore wholeness and mend human potential.

5. The shamans, sages, holy figures of other religions attest to the universal reality of our human condition and deepen our awareness of our own traditions more than they detract from them.

6. Religious sects that pursue their own agenda, apart from the historical and theological safeguards that have been advanced over the centuries to ensure a responsible Christian story, along with the world's declining respect for the mystery of God, should inspire our hunger for the truth about Jesus, rather than discourage or fragment our witness. Indeed, the latter is worthy of proclamation and in need, itself, of reassessment, reformation, and unity, as all Christians know.

7. Christianity is unique. In spite of its claim to exclusivity, it shares with other religious traditions the awareness that the Transcendent is ever present, ever open to all who empty their hearts to hear what the Spirit of God has to say. It has to do with our inner life, as well as with the incarnation of that transforming vision that leads to inner peace and outer world concord.

Bibliography

Arndt, William & Gingrich, F. Wilbur. *A Greek-English Lexicon of the New Testament*. 1957. Chicago, Illinois: The University of Chicago Press.
Augustine, Aurelius. *Confessions*. In *Augustine: Confessions and Enchiridion*. 1955. Philadelphia: Westminster Press.
Baigent, Michael, Richard Leigh, & Henry Lincoln. *Holy Blood, Holy Grail*. 1983. New York: A Dell Book.
_____. *The Jesus Papers*. 2006. HarperSanFrancisco.
Barnstone, Willis, ed. *The Other Bible*. 2005. HaperSanFrancisco.
Barnstone, Willis & Marvin Meyer. *The Gnostic Bible*. 2006. Boston: New Seeds.
Barth, Karl. *Church Dogmatics*. Vols. I & II. 1976. Edinburgh: T & T Clark Ltd.
_____. *The Faith of the Church*. 1958. New York: Living Age Books; Meridian Books, Inc.
Borg, Marcus J. *Meeting Jesus Again for the First Time*. 1994. HarperSanFrancisco.
Bornkamm, Gunther. *Jesus of Nazareth*. 1960. New York: Harper & Row.
Bruce, F. F. *Paul: Apostle of the Heart Set Free*. 1977. Grand Rapids: Wm. B. Eerdmans Publishing Company.
Brunner, Emil. *The Mediator*. 1947. Philadelphia: Westminster Press.
Buber, Martin. *Eclipse of God*. 1952. New York: Harper Torchbooks.
_____. *Hasidism and Modern Man*. 1958. New York: Harper Torchbooks.
_____. *Tales of the Hasidim*. 1991. New York: Schocken Books.
Bulfinch, Thomas. *The Age of Fable*. 1853. *Bulfinch's Mythology*. New York: The Modern Library. Random House, Inc.
Burkert, Walter. *Greek Religion*. 1985. Cambridge, Massachusetts: Harvard University Press.
Bultmann, Rudolf. Ed. by Hans W. Bartsch. *Kergyma and Myth*. 1961. New York: Harper Torchbooks.
Calvin, John. *Institutes of the Christian Religion*. Vols. I and II. 1957. Grand Rapids: Wm. B. Eerdmans Publishing Company.
Cameron, Ron. Ed. *The Other Gospels*. 1982. Philadelphia: The Westminster Press.
Campbell, Joseph. *An Open Life*. 1988. Burdette, New York: Paul Brunton Philosophic Foundation.
_____. *Myths to Live By*. 1988. New York: Bantam Books.
_____. *The Hero With A Thousand Faces*. 1949. Bolligen Series XVII. Princeton: Princeton University Press.
_____. *The Power of Myth, with Bill Moyers*. 1991. New York: Anchor Books.
Celsus: On the True Doctrine, trans. by R. J. Hoffmann. New York: Oxford University Press. 1987.
Cleary, Thomas. Ed. and Trans. *The Dhammapada: Sayings of the Buddha*. 1995. New York: Bantam Books.

Bibliography

Crossan, John Dominic. *The Birth of Christianity: Discovering What Happened in the Years Immediately After the Execution of Jesus.* 1998. HarperSanFrancisco.
_____. *The Historical Jesus: The Life of a Mediterranean Jewish Peasant.* 1991. HarperSanFrancisco.
_____. *Who Killed Jesus?* 1995. HarperSanFrancisco.
Dandby, Herbert. *The Mishnah.* 1985. New York: Oxford University Press.
Didache. In *Early Christian Fathers.* 1953. Philadelphia: Westminster Press.
Eisler, Riane. *The Chalice and the Blade: Our History, Our Future.* 1988. HarperSan Francisco.
Epictetus. *The Discourses of Epictetus,* in *The Stoic and Epicurean Philosophers.* 1940. New York: Random House.
Farley, Benjamin W. *Son of the Morning Sky.* 1999. New York: University Press of America.
Funk, Robert. Hoover, Roy. *The Five Gospels: The Search for the Authentic Words of Jesus.* 1993. HarperSanFrancisco.
Greek New Testament. 1966. Ed. by Aland, Black, Metzger & Wikgren. New York: American Bible Society.
Hall, Calvin S. and Nordby, V. J. *A Primer of Jungian Psychology.* 1999. New York: A Meridian Book.
Hamilton, Edith. *Mythology.* 1940, 1942. New York: A Mentor Book.
Heidegger, Martin. *Poetry, Language, Thought.* 2001. New York: Perennial Classics.
Hesiod. *Hesiod and Theognis,* trans. By D. Wender. 1973. New York: Penguin Books.
Hick, John. *Classical and Contemporary Readings in the Philosophy of Religion.* 3rd ed. 1990. Englewoods Cliffs: New Jersey: Prentice Hall.
Horney, Karen. *Neurosis and Human Growth: The Struggle Toward Self-Realization.* 1950. New York: W. W. Norton & Co., Inc.
Humphreys, Christian. *Buddhism.* 1972. Baltimore, Maryland: Penguin Books.
Ignatius of Antioch. *Letters.* In *Early Christian Fathers.* 1953. Philadelphia: Westminster Press.
Jaspers, Carl. *Way to Wisdom.* 1954. New Haven: Yale University Press.
Josephus, Flavius. *The Antiquities of the Jews.* 1987. Peabody, MA: Hendrickson Pub.
Jung, Carl. *Aion.* 1959. Bollingen Series XX. The Collected Works of C. C. Jung. Vol. 9. Part 2. Princeton: Princeton University Press.
_____. *The Archetypes and the Collective Unconscious.* 1969. Bollingen Series XX. The Collected Works of C. C. Jung. Vol. 9. Part 1. Princeton: Princeton University Press.
Kaufmann, Walter. *Tragedy and Philosophy.* 1992. Princeton: Princeton University Press.
Kierkegaard, Soren. *Philosophical Fragments.* 1971. Princeton: Princeton University Press.
King, Karen. *The Gospel of Mary of Magdala.* 2003. Santa Rosa, Calif.: Polebridge Press.
Lao Tzu. *Tao Te Ching.* 1972. Trans. D. C. Lau. Baltimore, Maryland: Penguin Books.
Leith, John Haddon. *Basic Christian Doctrine.* 1993. Louisville, Kentucky: Westminster/ John Knox Press.
Lempriere's Classical Dictionary. 1972. Boston: Routledge & Kegan Paul Ltd.
Long, Edward LeRoy, Jr. *A Survey of Christian Ethics.* 1967. New York: Oxford.
Martin, Luther. *Hellenistic Religions.* 1987. New York: Oxford University Press.
Matt, Daniel C. *The Essential Kabbalah: The Heart of Jewish Mysticism.* 1977. Edison, New Jersey: Castle Books.
_____. The *Zohar.* Vol. 1. 2004. Stanford, Calif. Stanford University Press.
Neihardt, John G. *Black Elk Speaks.* 1993. Lincoln, Nebraska: University of Nebraska Press.

Bibliography

Nikhilananda, Swami. *The Upanishads*. 1962. New York: Harper Torchbooks.

Noss, David. *A History of the World's Religions*. 10th ed. Upper Saddle River, NJ: Prentice Hall.

Ovid, Publius Naso. *The Metamorphoses*. 2005. New York: Barnes & Noble Classics.

Pliny, the Younger. *Pliny:Letters and Panegyricus*. Vol. 2. 1969. LCL. Cambridge: Harvard University Press. 1969.

Rogers, Carl. *On Becoming a Person*. 1961. Boston: Houghton Mifflin Company.

Sangharakshita. *The Three Jewels*. 1970. Garden City, New York: Anchor Books.

Schaff, Philip. *The Creeds of Christendom*. Vol. II. 1919. New York: Harper & Brothers.

Schweitzer, Albert. *The Quest of the Historical Jesus*. 1964. New York: The Macmillan Company.

Seutonius, Gaius. *The Twelve Caesars*. 1979. New York: Penguin Books.

Shibayama, Zenkei. *Zen Comments on the Mumonkan*. 1974. New York: New American Library.

Tacitus. Publius Gaius. *The Annals of Imperial Rome*. 1956. Trans. by Michael Grant. Baltimore, Maryland: Penguin Books.

Thiering, Barbara. *Jesus and the Riddle of the Dead Sea Scrolls*. 1992. New York: Harper Collins.

Tillich, Paul. *Systematic Theology*. Vols. *I & II*. 1957. Chicago: The University of Chicago Press.

Van Voorst, Robert E. *Anthology of World Scriptures*. 3rd ed. 2000. Belmont, California Wadsworth Publishing Co.

Whitehead, Alfred North. *Religion in the Making*. 1974. New York: New American Library.

Scripture Index

Old Testament

Genesis
1:2	55
2:24	94
4:4	133
5:21–24	119
12:4	175
27:38–40	69

Exodus
20–23	49
24:8	174

Leviticus
17–25	49

1 Samuel
8:12	161

2 Samuel
7:11, 14, 16	104
7:14	138

1 Kings
4:33	150
17:22	119

2 Kings
2:11	119
4:35	119

Job
25:4–6	140
35:7	176

Psalms
1:2–3	204
2	175
2:1	112, 114
2:2–4	190
2:7	137–38
2:2–7	106
8:3	140
8:5	138
16:10	123
22:1	112, 114
22:18	112
23	142
29	135
34:10, 17–18	157
69:21	112
89:35, 37	190
110:4	190
118:22	146, 165
118:176	69
119:50, 52	155
119:76	155
130:1, 3	56
139:9–10	56

Isaiah
2:58	170
5:2	144
5:7	144
6:3	29, 46
6:3, 8	160
7:14	103
8:14	146
9:6	131, 155
11:1	132
28:16	146
29:14	176
40:1	155
40:11	133
40:13	176
42:1	137–38
44:1–2	108
50:6–7	112
51:2	155
53	165, 174–75
53:5	115
53:7, 8	108, 133
53:12	112
55:7	112
57:18	155
58:8	45
61:1	170
61:2	190
61:1–3	155
66:13	156

Jeremiah
2:21	144
31:13, 31	155, 174

Scripture Index

Ezekiel
1:1–28   140
19:10–14   144
34:4   69
34:23–24   142
37:25   155

Daniel
2:44   190
7:13–14   140

Joel
2:28   190

Amos
8:9   112

Micah
2:2   157
5:2   103
5:2–5   142
5:4   143

Habakkuk
2:4   175

Zechariah
1:10   136
12:10   112
13:7–9   143
34:16   143
34:35–36   143

Malachi
4:5   106

Apocrypha

Tobit
6:5   151
10:7   69
11:11–14   151

Wisdom
6:1–3   163

Baruch
3:29–32   60

2 Maccabees
7:1–42   123
7:9   124

New Testament

Matthew
2:23   132
4:11   129
4:24   151
5:3   156
5:4   156
5:5   162
5:6   156
5:7   162
5:9   162
5:14   24
5:20   166
5:22   162
5:27   162
5:33   162
5:39   35, 162
5:42   83
5:44   23, 162
5:45   35
5:48   54
5:48   162
6:6   26, 36, 74
6:19   24
6:20   162
6:25–34   156
6:28–29   55
6:28–30   26
6:33   26
6:34   162, 172
7:1   162
7:7–8   157, 184
7:10   59f
7:12   162
7:13   23, 35, 162
7:24   162
8:20   141, 156
8:23   58
8:28   58
9:22   153
9:35   170
9:35–36   151
9:36   133, 157
10:10   173
10:26   73
10:34   160
10:39   69
11:28–39   157
12:1–14   171
12:9   170
12:10   171
12:11   171
12:23   142
13:31–32   62
13:44   63
13:45–46   62
13:47   60
13:54   170f
14:14   157
14:22–27   58
14:28–31   59

Scripture Index

15:10–11	70	6:2	170	6:24	156
15:17–18	70	6:3	6	6:25	156
15:32	157	6:34	133, 157	6:27–30	162
16:6	166	7:14–15	70	6:28	173
17:1–8	106	8:2	157	6:30–31	83, 162
17:27	59	8:27	158	6:32–34	83
18:13	166	8:34–35	113	6:34	83
18:12–14	68	8:35	8, 34, 69	6:35, 37–38	82, 162
18:15	173	9:2–13	106	7:13	157
19:4–6	94	10:11	173	7:29–30	82
19:14	76	10:14	76	7:36–50	160, 168
20:30–31	142	10:15	76	7:37–50	82
20:34	157	10:47–48	142	8:2–4	78
21:31–32	82	10:51	148	8:17	73
21:33–39	145	11:10	142	8:48	153
22:21	26	12:1–8	145	9:28–36	106
22:37–40	173	12:10	147	9:35	2
23:25–26	70	12:17	173	9:49	149
23:37	156	14:12	134	9:51	125
24:20	170	15:34	114	9:58	141, 156
25:31–46	158	15:43, 45	197	10:7–8	173
25:35–36	159	16:1	169	10:38–42	77
26:17	134			11:9–10	157
28:1	169	**Luke**		11:11	59f
28:9	119	1:27, 32	142	11:14	149
28:18–20	130	1:35	2, 104	11:40–41	71
		2:4	142	12:2	73
Mark		2:8	143	12:15	171
1:21	137, 170	3:9, 17	161	12:20	24
1:22	137	3:16	161	12:22–31	156
1:24	137	3:38	138	12:39	173
1:24–25	150	4:16	170	12:51	161
1:35	55	4:18–19	170	13:10	77, 170
1:41–43	151	4:22	170	13:10–17	77
1:43	152	4:31	170	13:18–19	62
2:23–24	171	6:1–11	171	13:32	149
3:4	171	6:4	171	13:34	156
4:22	73	6:9	171	15:4–6	68
4:30–32	62	6:20	156	15:8–9	68
5:34	153	6:21	156	15:11–32	68

15:20	157	6:63	126	2:44–46	157
15:23	69	7:23–24	171	3:15	122
15:30	82	8:6, 8	151	3:22–26	123
16:22	201	8:23	126	4:10	123
17:20–21	16	8:44, 49	126	4:11	147
17:27	59	9:6	151	4:12	139
17:33	23, 69	9:22	166	4:25	142
18:16–17	76	10:9	143	4:32–35	122
18:38–39	142	10:14	143	4:32–37	168
18:42	153	11:25–26	94	5:19	130
20:9–15	145	11:43–44	128	5:34	168
22:7	134	12:24	34, 113	6:1–6	122, 168
23:43	201	12:31	126	8:9–24	149
23:46	48	12:35	126	8:32–33	108, 133
23:56	169	13:1	134	8:35	108
24:13–21	122	14:6–7	27, 45	10:34–41	89
24:31–37	119	14:9	92	10:38	149, 157
24:44, 52	122	14:17–20	96	13:7	149
		14:27	163	13:9–13	149
John		15	144	13:30	123
1:1	27	16:13	126	14:12	106
1:3	127	17:2–3	126	16:37	178
1:3–4	126	17:3	61	19:11	149
1:11, 12, 14	90	18:36	126	22:25–29	178
1:14	127, 139, 191–92	19:25	80	24:43–47	168
1:16	126	19:39	91		
1:18	139	20:14, 19, 26	119	**Romans**	
1:29, 35	133	20:15–16	90	1:3	142, 174, 192
1:38	148	20:15–19	143	1:16	160
3:1–10	57	20:16	148	1:16–17	59, 174
3:5	76	21:5–13	61	3:21–26	174
3:6	126			5:1	124
3:7	57	**Acts of the Apostles**		5:1–21	174
3:12	126	1:3, 9, 22	123	5:6–11	174
4:7–15	57	1:8	130	6:5–10	124
4:14	57	1:9–11	119	7:14–25	174
5:2–9	73	2:24	123	7:21	54
5:18	171	2:29–31	142	8:18–25	174
6:9–11	61	2:41–44	144	8:22	118
6:25–26	61	2:42	122	8:39	57, 159

8:39–40	159
9:33	147
10:6–7	92
11:33	176
12:2	52, 107
12:14	173
13	60
13:3–4	178
13:7	173
13:10	173

1 Corinthians

1:12	177
1:19	176
1:21	176
1:22	176
1:24	176
1:25	176
1:30	176
2:1, 4–5	177
2:6–7	176
3:19	176
4:9	176
7:10	173
9:14	173
10:27	173
11:23	173
12:8	177
13:12	174
14:1	167
14:33	81
15:3	173
15:5–8	119
15:28	121
15:42–44	111
15:42–56	174
15:43–44	124
15:51–52	111
15:55	90

2 Corinthians

1:12	177
3:18	107
5:16–18	178, 192
5:19	192

Galatians

2:2	119
2:19–21	174
2:20	117
3:27	81
4:4	174
5:1	134
5:22–23	159, 177
6:1	173
6:2	159

Ephesians

1:8	176
1:19	175, 177
1:25	121
2:4–10	174
2:8	114
3:10	176

Philippians

2:5–8	174
2:6–8	93
2:8–11	174
3:13	159
4:6–7, 11–12	159

Colossians

1:19	121
1:28	176–77
2:3, 8	176
2:9	121
2:23	177
3:2	46
3:11–15	93, 121, 159

3:16	177
4:6	121

1 Thessalonians

4:13–18	174
4:17	124
5:2–5	173

1 Timothy

2:5	189
2:11–12	81
3:9, 16	175
6:16	92

2 Timothy

1:8	142

2 Peter

1:16–21	107–8, 111

1 John

3:17	144

Revelation

5:6—6:17	134

Rabbinical (Mishnah)

Ketuboth 3.8	76
Kiddushin 4.13	76
Sanhedrin 7.7.11	151
Sotah 3.8	76, 81

Non-Canonical Writings

Acts of Pilate	198
Dialogue of the Savior	120–21, 125

Scripture Index

Didache	37–38, 83	37	120
1 Enoch	203	49–51	120
Gospel of Mary	80	54:1	156
Gospel of Peter	165–66	58, 61–62	120
Gospel of Philip	80, 198	65:1–7	145
		66	146
Psalm of Solomon		69:2	120, 156
17	140–41, 174, 204	70	120
		76	62

Gospel of Thomas

1	119	77	120
2:1	157	79	120
3:1–4	60	82	120
3:4	119	84	120
4:3	94	85:2	120
5:2–3	73	86:1–2	141
6:5–6	73	86:2	156
8:1–2	59	89:1–2	70
8:1–4	61	90:2	157
11	94	92:1	157
11:4	94	94:1	157
13:1–4	158	95	83
14:5	70	96:1–2	78
16:2	161	97:1–4	78–79
18:3	120	101:3	120
19	120	106:1	94
19:4	120	107:1–3	68
20	62	108	120
22	56	109	63
22:1–2	76	111:2	120
22:4–6	82	113	16, 120
22:4–7	94		
23:1	94		
24	120		
26	23		
29	56		
30	120		
32	24		
36	55		
36:1–3	156		

www.ingramcontent.com/pod-product-compliance
Lightning Source LLC
Chambersburg PA
CBHW070314230426
43663CB00011B/2131